CW00677956

THE ZULU WAR

DESPATCHES FROM THE FRONT
*The Commanding Officers' Reports from
the Field and at Sea*

THE ZULU WAR

Introduced and compiled by
Martin Mace and John Grehan

with additional research by
Sara Mitchell

Pen & Sword
MILITARY

First published in Great Britain in 2013 by
PEN & SWORD MILITARY
An imprint of
Pen & Sword Books Ltd
47 Church Street
Barnsley
South Yorkshire
S70 2AS

Copyright © Martin Mace and John Grehan, 2013

ISBN 978-1-78159-322-6

The right of Martin Mace and John Grehan to be identified as the authors of this work has been asserted by them in accordance with the Copyright, Designs and Patents Act 1988.

A CIP catalogue record for this book is available from the British Library.

All rights reserved. No part of this book may be reproduced or transmitted in any form or by any means, electronic or mechanical including photocopying, recording or by any information storage and retrieval system, without permission from the Publisher in writing.

Typeset by Concept, Huddersfield, West Yorkshire, HD4 5JL.
Printed and bound in England by CPI Group (UK) Ltd, Croydon CR0 4YY.

Pen & Sword Books Ltd incorporates the imprints of Pen & Sword Archaeology, Atlas, Aviation, Battleground, Discovery, Family History, History, Maritime, Military, Naval, Politics, Railways, Select, Social History, Transport, True Crime, Claymore Press, Frontline Books, Leo Cooper, Praetorian Press, Remember When, Seaforth Publishing and Wharncliffe.

For a complete list of Pen & Sword titles please contact
PEN & SWORD BOOKS LIMITED
47 Church Street, Barnsley, South Yorkshire, S70 2AS, England
E-mail: enquiries@pen-and-sword.co.uk
Website: www.pen-and-sword.co.uk

Contents

List of Plates

A Sketch of Lord Chelmsford (31 May 1827 to 9 April 1905) made by an officer shortly before the battle of Ulundi.

The Battle of Isandlwana from 'Zulu War pictures from the *Illustrated London News* and *The Graphic*', 1879.

Cetshwayo ka Mpande.

The defence of Rorke's Drift 1879.

The battlefield at Rorke's Drift.

The Relief Column arriving at Rorke's Drift.

Present day view of the battle site at Rorke's Drift.

Anthony William Durnford (24 May 1830 to 22 January 1879).

A contemporary illustration showing soldiers being attacked during an attempt by the Relief Column to reach Rorke's Drift.

The burning of Ulundi.

Field-Marshal Sir Evelyn Wood, VC.

The Battle of Kambula.

Lieutenant-Colonel John Rouse Merriott Chard VC (1847–1897).

The Battle of Intombe.

Field-Marshal Viscount Garnet Wolseley.

A Zulu *Impi* on the march.

Introduction

On 11 January 1879, a British force crossed the Buffalo River to invade Zululand at the start of one of the most famous campaigns in British military history. The story of the subsequent Zulu War has been told very many times and this book does not attempt to tell that story again. Instead what are presented here are the original despatches sent back to the United Kingdom by the commanding officer of the British force, Lieutenant General Frederic Augustus Thesiger, 2nd Baron Chelmsford and the man that superseded him General Sir Garnet Wolseley.

In many cases these despatches, when published in *The London Gazette*, represented the first detailed knowledge the British people had of the campaign and its progress. These despatches include reports submitted to Lord Chelmsford from other officers under his command explaining their participation in the key events of the war.

Amongst those key events was the massacre at Isandlwana, regarded as being the British Army's worst defeat to a technically inferior enemy, following which Lord Chelmsford held a court of inquiry. The details of the inquiry were also sent back to the UK and were published in *The London Gazette* alongside his other despatches on 15 March 1879.

If Isandlwana was a shocking defeat, Rorke's Drift was a memorable victory. The citations for the eleven Victoria Crosses to the men of the 24th Foot, the Royal Engineers, the Army Medical Department, the Commissariat and the Natal Native Contingent were also appended to Lord Chelmsford's despatches and they too are reproduced here. Some of the Victoria Crosses awarded for actions in the Zulu War were not awarded until later in 1879, after the end of the campaign, but, for completeness, the citations for these have also been included. Two of the recipients, Nevill Coghill and Teignmouth Melville, were the first soldiers to receive the Victoria Cross posthumously.

The despatches of Lord Chelmsford have not been edited, added to or truncated in any way. We have not commented on them or attempted to interpret them. That is not the purpose of this book. They are reproduced here just as they were when they were first made public more than 130 years ago, nothing more or less.

The comparatively short duration of the conflict has allowed us to find space to reproduce every one of Lord Chelmsford's despatches, enabling the reader to follow the course of the campaign in detail. The despatches are displayed in the order that they were received in London, however the events referred to in the despatches do not always follow chronologically. This is because there was occasionally some delay in reports being received at Lord Chelmsford's headquarters, made more acute by the poor roads. This is exemplified by the observation of Colonel Wood who, in one of his communications wrote, "It is perhaps needless to state that the track has been termed a road because a few wagons have at some time passed over it."

Though it was Lord Chelmsford who finally defeated the Zulus under their King, Cetshwayo, at the Battle of Ulundi on 4 July 1879, the disaster at Isandlwana had already sealed Chelmsford's fate. General Garnet Wolseley had been sent to replace Chelmsford and it was he that oversaw the capture of Cetshwayo. Though the war was effectively over after the Battle of Ulundi, small bands of Zulus continued to resist until November 1879, when the last of these under Chief Sekuuni was broken up. The Admiralty also published the actions of the Naval Brigade during the conflict. Those despatches are also reproduced here in their original form.

Readers will note that many of the place names are spelt a number of different ways. Isandlwana, for instance is variously spelt Sandhlwana, Isandlana, Isandhlwana, Insalwana, Insilwana and Isandklwana; Gingindhlovo, as another example, is also Gingilovo. Sometimes different spellings are used even in the same despatch. The names of a few individuals also differ. Cetewayo is also Cetywayo, Captain Forster of the Buffs is also Foster. None of these have been changed, nor have any of the obvious spelling mistakes, such as 'presumptous', 'galop', 'Battation', 'reconnaissances', 'were' instead of 'where', and many more. Though we could have corrected these, we have sought to retain not just the content of the original despatches but also the authentic nature of these historically important documents.

The great value of these despatches is that they were written as the events they describe were unfolding, the authors unaware of what would happen next. As Lord Chelmsford himself wrote on 14 April 1879, when discussing the Battle of Hlobane, "the full value of this success is yet to be known," and that is exactly why these despatches are so intriguing.

Martin Mace and John Grehan
Storrington, 2013

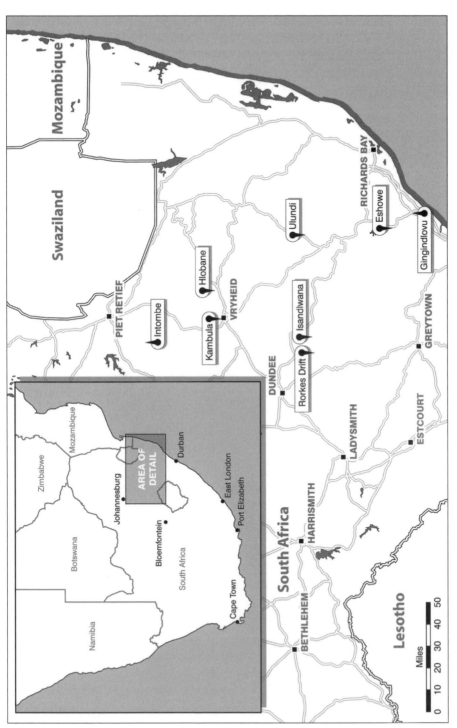

Map of the Battles of the Zulu War.

CHELMSFORD'S DESPATCHES PUBLISHED ON 20 FEBRUARY 1879

The Secretary of State for War has received the following Despatches from Lord Chelmsford, Commanding the Forces in South Africa:-

From the Lieutenant-General Commanding in South Africa
to the Right Honourable the Secretary of State for War.

Head Quarter Camp, Helpmakaar,
9th January, 1879.

SIR,

1. I have the honour to forward for your information the enclosed notification published by His Excellency the High Commissioner, together with a copy of his letter enclosing it to me, by which it will be seen the British Government declares itself in a state of war with the King of the Zulus.

Since the date of my last despatch I have personally visited Durban, the base of supplies and port of disembarkation. Thence I proceeded to the Lower Tugela, inspecting the various posts and troops on that line, the forces of which form the column under Colonel Pearson – this will be known as No. 1 Column. I have not yet received intelligence from that officer as to his movements since the 2nd January, but I instructed him to be deliberate in his movements, as from many reasons it is not desirable to bring on any collision before the full completion of the 30 days allowed Ketchwayo for the acceptance of our demands.

2. I visited the Native Contingent assembled in the neighbourhood of Krantz Kop, under Lieut-Colonel Durnford, R.E. – known as No. 2 Column: That officer reported yesterday that an excellent spirit pervaded his native battalions, which in a few days will be complete in numbers. I had always intended this column to act in a defensive manner until our advance into Zululand was made, and our footing there well established.

From my personal observations in this district (Umainga), and from the information I have received, I have issued orders to this officer to move two regiments of his command to this direction. It would appear that portions of the Zulu forces on the frontier between Rorke's Drift and Kranz Kop have received orders to raid into Natal. This portion of the frontier is a native location, and there is, therefore, a paucity of white persons to assist in its defence. I trust that the presence of portions of No. 2 Column on this part of the border will give confidence to our own natives, and deter such raids being made.

3. Halting one day at Greytown to communicate with His Excellency the High Commissioner, I arrived here on the 4th inst., where the head quarters of Colonel Glyn's column – known as No. 3 – is at present located. I visited the same day the various camps which extend down to Rorke's Drift, where this column will probably cross into Zululand on the 11th inst.

4. On the night of the 6th information came in from Colonel Wood, V.C., C.B., that his column – known as No. 4 – had crossed the Blood River from Utrecht that day, and was at Bemba's Kop (vide Durnford's map). He is aware of the date of advance of No. 3 Column.

5. The weather has been very wet, which has materially increased my difficulties of transport and the passage of stores up to this place.

6. Usirayo, the Zulu Chief before referred to in my despatches, resides opposite Rorke's Drift, and there seems to be every probability that he will attack No. 3 Column on its crossing the Buffalo. I have directed Colonel Wood to co-operate, if possible, with the movements of this column, which will, before a further advance, clear this Chief from the district. Colonel Wood, from whom I have just heard, is about 25 miles from this point; his information confirms my impression that Usirayo will, with all the forces at his disposal, attack No. 3 Column.

7. The disembarkation of the reinforcements is going on satisfactorily at Durban, and if the weather does not impede their movements, I hope before a week is past to have No. 1 Column reinforced by 6 companies of the 99th and a Company of Royal Engineers, and No. 3 Column by three companies of the 1–24th and a company of Royal Engineers; and, later on, five companies of the 2–4th will move to this spot; –Greytown, Pietermaritzburg, Stanger, and Durban being also garrisoned by single companies of Imperial Infantry.

8. Colonel Pearson (No. 1 Column) has been instructed to push on at once to Ekowe, after crossing the border.

I have, &c.
(Signed) CHELMSFORD,
Lieutenant-General.

Government House, Pietermaritzburg,
4th January, 1879.

SIR,

I have the honour to forward the Notification I have felt obliged to issue, declaring a state of war between Her Majesty's Government and the Zulu Xing, consequent on his non-compliance with the demands made on him, urging reparation and redress for violations of British territory.

I have, &c.
(Signed) H.B. FRERE,
Her Majesty's High Commissioner.

His Excellency, Lieut-General Lord Chelmsford, K.C.B.,
Commanding in South Africa.

NOTIFICATION
By His Excellency the High Commissioner.

1. Towards the latter end of July last two large armed bodies of Zulus, retainers of the Chief Sirayo, and led by three of that Chief's sons, and by one of his brothers, entered Natal, and took away by force and violence out of Natal territory two refugee women from two different kraals, one of them belonging to a Border Police Guard of the Magistrate of the Umsinga Division. The women were dragged across the border into Zululand, and there, it is reported, murdered.

2. These two separate acts of outrage were promptly brought to the notice of Cetywayo on the 1st and the 16th August by separate messengers from His Excellency the Lieutenant-Governor of Natal; and explanation, and redress by the surrender of the offenders for trial by the Colonial Courts of Law, were then and afterwards demanded from Cetywayo.

3. In the place of complying with this just demand, Cetywayo replied excusing the outrage as a boyish excess, and offering a sum of money as a solatium for the violation of British territory.

4. This offer of money was declined, with a repetition of the demand for the surrender of the offenders, but they were not surrendered, and on the 11th December a final demand was made on the Zulu King, in the name of the High Commissioner, that the three sons and brother of Sirayo should, be given up for trial, and that a fine of cattle for non-compliance with the demands already made should be paid within twenty days from the date of demand.

5. Those twenty days expired on the 31st December, 1878, and, the demand not having been complied with, the High Commissioner entertains no hope that it is the intention of the Zulu King to afford the redress Her Majesty's Government has a right to demand.

6. It appears clear to the High Commissioner, from Cetywayo's omission to comply with his demands, that the Zulu King's intentions are not friendly to the British Government, nor calculated to ensure the preservation of peace between the Zulus and the subjects of Her Britannic Majesty in South Africa.

7. I therefore hereby make known, for the information of Cetywayo and all the Zulu people, that I have placed the further prosecution of this and all other demands for redress and reparation in the hands of His Excellency Lieutenant-General Lord Chelmsford, Commanding Her Majesty's forces in South Africa, with a request that His Excellency will take such steps as he finds necessary to protect the British territory from further aggression, and to compel the Zulu King to comply with all the demands made on him, whether for satisfaction due to the British Government, or for the greater security of British territory, or for the better and more peaceable government of the Zulu people.

8. Lieutenant-General Lord Chelmsford will carefully notify to all Zulu Chiefs and people who may come within his reach for making such communication, that the demands of the British Government are made on Cetywayo, as much in the interests of the Zulu people as of the English nation, and that till the 11th January, the Lieutenant-General will be willing to receive and to transmit to me any intimation of the unqualified and complete acceptance by Cetywayo of all the terms offered him on the 11th December.

9. If such intimation of unqualified and complete acceptance be received by the Lieutenant-General before the 11th January, no further hostile movements will be made unless they should be rendered necessary by the action of the Zulu forces. Lord Chelmsford will place his own forces in such positions as shall best ensure compliance with all his demands, and up to the 11th January, he will be ready to consider any steps the Zulu King may propose to take for the purpose of giving real and permanent effect to the demands of the British Government.

10. But unless such unqualified and complete acceptance of the terms imposed be intimated to the Lieutenant-General on or before the expiration of the time specified, namely, the close of the 11th of January, the Lieutenant-General will no longer be bound by any of the terms offered on the 11th December for Cetywayo's acceptance, but will take such measures as the forces at his

command will permit for compelling the submission of the Zulu King – always bearing in mind that the British Government has no quarrel with the Zulu nation, and that the future good government and well-being of the Zulus is as much an object of the steps now taken, as the safety and protection of the British territories of Natal and the Transvaal.

11. And I do hereby warn all residents and inhabitants of Her Majesty's Possessions and Colonies in South Africa, of whatever race, to be guided by this my Notification, and I do strictly charge and command all Her Majesty's officers, ministers, and subjects, and all others whom it may concern, to govern themselves, and to act accordingly, and to take due notice of, and to pay due regard to, the tenour hereof.

H.B. FRERE, High-Commissioner.
Pietermaritzburg, Natal,
4th January, 1879.

From the Lieut.-General Commanding in South Africa,
to the Right Honourable the Secretary State for War.

Headquarter Camp, Zululand,
near Rorke's Drift, 14th January, 1879.

SIR,

1. On the 11th January the day after the expiration of the full period for the Zulu King to meet the whole of the demands of Her Majesty's Government – No. 3 Column, under the command of Colonel Glyn, C.B., crossed the Buffalo River into Zululand.

Owing to the very heavy rains, which have been of daily occurrence, the river was much swollen, and the operation was not an easy one. A barrel raft, a pont, and a small boat were used for the passage of the European Infantry and the arms of the mounted men: these latter troops together with the Native Contingent crossed at the ford lower down. The river has been unfordable since the 11th, and had been so for some time previously. On this occasion Captain Hayes of the Native Contingent, behaved in such a gallant manner as to cause my mentioning his name in General Orders, a copy of which I have the honour to enclose. A heavy mist shrouded the crossing of the ford, which was completed, as far as the troops were concerned, by 6.30 a.m.

2. There had been reason at one time to believe in the probability of our being opposed at this point, but from some cause or other the Zulu King appears, at the last moment, to have given instructions not to oppose our advance. It was well known, however, that the Chief Usirayo, whose sons had been demanded by the British Government, had expressed his intention of fighting:

his country lay immediately in our front, and his own kraal was within four miles of the Drift.

3. In the meantime Colonel Wood, V.C., C.B., Commanding No. 4 Column, had been halted at Bemba's Kop since the 6th instant, about 35 miles from Rorke's Drift. I had sent instructions to him to meet me with his mounted men on the 11th, in the direction of the Itelezi Hill, which I calculated would prove to be about halfway. Taking with me the bulk of the mounted men of No. 3 Column, consisting of the Imperial Mounted Infantry, Natal Carabineers, Natal Police, Newcastle Rifles, and Buffalo Border Guard, I rode in that direction. The heavy mist soon after lifted, and we traversed an open, undulating country. At about 15 miles Colonel Wood met us, accompanied by the Frontier Light Horse and some natives, mounted and foot, called 'Wood's Irregulars.' He had marched the day previously 12 miles, and moved a portion of his force on the 11th in my direction, thinking the first reports might not prove groundless, viz., that a strong Zulu force would attack Colonel Glyn's (No. 3) Column as it crossed.

4. I was completely satisfied with the account Colonel Wood gave me of the efficiency of his column with respect to its transport and commissariat arrangements, and its ability to move forward at once. I attribute the satisfactory state of this column to Colonel Wood's energy and military knowledge.

5. Colonel Wood returned to his camp the same day. I have not heard since from him, but I sent him an express yesterday, the 13th. I returned the same day to the camp of No. 3 Column, which is pitched on the rising ground on the left bank of the Buffalo River. Several hundred head of cattle, &c., were taken by Nos. 3 and 4 Columns on thy 11th: this I considered desirable on political grounds, as they all belonged to Usirayo, as well as from military necessities.

6. Lieut.-Colonel Durnford, R.E., commanding No. 2 Column, met me on my return to camp, as he wished personally to report on certain matters connected with his command. He informed me the country in his front was quite quiet – the women and old people in their kraals, but the army with the King. This information is confirmed up to date. I directed this officer to move one of his three battalions to watch, and eventually cross at, the gates of Natal, between Rorke's Drift and the Umsinga Mountain, while he and the mounted men and Rocket Battery were to join me with No. 3 Column. I directed the remaining two battalions to cross at Middledrift, as soon as Colonel Pearson with No. 1 Column had reached Ekowe.

7. No. 1 Column, under Colonel Pearson, was to have commenced crossing on the 12th, at 4.30 a.m. The wet weather had seriously delayed the arrival of stores, but from reports received last night, I have reason to hope anxiety on this head is for the present at an end. The Tugela, had been in very heavy flood, and the difficulties in crossing thereby were seriously increased. Colonel Pearson states that a hawser with anchor was carried away during the night of the 8th instant, down the stream from where it had been deeply buried in the opposite bank, it required 500 men to haul it back by main force. In laying it across again I regret to say a seaman of the 'Active' (name not forwarded in report) was drowned; a boat's crew nearly shared the same fate, and Lieut. Craigie of the 'Active' having been sucked down by the current under the pont which had turned nearly over, was rescued by a Krooman. Small parties of armed Zulus came within range of No. 1 Column, but no act of hostility on their part had taken place up to date of last report (11th January).

8. Very great difficulty has been experienced from the same causes as have delayed the arrival of supplies with No.1 Column, in bringing up stores to No. 3 Column; and it cannot be permitted to move forward until one month's supplies are stored on the right bank of the Buffalo, in addition to the 15 days' supply with the Column itself. Between this Camp and Greytown alone, a distance of some 70 miles, three rivers are now impassable, and waggons have to be crossed by ferries – a laborious operation, requiring more skilled labour than we at present have available. The road at various points requires the most constant supervision, as in some parts the heavy rain frequently dislodges huge boulders from the hill sides overhanging the roadway, and in many places water-courses become torrents after an hour's rain. Beyond this camp towards Isepesi Hill (my first objective point) the road will require great labour to make it passable, but strong working parties had already been at work. The transport difficulties are augmented by the great mortality in oxen: this is inevitable, but it will probably decrease in a few weeks time.

9. The welcome reinforcements are all on their way, but I feel constrained to say that had the Commissariat and Transport Services been strengthened during the period of preparation we should not be so much delayed during that of execution. I have, however, only referred to those difficulties for the purpose of explaining the reasons for a very probable slow advance, which, otherwise, might not be understood, for it must be remembered that nothing but cattle can be obtained from the country itself.

10. On the day following the crossing of the 3rd Column at Rorke's Drift, I directed Col. Glyn, C.B., to make a reconnaissance with the mounted men in

the direction of Isepesi Hill, while the valley of the Bashee was to be traversed by a portion of the Infantry. The troops left camp at daylight, and on reaching the Bashee the mounted scouts reported that armed Zulus were observed leaving the kraals, driving cattle up under the precipices. I should observe that the Chief is himself with the King – that one of his sons, with 15 led horses, had been seen leaving this country by a party from Col. Wood's force several days ago. As, however, it was well known that we had made a distinct demand for the punishment of the sons of this Chief, and that his clan was one of the bravest and most warlike of the Zulu nation, I considered it very desirable to punish them at once by capturing their cattle. Accordingly, Col. Glyn directed three companies, 1–24th Regt. and the 1–3rd Regt., Natal Native Contingent, to advance and capture the cattle, while Lieut.-Col. Russell, 12th Lancers, in command of the mounted portion of the force, was directed to continue along the waggon track to the high ground above. By 8.30 a.m. the precipitous sides of the Ugudu Mountain were occupied by the Infantry, when fire was opened upon them by the Zulus, who were occupying very strong positions in the caves and rocks above. A fight ensued, which lasted for about half an hour. The mountain side was cleared, the cattle and horses were captured; the Zulus left behind to defend the cattle made, however, a stubborn resistance, and 10 dead bodies were counted in the rocks, and 9 prisoners taken, three of whom were wounded. This, however, probably does not represent their total loss: one man severely wounded was found yesterday and brought in. In the meantime, before the mounted men had quite reached the higher terrace of the mountain, they were fired upon by a force of Zulus concealed by rocks. These were attacked and dispersed with the loss of 16 found killed, among whom, it is said, was a son of Usirayo, Umkumbi-ka-Zulu. It is stated by a prisoner that another of the Chiefs sons was also killed on this occasion, but it has not been verified.

I have the pleasure of reporting that the behaviour of the Natal Native Contingent was on this occasion all that could be desired, and by their list of casualties it will be seen that they did not shrink from closing on the enemy.

I beg to enclose a detailed list of casualties. The cattle captured by this force up to date is 413 cattle, 235 sheep, 332 goats, and several horses. The division of such booty will be made agreeably to the Regulations sanctioned by His Excellency the High Commissioner, and reported by him for the sanction of Her Majesty.

I have, &c.,
(Signed) CHELMSFORD,
Lieutenant-General.

COPY OF GENERAL ORDER.

The Lieut.-General Commanding has received with the greatest satisfaction a report from the Lieut.-Colonel Commanding Mounted Corps, No. 3 Column, giving an account of the gallant conduct of Captain Hayes, 3rd Regiment N. N. Contingent. On the 11th instant this officer, at the risk of his own life, saved that of Private Price of the Imperial Mounted Infantry, who, when crossing the Buffalo River was, with his horse swept away by the rapid current, and would have been drowned had it not been for the gallantry, coolness, and determination of Captain Hayes.

The Lieut.-General has much pleasure in thus publicly bringing to notice this courageous act which reflects the highest credit on the officer concerned.

15th Jan., 1879.

Return of Losses inflicted on the Enemy by the Forces
quoted since the 10th January.

12th January, Bashee Valley, Ngudu Mountain, No. 3 Column, Mounted Corps, 1–24th Regiment, 1–3rd Regiment Native Contingent, 2–3rd Regiment Native Contingent; 30 killed, 4 wounded, 10 prisoners. Stock captured, 13 horses, 413 cattle, 332 goats, and 235 sheep.

The above is taken from certified returns received from the forces engaged.

(Signed) JOHN NORTH CREALOCK,
Lieut.-Colonel,
Assistant Military Secretary.
Head Quarter Camp,

15th Jan., 1879.

Return of Casualties in Column No. 3, under Colonel Glyn, C.B.,
in the affair at the Ngudu Mountain, on the 12th January, 1879.

1–3rd Regiment Natal Native Contingent. – 2 natives killed; Lieutenant Thomas Purvis, severely wounded; Corporal Jessy Major, slightly wounded; natives, 6 severely wounded, 6 slightly wounded. – Total wounded, 14.

The above has been compiled from certified returns forwarded by the Army Medical Department, and Officer Commanding Regiment.

(Signed) J. NORTH CREALOCK,
Lieut.-Colonel,
Assist. Military Secretary.
Head Quarter Camp, Zululand.,
15th Jan. 1879.

CHELMSFORD'S DESPATCHES PUBLISHED ON 1 MARCH 1879

War Office, 1st March, 1879.
The Secretary of State for War has received the following Despatch from Lord Chelmsford, K.C.B., Commanding the Forces in South Africa:-

From Lieutenant-General Lord Chelmsford, K.C.B.,
to the Right Honourable the Secretary of State for War.

Pietermaritzburg, Natal,
27th January, 1879.

SIR,

The Telegram I sent you to-day will have conveyed the sad intelligence of the misfortune which has occurred to a portion of the force under my command.

The Court of Inquiry which is about to assemble to collect sufficient evidence to explain what at present appears to me almost incomprehensible; but, from the account of the few who escaped, I am able to give you a narrative which, though perhaps not absolutely accurate as to facts, will convey to you a fair idea of the events of that melancholy day. On the 20th January, No. 3 Column, under Colonel Glyn, broke up from its camp on the left bank of the Buffalo River, and marched about ten miles along the wagon track which leads from Rorke's Drift to the Indeni Forest, and encamped with its back to an isolated, precipitous-sided hill of peculiar appearance, called Insalwana.

On the 20th, I myself made a reconnaissance about ten miles farther on the same wagon track, which skirts the Inhlazatye Mountain as far as a place called Matyana's stronghold – a deep valley, full of caves, with three precipitous sides, over one of which a small river falls, and, flowing along its bottom, enters the Buffalo River at a distance of about twelve or fifteen miles.

Not having time to properly examine the country round this peculiar stronghold, into which I had been told the enemy would very probably retire, I ordered that the next day two separate parties should move out from camp at an early hour, and bring me back a full description of it.

One, under Major Dartnell, consisting of the Mounted Police and Volunteers of which he is commandant, took the same road that I had taken, whilst another, consisting of two battalions Native Contingent under Commandant Lonsdale, worked round a flat-topped mountain, called Malakata, which is the southern part of the Inhlazatye range. The orders given to the commanders of these two parties were that they were to effect a communication along the open ground on the Inhlazatye range, and then return to camp with the information they had been able to obtain. At about 3 P.M. one of my own staff officers, who had accompanied Major Dartnell, returned to camp and reported that the latter had been unable to effect a complete reconnaisance of the country beyond the small river alluded to, as he had found it occupied by the enemy in some force, that he had called up the two Battalions Native Contingent, and that if I sent him three companies of British Infantry to give them confidence he would be able to attack. I did not consider it advisable to comply with this request as the day was far advanced and the distance great. Biscuit was sent out to the force which bivouacked on the northern edge of the Inhlazatye range. At 2.30 A.M. on the 22nd January, Colonel Glyn, having received a despatch from Major Dartnell, saying that the enemy was in great force in front of him, sent his senior staff officer to enquire what I would wish done.

Feeling that the position was rather critical, I ordered Colonel Glyn to move to his assistance with all the available men of the 2nd Battalion 24th Regiment, consisting of six companies, and also to take four guns and the Mounted Infantry.

An express was sent off to Lieutenant-Colonel Durnford, Royal Engineers, who was at Rorke's Drift with 500 natives, half of whom were mounted and armed with breech-loaders, to move up to strengthen the force which were left to guard the camp.

The strength of this force was as follows:-

Royal Artillery, 2 officers, 78 men, 2 guns.
Two Rocket Tubes, 1 officer, 10 men (Lieutenant-Colonel Durnford's force).
First Battalion 24th Regiment, 15 officers, 334 men.
Second Battalion 24th Regiment, 5 officers, 90 men.
Mounted European Corps, 5 officers, 204 men.
Natal Native Contingent, 19 officers, 391 men.
Natal Pioneers, 1 officer, 10 men.
Lieutenant-Colonel Durnford's force, 18 officers, 450 men.
Total Natives, 851 men.
Total Europeans (including officers), 772.

Lieutenant-Colonel Pulleine, 1st Battalion 24th Regiment, was left in charge of the camp, and received strict instructions that he was left there to defend it.

The reinforcement under Colonel Glyn moved off at day-break, and I accompanied it, pressing forward with a small escort of the Mounted Infantry. I reached Major Dartnell about 6.30 A.M., and at once ordered him to send out his mounted men to gain intelligence of the enemy, whose whereabouts did not appear to be very certain.

The enemy shortly after showed in considerable strength on some heights opposite to the Inhlazatye range, but at some distance, and appeared to be advancing to take possession of a projecting spur which ran out into the plain beneath, and completely commanded it.

I at once ordered the two battalions Native Contingent to move across and occupy the spur in question, and sent word to Colonel Glyn to move with the guns and 2nd Battalion 24th Regiment up a valley which lay to the left of the spur in question.

The Mounted Infantry looked after the left flank, and the Mounted Police and Volunteers guarded the right.

A general advance was then made, and the enemy retired without firing; on the extreme right, however, the Natal Carabineers, under Captain Shepstone, managed to cut off about 300, who took refuge on a difficult hill and in some caves. These were finally dislodged with the assistance of some of the Native Contingents, and fifty were killed.

The main force of the enemy retired to Isipisi Hill, which was about six miles off, on their flanks being threatened by the advance of the Mounted Corps.

Whilst these operations were going on, Colonel Glyn received, about 9 A.M., a short note from Lieutenant-Colonel Pulleine, saying that firing was heard to the left front of the camp, but giving no further particulars.

I sent Lieutenant Milne, R.N., my A.D.C., at once to the top of a high hill from which the camp could be seen, and he remained there for at least an hour with a very powerful telescope, but could detect nothing unusual in that direction.

Having no cause, therefore, to feel any anxiety about the safety of the camp, I ordered Lieutenant-Colonel Russell to make a sweep round with the Mounted Infantry to the main wagon track, whilst a portion of the Infantry went over the hill top to the same point, and the guns with an escort retraced their steps.

I, myself, proceeded with Colonel Glyn to fix upon a site for our new camp, which I had determined to shift the next day to ground near the Mangeni River, which runs into Matyana's stronghold.

One battalion of the Native Contingent was ordered to march back to camp across country, and to examine en route the different deep dongas, or water cuttings, which intersect the plain, and which might very possibly conceal some of the enemy.

Having fixed upon the situation for the camp, and having ordered the troops then on the ground to bivouac there that night, I started to return to camp with the Mounted Infantry under Lieutenant-Colonel Russell as my escort, when within about six miles of the camp I found the 1st Battalion Native Contingent halted, and shortly after Commandant Lonsdale rode up to report that he had ridden into camp, and found it in possession of the Zulus.

I at once sent word to Colonel Glyn to bring back all the troops, and I myself advanced with the Mounted Infantry and the Native Contingent battalion for about two miles, when I halted to wait the arrival of the rest of the force.

Lieutenant-Colonel Russell went forward to reconnoitre the camp, and fully confirmed all that Commandant Lonsdale had reported.

On the arrival of Colonel Glyn and his force, I at once formed them up into fighting order; guns in the centre, on the road with three companies; 2nd Battalion 24th Regiment on each flanks in fours: Native Contingent battalions, one on each flank of the 2nd Battalion 24th Regiment in line, Europeans and natives, armed with guns, forming a third rank in front: Mounted Infantry on the extreme right Natal Mounted Volunteers on the extreme left, Mounted Police in reserve.

We advanced in this order across the plain with great speed and in excellent order, but could not reach the neighbourhood of our camp until after dark.

The Artillery came into action on the road, and shelled the crest of the narrow neck over which our line of retreat lay, whilst the left wing under Major Black, 2nd Battalion 24th Regiment, moved forward to seize a small stony hill on the left of this neck, the occupation of which would secure our left flank.

Major Black seized the position without opposition, and the right wing then advanced and occupied the neck in question, the right flank being protected by the precipitous sides of the Insilwana Hill.

The whole force lay down amidst the debris of the plundered camp and the corpses of dead men, horses, and oxen fully expecting to be attacked in front, and most probably in rear also.

A few alarms occurred during the night, but it passed, however, without a shot being fired at us.

At early dawn the following morning I ordered the troops to move off with all speed to Rorke's Drift, about which post I was in some anxiety.

The troops had no spare ammunition and only a few biscuits, a large portion of them had had no other food for 48 hours. All had marched at least 30 miles the day before, and had passed an almost sleepless night on the stony ground. No one, therefore, was fit for any prolonged exertion, and it was certain that daylight would reveal a sight which could not but have a demoralizing effect upon the whole force.

I determined, therefore, to reach our nearest supply depôt at Rorke's Drift, as quickly as possible, and, as I have already said, moved off before it was fairly light.

On sighting the post at Rorke's Drift, heavy smoke was seen to be rising from the house, and the Zulus were seen retiring from it.

It appeared as if our supplies at that post were lost to us, and I felt that those at Helpmakaar, some 12 miles further off, must have shared the same fate.

To our intense relief, however, on nearing the Buffalo River the waving of hats was seen from the inside of a hastily erected entrenchment, and information soon reached me that the gallant garrison of this post, some 60 of the 2nd Battalion 24th Regiment, under Lieutenant Bromhead, and a few Volunteers and Departmental Officers, the whole under Lieutenant Chard, R.E., had for 12 hours made the most gallant resistance I have ever heard of against the determined attacks of some 3,000 Zulus, 370 of whose dead bodies surrounded the post.

The loss of the garrison was 13 killed and 9 wounded.

On reaching Rorke's Drift, I, for the first time, heard some particulars of the attack upon the Insalwana Camp, and am thus able to furnish the following narrative, the absolute accuracy of which, however, I cannot vouch for:-

Shortly before the arrival of Lieutenant-Colonel Durnford in camp with his 450 natives, information had reached Lieutenant-Colonel Pulleine from the left picquets that a number of Zulus had been seen on that flank.

On receiving this information, Lieutenant-Colonel Durnford asked Lieutenant-Colonel Pulleine to give him two companies of British Infantry, in order that he might move up the heights on the left and attack them. Lieutenant-Colonel Pulleine at once stated that his orders were to defend the camp, and that without a positive order he could not allow the companies to leave.

Lieutenant-Colonel Durnford then took his 450 natives up the heights, and went, so far as I can learn, about five miles from camp, when he found himself in front of a very large army of Zulus.

He at once sent back word to Lieutenant-Colonel Pulleine, and with his Mounted Basutos retired slowly before the Zulus, who advanced to attack him.

The Mounted Basutos, I hear from many quarters, behaved remarkably well, and delayed the advance for a considerable time.

Their ammunition, however, began to run short and they were at last obliged to retire quickly on the camp.

Being unable to find a fresh supply of ammunition, it appears they disbanded themselves and made the best of their way to the Buffalo, where they swam the river and recrossed into Natal, assisting, however, as far as they could, many of our fugitives from the camp to escape.

As regards the proceedings of the six companies British Infantry, two guns, and two rocket tubes, the garrison of the camp, I can obtain but little information.

One company went off to the extreme left and has never been heard off since, and the other five, I understand, engaged the enemy about a mile to the left front of the camp, and made there a most stubborn and gallant resistance.

So long as they kept their faces to the enemy the Zulus were, I am told, quite unable to drive them back, and fell in heaps before the deadly fire poured into them.

An officer who visited this part of the field of battle on the following morning reported that the loss of the Zulus in killed could not be less than 2,000.

When, however, the Zulus got round the left flank of these brave men they appear to have lost their presence of mind, and to have retired hastily through the tents which had never been struck

Immediately the whole Zulu force surrounded them, they were overpowered by numbers, and the camp was lost.

Those who were mounted, ran the gauntlet and some small portion managed to reach the river, which, however, at the point of crossing was deep and rapid.

Many were shot or assegaied, and many were swept away by the current, and it is presumed have been drowned.

Had the force in question but taken up a defensive position in the camp itself, and utilized there the materials for a hasty entrenchment which lay near to hand, I feel absolutely confident, that the whole Zulu army would not have been able to dislodge them.

It appears that the oxen were yoked to the wagons three hours before the attack took place, so that there was ample time to construct that wagon laager which the Dutch in former days understood so well.

Had, however, even the tents been struck and the British troops placed with their backs to the precipitous Insalwana Hill, I feel sure that they could have made a successful resistance.

Rumours reached me, however, that the troops were deceived by a simulated retreat, and in their eagerness to close with the enemy allowed themselves to be drawn away from their line of defence.

Our actual loss cannot as yet be correctly ascertained, but I fear that it cannot be less than 30 officers and about 500 non-commissioned officers, rank and file, belonging to the Imperial troops, and 21 officers and 70 non-commissioned officers, rank and file of the Colonial forces.

The effect of this disaster throughout the Colony has already shown itself, and the European colonists generally are in great alarm.

The result of this has been to produce a similar effect upon the native mind, and our Native Contingents are beginning to lose heavily by desertion.

This will, I trust, be checked with a firm hand by the Natal Government, as the natives were ordered out by their supreme chief, the Lieutenant-Governor of Natal, and have no right to leave their corps until released by his order.

The fact remains, however, that the Natal native allies are no longer to be depended upon, and additional British reinforcements must be sent out if the operations against the Zulus are to be carried to a successful issue.

The country is far more difficult than I had been led to expect, and the labour of advancing with a long train of wagons is enormous.

It took seven days hard work, by one half of No. 3 Column, to make the ten miles of road between Rorke's Drift and Insalwana Hill practicable, and even then had it rained hard I feel sure that the convoy could not have got on.

The line of communication is very much exposed, and would require a party of mounted men always patrolling, and fixed intrenched posts of infantry at intervals of about ten miles.

Under these circumstances I feel obliged to ask for the following reinforcements, viz.:- three British Infantry Regiments, two Cavalry Regiments, and one Company Royal Engineers.

The cavalry must be prepared to act as mounted infantry, and should have their swords fastened to their saddles, and their carbines slung, muzzle downwards, by a strap across the shoulder. The swords should, if possible, be somewhat shorter than the present regulation pattern.

At least 100 artillerymen, with farrier, shoeing smith, and collar maker, must be sent out at once to replace casualties in N-5th, Lieutenant-Colonel Harness' Battery. A dozen farriers or good shoeing smiths are urgently required for the several columns, and two additional veterinary surgeons for depôt duty would be very valuable.

If the reinforcements asked for are sent out at once they will arrive at the most favourable time for campaigning, namely, at the end of the rainy season.

I have, &c.,
(Signed) CHELMSFORD,
Lieutenant-General.

CHELMSFORD'S DESPATCHES PUBLISHED ON 5 MARCH 1879

War Office, 5th March, 1879.

The following Despatch has been received by the Secretary of State for War from Lieutenant-General Lord Chelmsford, K.C.B., Commanding the Forces in South Africa:-

From Lieutenant-General Lord Chelmsford, K.C.B.,
to the Right Honourable the Secretary of State for War.

Pietermaritzburg, Natal,
3rd February, 1879.

SIR,

1. Since the date of my last Despatch, I have received a copy of Colonel Pearson's report (No. 1 Column) on the occurrences of the 23rd January, when he defeated the Zulu forces with a loss of 300 killed. This report, addressed to his Excellency the High Commissioner, has been published for the information of the Colony, a copy of it I have the honour to enclose (marked A), likewise that furnished me by Admiral Sullivan from Captain Campbell. R.N., commanding Naval Brigade, with No. 1 Column (A A).

2. Colonel Wood (No. 4 Column), on the 24th January, dispersed the force of Zulus, with a loss of 50 men killed, that had been ordered to attack him. (Copy of his report attached, marked B).

News of the events of the 22nd ultimo had been conveyed to Colonel Wood at Utrecht, with great readiness, by Captain Allan Gardner, 14th Hussars. This officer had escaped from the camp of No. 3 Column, after conveying orders to the officer commanding there, from Colonel Glyn, C.B., 12 miles distant. Colonel Wood, in consequence took up a position covering Utrecht.

3. On my arrival here, I at once directed Colonel Pearson to act as seemed best, without reference to my previous instructions.

A copy of my telegram and his reply I forward marked B B.

4. The Zulus have, since the 24th ultimo, shown no signs of activity, and everything is quiet along the border.

I have no means of forming an opinion as to the reason of this. It is confidently stated by some that it is only preparatory to further energetic action; others again, who claim to be well-informed from native sources, declare that the losses inflicted on the Zulus at Isandhlwana alone were so enormous, as to make them disinclined to attack us again, unless they are fully assured they have an advantage.

It must be remembered that since our crossing the frontier, the Zulus have been five times defeated, and always with loss.

5. I append a return, showing the distribution of the forces under my command (marked C).

6. Colonel Pearson seems fully assured of his ability to hold his own against any number of Zulus. He has 1,200 British troops, with about 320 rounds per rifle and provisions for two months.

Major Barrow, 19th Hussars, reports well of the position of the post and its healthiness. The water is close to and under fire of the fort, and is very good.

The road to Ekowe from the Lower Tugela is reported by the same officer to be a good one, and with two exceptions the country is open.

I, therefore, feel that with the force within reach of him at the Lower Tugela, Colonel Pearson is authorised to hold his present position. I proceed to-morrow to that place, when I shall be better able to form an opinion as to the steps to be taken to organize the detachments at the Lower Tugela.

7. Of the seven battalions of Native Contingent, all but three have disbanded themselves; these three have not been engaged. The conduct of the two battalions under Commandant Lonsdale with No. 3 Column, up to the day following the disaster to the camp, was all that I could wish; those, however, who knew the natives foresaw that they would break up after hearing of the death of their chiefs (who had remained in camp on the 22nd ult.). I cannot, therefore, count on retaining the services of any Native Contingent with the columns across the border, beyond those of some two or three hundred mounted men. I am still in hopes, however, that the authority of the Colonial Government, will be asserted, and will prove sufficient to fill up these battalions, the officers and non-commissioned officers of which are still on the frontier, where they will be available for frontier defence at least.

8. Such is the position of affairs in the Colony. Every effort will be made to procure reinforcements.

Captain Buller, Rifle Brigade, one of my Aides-de-Camp, has started for the Free State with a letter to the President from H.E. the High Commissioner, with the view of procuring mounted men, both white and black. A force of 200 mounted men is already being raised at Port Elizabeth, and a draft of 50 mounted men from the Capo Colony for the Frontier Light Horse, arrived yesterday.

9. Mr. Sprigg, the Colonial Secretary, Cape Colony, has shown every desire to assist us at this emergency; he despatched at once the three Companies of the 2nd Battalion 4th Regiment from Cape Town, they have arrived at Durban and are on their march here. The head quarters and 4 companies of the 88th Regiment will shortly arrive from King William's Town, their place being taken by Volunteers.

10. Every effort will be made to reinforce Colonel Wood's Column, in view of enabling him to resume active operations from that side.

11. The refitting No. 3 Column will, of necessity, take some little time, as the road (160 miles) from this to Helpmakaar is very much cut up by the rains.

12. I have not yet received from Colonel Hassard, C.B., C.R.E., the proceedings of the Court of Enquiry ordered to assemble regarding the loss of the camp on the 22nd ultimo; neither have I received from Colonel Glyn, C.B., Commanding No. 3 Column, an official list of the casualties on that occasion.

I regret also to state that I am still without an official report from Colonel Glyn of the details of the gallant defence made on the 22nd and 23rd ultimo by the Company 2nd Battalion 24th Regiment of the post at Rorke's Drift.

> I have, &c.,
> (Signed) CHELMSFORD,
> Lieutenant-General.

Enclosure A.
THE ACTION AT INYEZANE.
COLONEL PEARSON'S OFFICIAL REPORT.

From Colonel Pearson, Commanding No. 1 Column to the Military Secretary to His Excellency the High Commissioner.

> Etshowe, Zululand,
> 23rd January, 1879.

SIR,

I have the honour to report my arrival here at 10 A.M. this day, with the column under my command, and, I am happy to state, without a casualty of any kind – except, of course, those which occurred in the engagement of yesterday, of which I have already duly informed you by telegram, despatched yesterday evening.

Yesterday morning, the mounted troops which preceded the column under Major Barrow, had crossed the Inyezane River – which is about four miles from our camping ground on the previous night – when I received a note from him to say that he had selected a fairly open space for a halting place, which he had carefully vedetted. I at once rode forward to reconnoitre, and found the ground covered with more bush than seemed desirable for an outspan; but as there was no water between the Inyezane and the places where we bivouacked last night – four miles further on, and with several steep hills to climb – I decided upon outspanning for a couple of hours, to feed and rest the oxen, and to enable the men to breakfast.

It was then just eight o'clock, and I was in the act of giving directions about the pickets and scouts required for our protection, and the wagons had already begun to park, when the leading company of the Native Contingent, who were scouting in front – personally directed by Captain Hart, Staff Officer to the Officer commanding that Regiment – discovered the enemy advancing rapidly over the ridges in our front, and making for the clumps of bush around us.

The Zulus at once opened a heavy fire upon the men of the company who had shown themselves in the open, and they lost one officer, four non-commissioned officers, and three men killed, almost immediately after the firing began.

Unfortunately, owing to scarcely any of the officers or non-commissioned officers of the Native Contingent being able to speak Kafir, and some not even English (there are several foreigners among them), it has been found most difficult to communicate orders, and it is to be feared that these men who lost their lives by gallantly holding their ground did so under the impression that it was the duty of the contingent to fight in the first line, instead of scouting only, and, after an engagement, to pursue.

I must add, however, that every exertion has been made by Major Graves, Commandant Nettleton, and Captain Hart, to explain to both the officers and men the duties expected of them. These officers, indeed, have been indefatigable in their exertions.

As soon as the firing commenced, I directed the Naval Brigade, under Commander Campbell, Lieutenant Lloyd's division of guns, and Captain Jackson's and Lieutenant Martin's companies of the Buffs, to take up a position on a knoll close by the road (and under which they were halted), and from whence the whole of the Zulu advances could be seen and dealt with.

Meanwhile, the wagons continued to park, and as soon as the length of the column had thereby sufficiently decreased, I directed the two companies of the Buffs, which were guarding the wagons about half way down the column, to clear the enemy out of the bush, which had been already shelled, and fired into with rockets and musketry by the troops on the knoll above-mentioned. These companies, led by Captains Harrison and Wyld, and guided by Captain

Macgregor, D.A.Q.M.G., whom I sent back for this purpose, moved out in excellent order, and quickly getting into skirmishing order, brought their right shoulders gradually forward, and drove the Zulus before them back into the open, which again exposed them to the rockets, shells, and musketry from the knoll.

This movement released the main body of the Mounted Infantry and Volunteers, who, with the Company of Royal Engineers, had remained near the Inyezane, to protect that portion of the convoy of wagons. The Royal Engineers happened to be working at the drift when the engagement began.

When thus released, both the Engineers and Mounted Troops, under Captain Wynne and Major Barrow, respectively moved forward with the infantry. Skirmishers on the left of the latter, the whole being supported by a half-company of the Buffs and a half-company of the 99th Regiment, sent out by Lieutenant-Colonel Welman, 99th Regiment, who, with the rear of the column, was now coming up.

About this time the enemy was observed by Commander Campbell to be trying to outflank our left, and he offered to go with a portion of the Naval Brigade to drive away a body of Zulus who had got possession of a kraal about 400 yards from the knoll, and which was helping their turning movement. The Naval Brigade was supported by a party of the officers and non-commissioned officers of the Native Contingent, under Captain Hart, who were posted on high ground on the left of the Etshowe Road, and who checked the Zulus from making any further attempt on our left.

Shortly afterwards, when the kraal was evacuated, Commander Campbell suggested that the enemy should be driven off still further, to which I at once assented, and I desired Colonel Parnell take Captain Forster's company, the Buffs, which up to this time had remained at the foot of the knoll, and assist the Naval Brigade to attack some heights beyond the kraal, upon which a considerable body of Zulus were still posted. The action was completely successful, and the Zulus now fled in all directions, both from our front and left, and before the skirmishers on the right.

I now ordered the column to be reformed, and at noon we resumed our march, and bivouacked for the night on the ground described in the first part of my letter.

The last shot I fired was about half-past 9 A.M.

I enclose a list of the killed and wounded, and, in addition, I beg to state that both Colonel Parnell and myself had our horses shot under us.

The loss of the enemy I can, of course, only approximately give. By all accounts, however – and I have taken every pains to verify and confirm the statements made – upwards of 300 Zulus were killed. The wounded, if there were any, were either carried off or hid in the bush, as only two were found.

The dead were lying about in heaps of seven and eight, and in one place ten dead bodies were found close together. At another 35 were counted within a very small space.

As far as I can ascertain, the numbers opposed to us were about 4,000, composed of the Umxapu, Umdhlanefu, and the Ingulubi Regiments, and some 650 men of the district.

I had already been warned, through Mr. Fynney, Border Agent, and other sources, that I might expect to be attacked at any moment after crossing the Umsindusi River, but the number of Zulus stated to be in the neighbourhood was estimated at about 8,000.

All the commanding officers speak highly of the behaviour of their men during the engagement, and of the coolness of the officers and the pains taken by them to control the expenditure of ammunition. This I can personally vouch for as regards troops on the knoll, as I was present with them the whole time. The practice made by Lieutenant Loyd's guns, and by the rockets of the Naval Brigade, directed by Mr. Cotter, boatswain of H.M.S. 'Active,' was excellent, and no doubt contributed materially to the success of the day.

Major Barrow particularly wishes me to mention the steadiness and good conduct under fire of the Natal Mounted Volunteer Corps. Those engaged were the Victoria and Stanger Mounted Rifles and the Natal Hussars.

Of the commanding officers themselves I have already spoken.

From the officers of my staff, Colonel Walker C.B., Captain MacGregor, and Lieutenant Knight, the Buffs, – my orderly officer – I have received every assistance, not only during yesterday's engagement, but ever since they joined me.

I cannot speak too highly of the energy and attention to their duties of Staff-Surgeon Norbury, R.N., my Senior Medical Officer, and his assistants. The field hospital was established in a convenient place, almost immediately after the firing began, and the wounded received every attention.

Lastly, I wish to report the good example shown to the Native Pioneers by Captain Beddoes and Lieutenant Porrington, who, throughout our march, under the direction of Lieutenant Main, R.E., repaired our road in front, and during the engagement remained on the knoll, fighting rifle in hand.

I must apologise for the great length of this letter; but as the present is the first campaign of British troops against the Zulus, and as the Natal natives were being tested as soldiers for the first time, I have purposely gone into details. Should we again be engaged with the enemy there will, of course, be no further necessity for describing everything so minutely.

To-morrow morning I propose sending two companies of the Buffs, two companies of the Native Contingent, and a small number of mounted men, to reinforce Lieutenant-Colonel Ely, 99th Regiment, who, with three companies of his regiment, left behind for the purpose, is now on his way to Etshowe, with a convoy of 60 commissariat wagons.

I have written to request Colonel Ely not to advance beyond the Umsindusi till reinforced.

On Saturday, Major Coates starts for the Tugela with 50 empty wagons, escorted by four companies infantry, two native companies, and a few troopers to bring up more stores.

I enclose a couple of sketches of the ground on which the engagement took place, made by Captain McGregor and Lieutenant Knight, from memory [*not enclosed*].

I have the honour to be, Sir,
Your most obedient servant,
C.K. PEARSON,
Colonel.

(Enclosure A A.)

'Active,' off Natal,
30th January, 1879.

MY LORD,

I have the honour to forward herewith a copy of the official report from Commander Campbell, Naval Brigade, of the action on 22nd instant for your information.

I have, &c,
(Signed) P.W. SULLIVAN,
Commodore.

Lieutenant-General, The Lord Chelmsford, K.C.B.,
Commanding Forces.

Naval Brigade, Ekowe,
24th January, 1879.

SIR,

I have to acquaint you with the distribution of the Naval Brigade at this moment.

A and B Companies 'Active,' encamped here with 1st Division of No. 1 Column, also Gatling gun and crew, also rockets and their crews, also Royal Marines.

The above march in 1st Division 1st Column, A and B Companies, in front with rockets, Marines and Gatling in rear, while marching three to four miles separate the front and rear of 1st Division, the interval being filled with wagons and other troops.

2. Sub-Lieutenant Heugh, with two 7-pr. Guns and their crews are attached to the rear of the 2nd Division of No. 1 Column, they are here but occupy a different position.

3. The men of 'Tenedos' except one who is attached to the 'Active's' men, are stationed at Lower Tugela.

4. Staff-Surgeon Norbury, is Principal Medical Officer of the Column, and with Surgeon Thompson, 1 sick berth steward, 1 attendant, and 1 marine servant, are attached to the Field Hospital, the sick of the Naval Brigade are treated by them, as well as I believe the greater part of the 1st Division of the Column, they are encamped here.

Order of March for 1st Division of 1st Column generally preserved from Tugela to Ekowe.

Cavalry.
Detachment Royal Engineers.
1 cart.
Half Company Natal Native Pioneers.
1 cart.
2 Companies Buffs.
Royal Artillery.
2 guns.
2 Companies Buffs.
H and B Companies Naval Brigade, with
    2 24-pr. rockets and crews.
Company Royal Engineers.
Wagons.
Rear Guard.
3 Companies Native Contingent.
Gatling and Crew.
Royal Marines.
2 Companies Buffs.

Left flank: Cavalry. Company Native Contingent. Company of Buffs. Company Native Contingent.

Right flank: Company Native Contingent. Company of Buffs. Company Native Contingent.

5. The 1st Division of the Column marched from the Tugela at 6 A.M. of 18th January, camping that night at Inyoni River.

The 2nd Division was ordered to march at same time the following morning.

On the afternoon of 19th the 1st Division camped north of Umsimdusi River, and was joined there by the 2nd Division.

The 20th was spent preparing for the passage of the Matakula River.

At 5 A.M. of 21st the whole Column, accompanied by 130 wagons with other vehicles, marched from camp, the whole day spent on the passage of the Matakula River, in evening encamped 4" north of river.

An expedition composed of half of the Naval Brigade, 2 Companies Buffs and other troops, destroyed a large military kraal 5" E. by S. of camp.

Order of March.

2 Companies Native Contingent.

1 Company 99th Regiment.

2 Companies Native Contingent.

Cavalry.

2nd Division No. 1 Column.

20 Natal Native Pioneers.

2 Companies 99th Regiment.

1 Company Native Contingent.

Wagons.

Wagons.

1 Company Native Contingent.

2 7-pr. Naval Brigade.

Guns with crews.

1 Company 99th Regiment.

2 Companies Native Contingent.

1 Company 99th Regiment.

2 Companies Native Contingent.

Cavalry.

22nd, 5 A.M. marched. After passing 5 miles along a fertile valley the path turns suddenly to the left, and the ascent of the high land on which Ekowe is situated commences, the head of the column reached this turning, and was preparing to halt for breakfast, when it was suddenly attacked along the entire right flank and on both fronts by the enemy, who had evidently been lying concealed in the bushes; they boldly advanced to within 150 yards in extended order rushing from bush to bush and firing with great rapidity. Two 7-prs. Royal Artillery and two 24-prs. Naval Brigade rockets were placed on an knoll at the foot of the pass, but commanding the valley from which the flank attack was proceeding, these supported by two companies of the Buffs and A and

B Companies of Naval Brigade opened a heavy fire on the enemy, checking their advance. This knoll continued to be the head quarters of the column during the engagement.

From head quarters to the head of the pass, the road or path to Ekowe leads along the top of a low ridge for about a mile; this ridge is commanded on both sides by two higher ridges running parallel to it and distant 800 to 1,000 yards.

On these high ridges the enemy were posted in large numbers, they also occupied a position B, 300 yards from head quarters on the same ridge, and had commenced to open fire from this latter post when a well-directed rocket from the Naval Brigade was driven right through the Kraal B instantly expelling the enemy.

6. Having been instructed to defend this part of the position I advanced A and a part of B Companies of the 'Active's' men in skirmishing order along the ridge above-described, leaving the remainder of B Company with the rockets, to assist in protecting the head quarter position, which throughout the day was exposed to an irritating fire from the bushes on the sides of a mountain opposite, as well as from the enemy in the plain, the colonel commanding having already had a horse killed under him.

7. My attention was now wholly directed to the advance along the ridge (see sec. 6, par. 1), along the top of which runs the track to Ekowe. Not-withstanding the heavy fire directed against our small party from front and both flanks, steady progress was made, and the enemy driven back step by step for about three-quarters of a mile, when he posted his troops for a final stand in a strong position perpendicular to the road parallel to which the Naval Brigade were slowly advancing. By this time four men of the Naval Brigade had been sent to the rear badly wounded, and another temporarily stunned by a bullet passing through his helmet, when the arrival of a company of Buffs under Colonel Parnell enabled the attack very rapidly to be pushed to within 100 yards of the Zulu position. A final rush was then made, headed by the Naval Brigade, and the position carried by assault. The first un-mounted man in the enemy's position was Thomas Harding, Ordinary of H.M.S. 'Active,' closely followed by the remainder of A Company, under Lieutenant Hamilton.

Two other hills were carried as soon as the men had recovered breath, thus breaking through and driving back the right horn of the Zulu army, dispersing it in all directions, and clearing the road to Ekowe, along which the column shortly after advanced without molestation, camping for the night five miles south of that place.

The action lasted nearly three hours, and resulted in the enemy being driven back on all sides with a loss of 300 dead; only one wounded Zulu was found on the field, so it is to be presumed the wounded were removed by their companions.

The loss of Europeans in the engagement was eight killed and sixteen wounded, one of whom has since died; out of the killed six were officers or non-commissioned officers of the Native Contingent; these men fought, as far as came under my notice, with great bravery, being, of course, unsupported by their men, one out of ten of whom only have fire-arms, while the Zulus appear all to be possessed of them.

I enclose the reports of Lieutenant Dowding, commanding Royal Marine Light Infantry, and Midshipman Coker, in charge of the Gatling, both of whom were placed so far in rear that I had no opportunity of observing their movements.

It is with greatest gratification I report the splendid behaviour of the Naval Brigade in action of 22nd instant; all were remarkably steady under fire; those employed on the ridge were exposed to a cross fire for nearly two hours, after which they responded to my call for the final assault with alacrity, and led the rush till success was secured.

I particularly recommend Lieutenant Hamilton, whose company was in front during the action.

Sub-Lieutenant Fraser also did good service in command of the Reserve, being under fire the whole time.

Boatswain Cotter was most successful with the rockets I placed in his charge.

Lieutenant Craigie, Gunnery Lieutenant, rendered valuable services as Acting Adjutant.

Ekowe was reached early on 23rd, and the head quarters are expected to remain for eight or ten days before any further advance is made.

200 men marched in the direction of the Tugela this morning, and 400 more leave tomorrow, to escort convoys; reports have reached that attacks have been made on these.

The force lately beaten by the 1st Division of the Column are said to be assembled in the bush at Umlatoo River, there to attack us on advancing. It seems probable that they will not be dispersed without some loss on our side. The Zulus seem adepts at skirmishing, always in extended order; they rush from one bush to another, delivering their fire, and then retiring under cover to load. It requires a good marksman to bring them down. Nothing like the masses of men spoken of as composing their armies has been seen, and they show no disposition to meet us in the open, but confine themselves to taking us at a disadvantage as on the 22nd instant.

The enemy have unfortunately carried off the six Martini-Henry rifles and ammunition of the Europeans of the Native Contingent killed; doubtless these will be used against us with effect in the next action.

I trust my proceedings may meet your approval.

I have &c.,

(Signed) H. FLETCHER CAMPBELL,

Commanding Naval Brigade.

I beg to recommend to your notice, E. White, Principal Officer First Class, who continued to fight after having been struck by a ball.

E. Futcher, Principal Officer First Class, took a leading part in the movements. Thomas Harding, Ordinary, the first un-mounted man in enemy's position.

Inyezana, 23rd January, 1879.

SIR,

I have the honour to report that in accordance with orders, I marched the Marines from the camping ground near the Amatikulu, on the morning of the 22nd inst. in rear of the Gatling gun. After marching about 2½ hours we heard rapid firing commencing at the front of the column; almost at the same instant an officer of the Native Contingent rode up to me, reporting that the enemy were in large numbers on our right. Immediately told Captain Forster of the Buffs, who was in command of the rear guard.

He ordered us to extend on the right flank of the wagons, at the same time the Gatling gun was brought into action.

I advanced the Marines in line with a Company of the Buffs under Captain Foster, but owing to the height of the reeds and bush we only occasionally got a glimpse of the enemy about 400 yards in front of us, and apparently, in large numbers. They appeared to be trying to get round the rear of the column. I was able occasionally to open fire at them on arriving at the edge of the reeds.

After advancing in this way about a quarter of a mile, we found another company of the Buffs, moving from the front of the column, and some 300 yards to our front. I therefore at once moved my men back on the Gatling gun, and made my way at once to the Head Quarter Staff, and reported my arrival to Colonel Pearson.

He ordered Mr. Coker to bring up the Gatling gun at once. 1 was told to place my men at the top of the hill to the left of the Gatling gun, when I at once opened fire on the enemy, who were keeping up a fairly continuous fire in our direction. The Gatling gun shortly opening fire on our right; after about a quarter of an hour Mr. Craigie rode up with half of 'B' Company, saying he had orders to bring up the rest of the Naval Brigade to support 'A' Company, and as the Gatling gun was now well guarded, I at once joined him with the Marines.

We moved rapidly along to the kraal on the top of the hill that had been already taken, where we found the remainder of 'B' Company, keeping up a continuous fire at the enemy on our left, and then advanced on the main road, up a steep hill, until we joined Mr. Hamilton's men.

The men behaved well and steadily under fire. The marching at the commencement in extended order being very heavy through the thick bush and reeds.

The amount of ammunition expended was between 500 and 600 rounds.

I have, &c.
(Signed) TOWNLY W. DOWDING,
Lieut. Comdg. R. Marines.
H.M.S. 'Active.'

·

A. Campbell, R.N., Comdg. Naval Brigade.

Inyizaua, 23rd January, 1879.

SIR,

I have the honor to report I was placed in rear of the leading column with Gatling gun. About two and a half hours after leaving the camping grounds, the head of the column was engaged. A report having come in that the Natives were threatening the rear of the column, I placed my gun on a hill, in a good position for firing if necessary.

I brought my gun into action, but through the clumsiness of my driver, my dissleboom carried away. I repaired it as quickly as possible; no natives appearing, I moved on with the wagons; owing to the dissleboom I was very much delayed.

On arriving at the foot of the hill, where the head quarters were, I was ordered by Colonel Pearson to bring the gun up and place it opposite a hill where some natives had taken up a position.

I immediately opened fire on them, they retiring into the bush I ceased firing, having expended about 300 rounds, and stationed my men to try and pick off a few natives who were annoying us considerably.

The men behaved well under fire and worked hard to bring the gun into action.

I have, &c.
(Signed) LEWIS C. COKER.

Enclosure B.

Fort Tinta, 9 a.m., 25/1/79.

D. A. GENERAL,

I fear you will not be able to gather where No. 4 Column has been from any of the maps, as all are inaccurate.

After clearing the Tunguin Range, on the 22nd, the Zulus retiring hastily leaving cattle and sheep as already reported, the Column halted on the 23rd, the Artillery having had with the F. L. Horse hard work, while the 90th Light Infantry were 19 hours under arms in 24.

The F. L. Horse had scarcely been off-saddled for 48 hours.

Yesterday, the 24th, the Column moved in the direction of the road indicated in Durnsford's map, as passing between the Tunguin's Nek and Ityenteka Range. It is perhaps needless to state that the track has been termed a road because a few wagons have at some time passed over it.

About 7.30 a.m., when the Column had marched eight miles, some Zulus ran forward towards a stony hill in our front, but were anticipated by Colonel Buller with a troop of the F.L. Horse. The morning was misty, and our advance was apparently unperceived, as the Zulus were only forming up when two guns opened on them, and caused them to scatter in all directions.

Finding we could not advance where our guide thought the track existed, I ordered the Column to turn to the left and pass round a high hill on our left, and there outspan. Before I reached this position, however, the 90th Light Infantry, with 2 guns, moved down into a valley and up the opposite hill, on which the Zulus fled hastily, the F. L. Horse and Mr. P. Uy's men pursuing them.

It was at this time I received the first intimation of the Zulu attack on No. 3 Column camp, and I therefore halted for 2½ hours, and then retraced our steps towards the Umvolosi, where the column arrived at 7 a.m. this day.

I append a return of the casualties, and I believe about 50 Zulus were killed from the different bodies, counting 10 in one group, 15 in another, 6 in another, while 5 men were killed by one shell, besides single men.

As I learn from Colonel Crealock's letter, No. 3 Column will go Helpmakaar, I shall move tomorrow, towards the Ugaba Ka Hawane, in the kloofs of which I hope to get wood, and where I shall be in position to cover Utrecht, and yet able to move towards the Bagalususi.

You may probably know, but I think it well to inform you, that the force attacking No. 3 Column camp was composed of Ubonambi, Umcetya, Undi, Nodwengu and Takobamakosi regiments, commanded by, as No. I, Umdabulamanzi, Cetewayo's brother, second senior Umbumengwana, third senior Fatyingwayo.

Unsebe commanded the 3,000 to 4,000 men who yesterday fled before No. 4 Column, which they had undertaken to attack.

If No. 3 Column is to be stationary some time I should be glad of the loan of all its horsemen, as if I can burn the Bagalususi Kraal the effect in North Zulu-land will be good.

(Signed) EVELYN WOOD,
Colonel.

B.B.
Telegram.

From Lord Chelmsford to Colonel Pearson,
Lower Tugela Drift.

Pietermaritzburg,
27th January, 1879.

Consider all my instructions as cancelled, and act in whatever manner you think most desirable in the interests of the Column under your command. Should you consider the Garrison of Ekowe as too far advanced to be fed with safety, you can withdraw it.

Hold, however, if possible, the post on the Zulu side of Lower Tugela. You must be prepared to have the whole Zulu force down upon you. Do away with tents, and let the men take shelter under the wagons, which will then be in position for defence and hold so many more supplies.

The following is an answer to the above telegram:-

From Lieut. Kingscote, Tugela, to Lord Chelmsford,
Pietermaritzburg.

When your telegram arrived at 11 A.M. yesterday, I assembled Commanding Officers, and we determined to hold our ground here. At once sent off mounted men and two battalions Native Contingent to Lower Tugela. Hope both reached there early this morning; this will give us more food and ammunition.

Colonel Ely's convoy arrived last night; had to abandon seven wagons about seven miles from here – six with food, one with forage – disselbooms broken, oxen dead-beat, &c. The oxen were brought on; remainder of convoy – seventy-two wagons – arrived safely. All food and ammunition off loaded and under cover. So many oxen of convoy a great nuisance; laagered some and put remainder into ditch. Will try to improve matters to-day.

We are already well entrenched, but shall work away till we are safe at every corner. My only fear is the water not lasting: making every effort to economise it.

C.
Return of Troops.

Pietermaritzburg. – 1 Company 88th Foot, Fort Napier; 1 Company General Depôt; 1 Company Natal Native Pioneers – Lieutenant-Colonel Hopton.

Greytown. – 3 Companies 2nd Battalion 4th Regiment—Major Twentyman.

Helpmakaar. – 2 Companies 1st Battalion 24th Foot; 2 Companies 2nd Battalion 24th Foot; N Battery, 5th Brigade Royal Artillery (4 guns) – Colonel Hassard, C.B.

Helpmakaar – 1 Squadron Mounted Infantry; Natal Mounted Police, 1 Troop; Natal Carbineers, ½ Troop; Newcastle Mounted Rifles, Buffalo Border Guards, ½ Troop; 2nd Battalion 1st Regiment Natal Native Contingent – Lieutenant-Colonel Russell.

Rorke's Drift. – No. 5 Company Royal Engineers, 7 Companies 2nd Battalion 24th Regiment – Colonel Glyn, C.B.

Krantz Kop. – 1st Battalion 1st Regiment Natal Native Contingent, 3rd Battalion 1st Regiment Natal Native Contingent, 3rd Battalion Natal Native Pioneers – Captain Barton.

Durban – ½ Company 99th Regiment, 1 Troop Mounted Volunteers – Major Huskisson.

Stanger – 1½ Companies 99th Regiment – Major Walker.

Lower Tugela, Fort Pearson, Camp right bank – ½ Company 99th Regiment; Guns, 1 12-pounder; No. 2 Squadrons Mounted Infantry; Natal Hussars, ½ Troop; Durban Mounted Rifles, 1 Troop; Alexandra Mounted Rifles, 1 Troop; Stanger Mounted Rifles, 1 Troop; Victoria Mounted Rifles, 1 Troop – Major Barrow.

Fort Tenedos, left bank – 2½ Companies 99th Regiment; 2 Companies Buffs; Naval Brigade (43); 1 12-pounder gun.

Ekowe – 6 Companies 2nd Battalion 3rd Regiment; 3 Companies 99th Regiment; Naval Brigade 128, 2 7-pounders, 1 Gatling, 1 rocket tube; Royal Artillery (23) 2 7-pounder muzzle-loading guns; No. 2 Company Natal Native Pioneers – Colonel Pearson.

Ekowe – Royal Artillery 1st Battalion 13th Regiment Light Infantry; 90th Regiment Light Infantry; Frontier Light Horse, 2 Squadrons; Wood's Irregular Natives – Colonel E. Wood, V.C., C.B.

RETURN of such Casualties as have been officially reported up to date, from 12th to 24th January, 1879.

12th January, 1879, at Isipezi.
KILLED.
Privates Two, N.N.C.

WOUNDED.
Lieutenant Purvis, N.N.C.
Corporal Mayor, N.N.C.
Private Twelve, N.N.C.

18th January, 1879, in Zululand, on march with Colonel Wood's column.
WOUNDED.
Private Jack, Wood's Irregulars.
Private Slanyola, Wood's Irregulars.

20th January, 1879, in Zululand, on march with Colonel Wood's column.
WOUNDED.
Trooper J. Berry, F.L. Horse.
Trooper Randall, F.L. Horse.

22nd January, 1879, at Inyanzani.
KILLED.
Private J. Bough, 2nd Battalion 3rd Foot.
Private J. Kelleher, 2nd Battalion 3rd Foot.
Lieutenant J. L. Raines, N.N.C.
Lieutenant G. Platterer, N.N.C.
Sergeant Emil Unger, N.N.C.
Corporal W. Tieper, N.N.C.
Corporal E. Miller, N.N.C.
Corporal Carl Goesch, N.N.C.

WOUNDED.
Private Peter Dunn, 2nd Battalion 3rd Foot, since dead.
Private J. Corteel, 2nd Battalion 3rd Foot.
Private F. Smith, 2nd Battalion 3rd Foot.
Private F. Clifford, 2nd Battalion 3rd Foot.
Private H. Walker, 2nd Battalion 3rd Foot.
Quartermaster-Sergeant Kelly, Musketry Instructor, 90th Foot.
Private W. Devenport, Musketry Instructor, 2nd Battalion 24th Foot.
H. Gosling, A.B., Naval Brigade.

G. Berryman, O.S., Naval Brigade.
G. Doran, O.S., Naval Brigade.
T. Butler, A.B., Naval Brigade.
E. White, O.S., Naval Brigade.
Krooman, Jack Ropeyarn, O.S., Naval Brigade.
Ducklewis, O.S., Naval Brigade.
Lieutenant H. Webb, N.N.C.
Sergeant O. Aeydenburg, N.N.C.

22nd January, 1879, Isandhlawana.
KILLED.

Colour-Sergeant M. C. Keane, Staff Clerk to Military Secretary.
Farrier Wright, Army Service Corps.
Sergeant Thompson, 80th Foot.
Private Fitzpatrick, 25th Foot.
Private Williamson, 2nd Battalion 24th Foot.
Private Watson, 31st Foot.
Private Hughes, 1st Battalion 24th Foot.
Signalman Aynesley, Royal Navy.
Mr. Laparra, General's Cook.
All attached to the personal Staff of the Lieutenant-General as servants.

23rd January, at Rorke's Drift.
WOUNDED.

Private Beckett, 1st Battalion 24th Foot, since dead.
Private J. Waters, 1st Battalion 24th Foot.
Sergeant T. Williamson, 2nd Battalion 24th Foot.
Corporal J. Lyons, 2nd Battalion 24th Foot.
Corporal W. Allon, 2nd Battalion 24th Foot.
Private Hitch, 2nd Battalion 24th Foot.
Private Jones, 2nd Battalion 24th Foot.
Private Scammen, N.N.C.
Private F. Seliess, N.N.C.

24th January, at Zuukem Nek.
WOUNDED.

Private Budenback, Dutch Contingent.
Private Jelloame, Dutch Contingent.

W. BELLAIRS,
D.A.G.

Pietermaritzburg, Natal,
2nd February, 1879.

The Principal Medical Officer's return of nature of wound not received up to time of closing the Despatch.

J. N. CREALOCK,
A.M.S.

CHELMSFORD'S DESPATCHES PUBLISHED ON 15 MARCH 1879

War Office, 15th March, 1879.

The following Despatch has been received by the Secretary of State for War from Lieutenant-General Lord Chelmsford, K.C.B., Commanding the Forces in South Africa:-

From the Lieutenant-General Commanding in South Africa to the Right Honourable the Secretary of State for War.

Durban, Natal,
8th February, 1879.

SIR,

I have the honour to forward herewith the proceedings of the Court of Inquiry held to take evidence regarding the disastrous affair of Isandlana.

The Court has very properly abstained from giving an opinion, and I myself refrain also from making any observation or from drawing any conclusions from the evidence therein recorded.

I regret very much that more evidence has not been taken, and I have given instructions that all those who escaped, and who are able to throw any light whatever upon the occurrences of the day, should be at once called upon for a statement of what they saw.

I deem it better, however, not to delay the transmission of the proceedings, which will no doubt be awaited with anxiety.

I have directed my Military Secretary, Lieutenant-Colonel Crealock, to append a statement of the facts which came under his cognisance on the day in question, which may possibly serve to throw some additional light on what, I fear, will still be considered very obscure.

It will, I fear, be impossible to furnish an absolutely correct list of all those who perished on the 22nd January, as every record connected with the several corps belonging to No. 3 Column has been lost.

Colonel Glyn is doing his best to furnish what is required.

Since writing the above the printed list of killed and wounded has reached me, several copies of which I beg to enclose.

I have, &c.,
(Signed) CHELMSFORD,
Lieutenant-General.

Adjutant-General.

> Camp, Helpmakaar, Natal,
> 29th January, 1879.

Herewith proceedings of Court of Enquiry assembled by order of His Excellency the Lieutenant-General Commanding. The Court has examined and recorded the statements of the chief witnesses.

The copy of proceedings forwarded was made by a confidential clerk of the Royal Engineers.

The Court has refrained from giving an opinion, as instructions on this point were not given to it.

> (Signed) F.C. HASSARD, C.B.,
> Colonel Royal Engineers,

President.

Proceedings of a Court of Enquiry, assembled at Helpmakaar, Natal, on the 27th January, 1879, by order of His Excellency the Lieutenant-General Commanding the troops in South, Africa, dated 24th January, 1879.

President:
Colonel F.C. Hassard, C.B., Royal Engineers.

Members:
Lieutenant-Colonel Law, Royal Artillery,
Lieutenant-Colonel Harness, Royal Artillery.

The Court having assembled pursuant to order, proceeded to take the following evidence:-

1st Witness. – Major Clery states: I am Senior Staff Officer to the 3rd Column, commanded by Colonel Glyn, C.B., operating against the Zulus. The General commanding accompanied this Column from the time it crossed the border into Zululand.

On the 20th January, 1879, at the Camp, Isandlana, Zululand, the Lieutenant-General commanding gave orders to Commandant Lonsdale and Major Dartnell to go out the following morning in a certain direction from the camp with their men, *i.e.*, the Native Contingent, and the Police, and Volunteers, part of the 3rd Column. On the evening of the following day (the 21st) a message arrived from Major Dartnell that the enemy was in considerable force in his neighbourhood, and that he and Commandant Lonsdale would bivouac out that night. About 1.30 A.M., on the 22nd, a messenger brought me a note from Major Dartnell, to say that the enemy was in greater numbers than when he last reported, and that he did not think it prudent to attack them unless reinforced by two or three companies of the 24th Regiment. I took this note to Colonel Glyn, C.B., at once, he ordered me to take it on to the General. The General ordered the 2nd Battalion 24th Regiment, the Mounted Infantry, and four guns, to be under arms at once to march. This force marched out from camp as soon as there was light enough to see the road. The Natal Pioneers accompanied this column to clear the road. The General first ordered me to write to Colonel Durnford, at Rorke's Drift, to bring his force to strengthen the camp, but almost immediately afterwards he told Colonel Crealock that he (Colonel Crealock) was to write to Colonel Durnford these instructions, and not I. Before leaving the camp, I sent written instructions to Colonel Pulleine, 24th Regiment, to the following effect:- 'You will be in command of the camp during the absence of Colonel Glyn; draw in (I speak from memory) your camp, or your line of defence' – I am not certain which – 'while the force is out: also draw in the line of your infantry outposts accordingly; but keep your cavalry vedettes still far advanced.' I told him to have a wagon ready loaded with ammunition ready to follow the force going out at a moment's notice, if required. I went to Colonel Pulleine's tent just before leaving camp to ascertain that he had got these instructions, and I again repeated them verbally to him. To the best of my memory, I mentioned in the written instructions to Colonel Pulleine that Colonel Durnford had been written to to bring up his force to strengthen the camp. I saw the column out of camp and accompanied it.

2nd Evidence. – Colonel Glyn, C.B., states: From the time the column under my command crossed the border I was in the habit of receiving instructions from the Lieutenant-General Commanding as to the movements of the column, and I accompanied him on most of the patrols and reconnaissances carried out by him. I corroborate Major Clery's statement.

3rd Evidence. – Captain Alan Gardner, 14th Hussars, states: I accompanied the main body of the 3rd Column as Acting Staff Officer to Officer commanding 3rd Column when it left the camp at Isandlana on the 22nd January, 1879. I was sent back with an order from the General between ten and eleven A.M. that day into camp, which order was addressed to Colonel Pulleine, and was that the camp of the force out was to be struck and sent on immediately, also rations and forage for about seven days. On arriving in camp I met Captain George Shepstone, who was also seeking Colonel Pulleine, having a message from Colonel Durnford, that his men were falling back, and asking for reinforcements. We both went to Colonel Pulleine, to whom I delivered the order. Colonel Pulleine at first hesitated about carrying out the order, and eventually decided that the enemy being already on the hill on our left in large numbers, it was impossible to do so.

The men of the 24th Regiment were all fallen in, and the Artillery also, and Colonel Pulleine sent two companies to support Colonel Durnford, to the hill on the left, and formed up the remaining companies in line, the guns in action on the extreme left flank of the camp, facing the hill on our left. I remained with Colonel Pulleine by his order. Shortly after, I took the mounted men, by Colonel Pulleine's direction, about a quarter of a mile to the front of the camp, and left them there under the direction of Captain Bradstreet, with orders to hold the spruit. I went back to Colonel Pulleine, but soon after, observing the mounted men retiring, I went back to them, and, in reply to my question as to why they were retiring, was told they were ordered by Colonel Durnford to retire, as the position taken up was too extended This same remark was made to me by Colonel Durnford himself immediately afterwards.

By this time the Zulus had surrounded the camp, the whole force engaged in hand to hand combat, the guns mobbed by Zulus, and there became a general massacre. From the time of the first infantry force leaving the camp to the end of the fight about one hour elapsed. I estimated the number of the enemy at about 12,000 men. I may mention that a few minutes after my arrival in camp, I sent a message directed to the Staff Officer 3rd Column, saying that our left was attacked by about 10,000 of the enemy; a message was also sent by Colonel Pulleine.

The Native Infantry Contingent fled as soon as the fighting began, and caused great confusion in our ranks. I sent messages to Rorke's Drift and Helpmakaar Camp that the Zulus had sacked the camp and telling them to fortify themselves.

4th Evidence. – Captain Essex, 75th Regiment, states: I hand in a written statement of what occurred, I have nothing to add to that statement. This statement is marked A.

5th Evidence. – Lieutenant Cochrane, 32nd Regiment, states: I am employed as transport officer with No 2 Column, then under Colonel Durnford, R.E., on the 22nd January, 1879, the column marched on that morning from Rorke's Drift to Isandlana in consequence of an order received from the Lieutenant-General. I do not know the particulars of the order received. I entered the Isandlana camp with Colonel Durnford about 10 A.M., and remained with him as Acting Staff Officer. On arrival he took over command from Colonel Pulleine, 24th Regiment. Colonel Pulleine gave over to Colonel

Durnford a verbal state of the troops in camp at the time, and stated the orders he had received, viz., to defend the camp, these words were repeated two or three times in the conversation. Several messages were delivered, the last one to the effect that the Zulus were retiring in all directions – the bearer of this was not dressed in any uniform. On this message Colonel Durnford sent two troops Mounted Natives to the top of the hills to the left, and took with him two troops of Rocket Battery, with escort of one company Native Contingent, on to the front of the camp about four or five miles off. Before leaving, he asked Colonel Pulleine to give him two companies 24th Regiment. Colonel Pulleine said that with the orders he had received he could not do it, but agreed with Colonel Durnford to send him help if he got into difficulties. Colonel Durnford, with two troops, went on ahead and met the enemy some four or five miles off in great force, and, as they showed also on our left, we retired in good order to the Drift, about a quarter of a mile in front of the camp, where the mounted men reinforced us, about two miles from the camp. On our retreat we came upon the remains of the Rocket Battery which had been destroyed.

6th Evidence. – Lieutenant Smith-Dorrien, 95th Regiment, states: I am Transport Officer with No. 3 Column. On the morning of the 22nd I was sent with a Despatch from the General to Colonel Durnford, at Rorke's Drift, the Despatch was an order to join the camp at Isandlana as soon as possible, as a large Zulu force was near it.

I have no particulars to mention besides.

7th Evidence. – Captain Nourse, Natal Native Contingent, states: I was commanding the escort to the Rocket Battery, when Colonel Durnford advanced in front of the camp on the 22nd to meet the enemy. Colonel Durnford had gone on with two troops, Mounted Natives. They went too fast, and left us some two miles in the rear. On hearing heavy firing on our left, and learning that the enemy were in that direction, we changed our direction to the left. Before nearly reaching the crest of the hills on the left of the camp, we were attacked on all sides. One rocket was sent off, and the enemy was on us; the first volley dispersed the mules and the natives, and we retired on to the camp as well as we could. Before we reached the camp it was destroyed.

8th Evidence. – Lieutenant Curling, R.A., states: I was left in camp with two guns, when the remaining four guns of the battery went out with the main body of the column, on 22nd January, 1879. Major Stuart Smith joined and took command of the guns about twelve noon.

I hand in a written statement (marked B). I have nothing to add to that statement.

(Signed) F.C. HASSARD,
Colonel, Royal Engineers, President.
F.T.A. LAW,
Lieutenant-Colonel, R.A.
A. HARNESS,
Major R.A. and Lieutenant-Colonel.

A.

Captain Essex's Evidence.

Rorke's Drift,
24th January, 1879.

SIR,

I have the honour to forward for the information of the Lieutenant-General Commanding, an account of an action which took place near the Isandlana Hills on the 22nd instant.

After the departure of the main body of the column, nothing unusual occurred in camp until about eight A.M., when a report arrived from a picquet stationed at a point about 1,500 yards distant, on a hill to the north of the camp, that a body of the enemy's troops could be seen approaching from the north-east. Lieutenant-Colonel Pulleine, 1st Battalion 24th Regiment, commanding in camp, thereupon caused the whole of the troops available to assemble near the eastern side of the camp, facing towards the reported direction of the enemy's approach. He also dispatched a mounted man with a report to the column, presumed to be about twelve or fifteen miles distant. Shortly after nine A.M., a small body of the enemy showed itself just over the crest of the hills, in the direction they were expected, but retired a few minutes afterwards, and disappeared. Soon afterwards, information arrived from the picquet before alluded to, that the enemy was in three columns, two of which were retiring, but were still in view; the third column had disappeared in a north-westerly direction.

At about ten A.M. a party of about 250 mounted natives, followed by a rocket battery, arrived with Lieutenant-Colonel Durnford, R.E., who now assumed command of the camp.

The main body of this mounted force, divided into two portions, and the rocket battery were, about 10.30 A.M., sent out to ascertain the enemy's movements, and a company of 1st Battalion 24th Regiment, under command of Lieutenant Cavaye was directed to take up a position as a piquet on the hill to the north of the camp at about 1,200 yards distant, the remainder of the troops were ordered to march to their private parades when the men were to be down in readiness, at this time, about eleven A.M., the impression in camp was that the enemy had no intention of advancing during the daytime, but might possibly be expected to attack during the night. No idea had been formed regarding the probable strength of the enemy's force.

At about twelve o'clock, hearing firing on the hill where the company 1st Battalion 24th Regiment was stationed, I proceeded in that direction. On my way I passed a company of the 1st Battalion 24th Regiment, under command of Captain Mostyn, who requested me, being mounted, to direct Lieutenant Cavaye to take special care not to endanger the right of his company, and to inform that officer that he himself was moving up to the left. I also noticed a body of Lieutenant-Colonel Dunford's mounted natives retiring down the hill, but did not see the enemy. On arriving at the far side of the crest of the hill, I found the company in charge of Lieutenant Cavaye a section being detached about 500 yards to the left, in charge of Lieutenant Dyson. The whole were in extended order engaging the enemy, who was moving in similar formation towards our left, keeping at about 800 yards from our line.

Captain Mostyn moved his company into the space between the portions of that already on the hill, and his men then extended and entered into action. This line was then prolonged on our right along the crest of the hill by a body of native infantry. I observed that the enemy made little progress as regards his advance, but appeared to be moving at a rapid pace towards our left. The right extremity of the enemy's line was very thin, but increased in depth towards and beyond our right as far as I could see, a hill interfering with an extended view. About five minutes after the arrival of Captain Mostyn's Company I was informed by Lieutenant Melville, Adjutant 1st Battalion 24th Regiment, that a fresh body of the enemy was appearing in force in our rear, and he requested me to direct the left of the line formed, as above described, to fall slowly back, keeping up the fire. This I did; then proceeded towards the centre of the line. I found, however, that it had already retired. I therefore followed in the same direction, but being mounted had great difficulty in descending the hill, the ground being very rocky and precipitous. On arriving at the foot of the slope I found the two companies of 1st Battalion 24th Regiment drawn up at about 400 yards distant in extended order, and Captain Younghusband's company in a similar formation in echelon on the left. The enemy was descending the hill, having rushed forward as soon as our men disappeared below the crest, and beyond (?) the right of the line with which I was present had even arrived near the foot of the hill. The enemy's fire had hitherto been very wild and ineffective, now, however, a few casualties began to occur in our line. The companies 1st Battalion 24th Regiment first engaged were now becoming short of ammunition, and at the request of the officer in charge I went to procure a fresh supply with the assistance of Quartermaster 2nd Battalion 24th Regiment and some men of the Royal Artillery. I had some boxes placed on a mule cart and sent it off to the companies engaged, and sent more by hand, employing any men without arms. I then went back to the line, telling the men that plenty of ammunition was coming. I found that the companies 1st Battalion 24th Regiment before alluded to had retired to within 300 yards of that portion of the camp occupied by the Native Contingent. On my way I noticed a number of native infantry retreating in haste towards the camp, their officer endeavouring to prevent them but without effect. On looking round to that portion of the field to our right and rear I saw that the enemy was surrounding us. I rode up to Lieutenant-Colonel Durnford, who was near the right, and pointed this out to him. He requested me to take men to that part of the field and endeavour to hold the enemy in check; but while he was speaking, those men of the Native Contingent who had remained in action rushed past us in the utmost disorder, thus laying open the right and rear of the companies of 1st Battalion 24th Regiment on the left, and the enemy dashing forward in a most rapid manner poured in at this part of the line. In a moment all was disorder, and few of the men of 1st Battalion 24th Regiment had time to fix bayonets before the enemy was among them using their assegais with fearful effect. I heard officers calling to their men to be steady; but the retreat became in a few seconds general, and in a direction towards the road to Rorke's Drift. Before, however, we gained the neck near the Isandlana Hill the enemy had arrived on that portion of the field also, and the large circle he had now formed closed in on us. The only space which appeared opened was down a deep gully running to the south of the road into which we plunged in great confusion. The enemy followed us closely and kept up with us at first on both flanks, then on our right only, firing occasionally, but chiefly making use of the assegais. It was now about 1.30 P.M.; about this period two guns with which Major Smith and Lieutenant Curling, R.A., were returning with great difficulty, owing to the nature of the ground, and I understood were just a few seconds' late. Further on the ground passed over on our retreat would at any other time be looked upon as impracticable for horsemen to descend, and many losses occured, owing to horses falling and the enemy coming up with the riders; about half a mile from the neck the retreat had to be carried on in nearly single file, and in this manner the Buffalo River was gained at a point about five miles below Rorke's Drift. In crossing this river many men and horses were carried away by the stream and lost their lives; after crossing the fire of the enemy was discontinued, pursuit, however, was still kept up, but with little effect, and apparently with the view of cutting us off from Rorke's Drift. The number of white men who crossed the river at this point was, as far as I could see, about 40. In addition to these, there were a great number of natives on foot and on horseback. White men of about 25 or 30 arrived at Helpmakaar between five and six P.M., when, with the assistance of other men joined there, a laager was formed with wagons round the stores. I estimate the strength of the enemy to have been about 15,000. Their losses must have been considerable towards the end of the engagement.

I have, &c.,
(Signed) E. ESSEX,
Captain, 75th Regiment,
Sub-Director of Transports.

B.

From Lieutenant Curling to Officer Commanding No. 8.

Helpmakaar,
26th January, 1879.

SIR,
I have the honour to forward the following report of the circumstances attending the loss of two guns of N Brigade, 5th Battery Royal Artillery, at the action of Isandlana, on January 22. About 7.30 A.M. on that date, a large body of Zulus being seen on the hills to the left front of the camp, we were ordered to turn out at once, and were formed up in front of the 2nd Battalion 24th Regiment Camp, where we remained until eleven o'clock, when we returned to camp with orders to remain harnessed up and ready to turn out at a minute's notice. The Zulus did not come within range and we did not come into action. The infantry also remained in column of companies. Colonel Durnford arrived about ten A.M. with Basutos and the rocket battery; he left about eleven o'clock with these troops in the direction of the hills where we had seen the enemy. About twelve o'clock we were turned out, as heavy firing was heard in the direction of Colonel Durnford's force. Major Smith arrived as we were turning out and took command of the guns, we trotted up to a position about 400 yards beyond the left front of the Natal Contingent Camp, and came into action at once on a large body of the enemy about 3,400 yards off. The 1st Battalion 24th Regiment soon came up and extended in skirmishing order on both flanks and in line with us.

In about a quarter of an hour, Major Smith took away one gun to the right, as the enemy were appearing in large numbers in the direction of the Drift, in the stream in front of the camp.

The enemy advanced slowly, without halting; when they were 400 yards off, the 1st Battalion, 24th Regiment advanced about 30 yards. We remained in the same position. Major Smith, returned at this time with his gun, and came into action beside mine. The enemy advancing still, we began firing case, but almost immediately the infantry were ordered to retire. Before we could get away, the enemy were by the guns; and I saw one gunner stabbed as he was mounting on to an axle-tree box. The limber gunners did not mount, but ran after the guns. We went straight through the camp but found the enemy in possession. The gunners were all stabbed going through the camp with the exception of one or two. One of the two sergeants was also killed at this time. When we got on to the road to Rorke's Drift it was completely blocked up by Zulus. I was with Major Smith at this time, he told me he had been wounded in the arm. We saw Lieutenant Coghill, the A.D.C., and asked him if we could not rally some men and make a stand, he said he did not think it could be done. We crossed the road with the crowd, principally consisting of natives, men left in camp, and civilians, and went down a steep ravine leading towards the river.

The Zulus were in the middle of the crowd, stabbing the men as they ran. When we had gone about 400 yards, we came to a deep cut in which the guns stuck. There was, as far as I could see, only one gunner with them at this time, but they were covered with men of different corps clinging to them. The Zulus were in them almost at once, and the drivers pulled off their horses. I then left the guns. Shortly after this I again saw Lieutenant Coghill, who told me Colonel Pulleine had been killed.

Near the river I saw Lieutenant Melville, 1st Battalion 24th Regiment, with a colour, the staff being broken.

I also saw Lieutenant Smith-Dorrien assisting a wounded man. During the action, cease firing, was sounded twice.

I am, &c.
(Signed) H.T. CURLING,
Lieutenant R.A.

From the Lieutenant-General Commanding in South Africa
to the Right Honourable the Secretary of State.

Durban, Natal,
8th February, 1879.

SIR,
It is with much satisfaction that I have the honor to forward the report of the successful defence of Rorke's Drift Post on January 22nd and 23rd.

The defeat of the Zulus at this post, and the very heavy loss suffered by them, has to a great extent neutralized the effects of the disaster at Isandlana, and it no doubt saved Natal from a serious invasion.

The cool determined courage displayed by the gallant garrison is beyond all praise, and will, I feel sure, receive ample recognition.

As at the present moment the lesson taught by this defence is most valuable, I have thought it advisable to publish, for general information, the report in question, which I trust will meet with your approval.

I have,
(Signed) CHELMSFORD,
Lieutenant-General.

From reports received since the date of Lieut.- Chard's letter, it appears that the Zulu loss was greater than he knew of at that time.

Rorke's Drift,
25th January, 1879.

SIR,

I have the honour to report that on the 22nd instant I was left in command at Rorke's Drift by Major Spalding, who went to Helpmakaar to hurry in the company 24th regiment ordered to protect the ponts.

About 3.15 p.m. on that day, I was at the ponts when two men came riding from Zululand at a galop, and shouted to be taken across the river.

I was informed by one of them, Lieutenant Adenhdorff of Lonsdale's regiment (who remained to assist in the defence) of the disaster at Isandlana camp, and that the Zulus were advancing on Rorke's Drift. The other, a carabineer rode off to take the news to Helpmakaar.

Almost immediately I received a message from Lieutenant Bromhead, commanding the company 24th Regiment at the camp near the commissariat stores, asking me to come up at once.

I gave the order to inspan, strike tents, put all stores, &c., into the wagon, and at once rode up to the commissariat store and found that a note had been received from the 3rd column to state that the enemy were advancing in force against our post, which we were to strengthen and hold at all costs.

Lieutenant Bromhead was most actively engaged in loopholing and barricading the store building and hospital, and connecting the defence of the two buildings by walls of mealie bags and two wagons that were on the ground.

I held a hurried consultation with him and with Mr. Dalton, of the Commissariat (who was actively superintending the work of defence, and whom I cannot sufficiently thank for his most valuable services) entirely approving of the arrangements made. I went round the position, and then went down to the ponts and brought up the guard of 1 sergeant and 6 men, wagon, &c. I desire here to mention the offer of the punt-man Daniels and Sergeant Milne, 3rd Buffs, to move the punts in the middle of the stream, and defend them from their decks with a few men. We arrived at the post about 3.30 p.m. Shortly after an officer of Durnford's Horse arrived and asked for orders. I requested him to send a detachment to observe the drifts and punts and throw out outposts in the direction of the enemy and check his advance as much as possible, falling back upon the post when forced to retire and assist in its defence.

I requested Lieutenant Bromhead to post his men, and having seen his and every man at his post, the work once more went on.

About 4.20 p.m. the sound of firing was heard behind the hill to our south. The officer of Durnford's returned, reporting the enemy close upon us, and that his men would not obey his orders, but were going off to Helpmakaar, and I saw them, apparently about 100 in number, going off in that direction.

About the same time Captain Stephenson's detachment of Natal Native Contingent left us, as did that officer himself.

I saw that our line of defence was too extended for the small number of men now left us, and at once commenced a retrenchment of biscuit boxes.

We had not completed a wall 2 boxes high when, about 4.30 p.m., 500 or 600 of the enemy came in sight around the hill to our south, and advanced at a run against the south wall. They were met by a well-sustained fire but, notwithstanding their heavy loss, continued the advance to within 50 yards of the wall, when they were met with such a heavy fire from the wall and cross fire from the store that they were checked, but taking advantage of the cover afforded by the cookhouse, ovens, &c., kept up a heavy fire. The greater number, however, without stopping, moved to the left, around the hospital, and made a rush at our N.W. wall of mealie bags, but after a short but desperate struggle were driven back with heavy loss into the bush around the work.

The main body of the enemy were close behind, and had lined the ledge of rock and caves overlooking us about 400 yards to our south, from where they kept up a constant fire, and advancing somewhat more to their left than the first attack, occupied the garden, hollow road and bush in great force.

Taking advantage of the bush, which we had not time to cut down, the enemy were able to advance under cover close to our wall, and in this part soon held one side of the wall, while we held the other. A series of desperate assaults were made, extending from the hospital, along the wall, as far as the bush reached; but each was most splendidly met and repulsed by our men with the bayonet, Corporal Schiess, N.N.C. greatly distinguishing himself by his conspicuous gallantry.

The fire from the rocks behind us, though badly directed, took us completely in reverse, and was so heavy that we suffered very severely and about 6 p.m. were forced to retire behind the retrenchment of biscuit boxes.

All this time the enemy had been attempting to force the hospital, and shortly after set fire to its roof.

The garrison of the hospital defended it room by room, bringing out all the sick who could be moved before they retired. Privates Williams, Hook, R. Jones and W. Jones, 24th Regiment, being the last men to leave, holding the doorway with the bayonet, their own ammunition being expended. From the want of interior communication and the burning of the house it was impossible to save all. With most heartfelt sorrow I regret we could not save these poor fellows from their terrible fate.

Seeing the hospital burning and the desperate attempts of the enemy to fire the roof of the stores, we converted two mealie bag heaps into a sort of redoubt, which gave a second line of fire all round; Assistant Commissary Dunne working hard at this, though much exposed, and rendering valuable assistance.

As darkness came on we were completely surrounded, and after several attempts had been gallantly repulsed, were eventually forced to retire to the middle, and then inner wall of the Kraal on our East. The position we then had we retained throughout.

A desultory fire was kept up all night, and several assaults were attempted and repulsed; the vigour of the attack continuing until after midnight, and men firing with the greatest coolness did not waste a single shot; the light afforded by the burning hospital being of great help to us.

About 4 a.m. 23rd instant, the firing ceased, and at daybreak the enemy were out of sight over the hill to the south-west.

We patrolled the grounds, collecting the arms of the dead Zulus, and strengthened our defences as much as possible.

We were removing the thatch from the roof of the stores, when about 7 a.m. a large body of the enemy appeared on the hills to the south-west.

I sent a friendly Kafir, who had come in shortly before, with a note to the Officer Commanding at Helpmakaar asking for help.

About 8 a.m. the third column appeared in sight, the enemy who had been gradually advancing, falling back as they approached.

I consider the enemy who attacked us to have numbered about 3,000 (three thousand).

We killed about 350 (three hundred and fifty).

Of the steadiness and gallant behaviour of the whole garrison I cannot speak too highly.

I wish especially to bring to your notice the conduct of:-

Lieutenant Bromhead, 2nd Battalion 24th Regiment, and the splendid behaviour of his Company B 2nd Battalion 24th Regiment.

Surgeon Reynolds, A.M.D., in his constant attention to the wounded, under fire where they fell.

Acting Commissariat Officer Dalton, to whose energy much of our defences were due, and who was severely wounded while gallantly assisting in the defence.

Assistant Commissary Dunne.

Acting Store Keeper Byrne (killed).

Colour-Sergeant Bourne, 2nd Battalion 24th Regiment.

Sergeant Williams, 2nd Battalion 24th Regiment (wounded dangerously).

Sergeant Windridge, 2nd Battalion 24th Regiment.

Corporal Schiess, 2nd Battalion 3rd Natal Native Contingent (wounded).

1395 Private Williams, 2nd Battalion 24th Regiment.

593 Private Jones, 2nd Battalion 24th Regiment.

Private McMahon, Army Hospital Corps.

716 Private R. Jones, 2nd Battalion 24th Regiment.

Private H. Hook.

Private Roy, 1st Battalion 24th Regiment.

The following return shows the number present at Rorke's Drift, January 22nd, 1879:-

Staff, 1 Non-Commissioned Officer and Men, total 1.

Royal Artillery, 1 Non-Commissioned Officer and Men, 3 sick Non-Commissioned and Men, total 4.

Royal Engineers, 1 Officer, 1 Non-Commissioned Officer and Men, total 2.

3rd Buffs, 1 Non-Commissioned, Officer and Men, total 1.

1st Battalion 24th Regiment, 6 Non-Commissioned Officers and Men, 5 sick Non-Commissioned Officers and Men, total 11.

2nd Battalion 24th Regiment, B Company, 17 casuals sick, 1 Officer, 81 Non-Commissioned Officers and Men, 17 sick Non-Commissioned Officers and Men, total 99.

90th Light Infantry, Non-Commissioned Officer and man sick.

Commissariat and Transport Department, 3 Officers. 1 Non-Commissioned Officer and men, total 4.

Army Medical Department, 1 Officer, 3 Non-Commissioned Officers and Men, total 4.

Chaplains, 1 Officer, total 1.

Natal Mounted Police, 3 sick Non-Commissioned Officers and Men, total 3.

Natal Native Contingent, 1 Officer, 6 sick Non-Commissioned Officers and Men, total 7.

Ferryman, 1 Non-Commissioned Officer and Men, total 1.

Total. – 8 officers, 96 Non-Commissioned Officers and Men, 35 Non-Commissioned Officers and Men sick, total 139.

The following is a list of the killed:-

Sergeant Maxfield, 2nd Battalion 24th Regiment.

Private Scanlan.

Private Hayden.

Private Adams.

Private Cole.

Private Fagan.

Private Chick.

1398 Private Williams, 2nd Battalion, 24th Regiment.

Private Nicolls, 1st Battalion, 24th Regiment.

Private Horrigan, 1st Battalion, 24th Regiment.

Jenkins, 1st Battalion, 24th Regiment.

M. Byrne, Commissariat Department.

Trooper Hunter, Natal Mounted Police.

Trooper Anderson, N.N.C.

1 Private (Native) N.N.C.

Total 15.

12 wounded* of whom two have since died, viz.:-

Sergeant Williams, 2nd Battalion, 24th Regiment.

Private Beckett, 1st Battalion, 24th Regiment.

making a total killed of 17.

Herewith is appended a plan of the buildings, showing our lines of defence. The points of the compass referred to in this report are, as shewn in sketch, approximately magnetic.

* List already forwarded by Medical Officers.

I have, &c.,
(Signed) JOHN R.M. CHARD,
Lieutenant R.E.

To Colonel Glyn, C.B.,
Commanding 3rd Column.

Copy of Major Spalding D.A.A.G.'s Report.

1. At 2 p.m. on the 22nd inst. I left Rorke's Drift for Helpmakaar, leaving a second horse at Varmaaks. My intention was to bring up Captain Rainforth's Company 1st Battalion 24th Regiment to protect the ponts. Lieutenant Chard, R.E., on returning from the camp Isandlana, had observed Zulus on the neighbouring heights. I thought they might make a dash for the ponts during the night.

2. Between Varmaaks and Helpmakaar, where I arrived 3.45 p.m., I met two Companies 1st Battalion 24th Regiment under Major Upcher; on returning from Helpmakaar, I met Major Upcher, who informed me of the disaster at Isandlana.

3. We advanced as far as Varmaaks with the troops. I then pushed on to the foot of the Berg, accompanied by Mr. Dickson, of the Buffalo Border Guard. The road was covered with fugitives, chiefly Basutos and people in civilians' clothes, but there were one or two mounted Infantry. Several of these I ordered to accompany me, but all, except two, slipped away when my back was turned.

My object was to ascertain whether the post at Rorke's Drift still held out. In this case I should have sent word to Major Upcher to advance and endeavour to throw myself into it.

4. But every single white fugitive asserted that the Mission-house was captured; and at about 3 miles from the same I came across a body of Zulus in extended order across the road. They were 50 yards off – a deep (ravine) donga was behind them, capable of concealing a large force. They threw out flankers as if to surround the party.

Mr. Dickson agreed with me that they were Zulu, an opinion soon borne out by the 'horns' which they threw out. So we trotted back to the troops some two miles in rear.

5. On reaching the summit of a hill from which the Mission-house is visible, it was observed to be in flames. This confirmed the statement of the fugitives that the post had been captured. This being the case it was determined to save, if possible, Helpmakaar and its depôt of stores.

6. It was growing dusk: the oxen had already had a long trek; the hill had to be re-ascended, and the heights were said to be lined with Zulus. I examined

them with my glass, but could not observe the enemy. There may have been a few detached parties, however, as these were observed by competent witnesses. No attack was made by them: and the column reached Helpmakaar by 9 p.m., when wagon laager was formed around the Commissariat stores. Colonel Hassard, R.E., met us half way up the Berg and took over command from me.

7. The following morning a dense fog prevailed. About 9 a.m. a note arrived from Lieutenant Chard, R.E., stating that Rorke's Drift still held out and begging for assistance. It was considered imprudent to risk the safety of Helpmakaar by denuding it of its garrison, and probable that Rorke's Drift had already been relieved by the column under the General. It was determined to push down to the Drift some mounted men to gather intelligence. I was in command. A short distance from Helpmakaar Mr. Fynn was met, who communicated the fact that the General's column had relieved Rorke's Drift. At the top of the Berg I met Lieut.-Colonel Russell, who confirmed the news. At about noon I reached Rorke's Drift and reported myself to the General.

(Signed) H.S. SPALDING,
Major, D.A.A.G.

From the Lieutenant-General Commanding in South Africa
to the Right Honourable the Secretary of State for War.

Durban, Natal,
8th February, 1879.

SIR,

Since the date of my last Despatch the situation of military affairs has not changed. Colonel Pearson, commanding No. 1 Column, writes in good spirits from Ekowe, which is now a strongly entrenched position, with supplies until the end of the month. Zulus hover round him, but up to the date of last communication from him (the 4th) no attack has been made on him.

The arrival of the three companies 88th Regiment, about 350 men, will enable me to move to the Lower Tugela (Forts Pearson and Tenedos), the two companies at present between Durban and that point; two companies of the Buffs and five of the 99th will be then assembled there, and will be held in readiness to move in any direction at the shortest notice as soon as the necessary class of transport can be collected.

2. Durban, Stanger, Pietermaritzburg, and Greytown are now being placed (or are already so) in a position for defence, with garrisons which should prevent panic among those living around.

3. At Rorke's Drift and Helpmakaar the position is quite unchanged, and the frontier has been quite quiet and the road running from Greytown has been quite open. Colonel Glyn, C.B., reports that the bodies of Lieutenants Melville and Coghill, 24th Regiment, had been found five miles down the river, 300 yards from the banks, they lay close to each other, and a number of dead Zulus around them showed how they had stood their ground.

4. Uneasiness has been felt in the Colony at the prospect of a raid, but the latest information tends to an impression that our forces at Ekowe and Rorke's Drift are to be attacked first.

5. Colonel Evelyn Wood, commanding No. 4 Column, has forwarded me two reports, copies of which I have the honour to forward. He also expects to be attacked.

I beg to call your attention to the manner in which Lieutenant-Colonel Redvers Buller carried out Colonel Wood's instructions regarding the destruction of the Bagalusini Kraal. The energy and intrepidity shown by this officer and those under his command, deserves, in my opinion, warm commendation, and I have so expressed myself to Colonel Wood.

6. I regret to say that nearly half the volunteers serving under Lieutenant-Colonel Buller are now leaving him. They have done good service, but the loss of the services of mounted men, such as these, is much to be deplored at this moment. Mounted men are found to be an absolute necessity in this country, and I trust the efforts of His Excellency the High Commissioner to obtain them from the Free State and Cape Colony may be successful.

7. The Medical Department has lost the services of two valuable officers, Surgeon-Major Alcock, who has been invalided, and Surgeon-Major Shepherd, whose name, I regret to say, is among the list of killed on the 22nd January.

8. I have already brought to your notice the wants of the Royal Artillery: the casualty list shows the severe loss this arm has experienced.

9. I should be very glad if a Field Telegraph could be sent out. In a country of vast distances, with so few facilities for transmission of news, it would be of great value, and in the future will supplement the main lines of telegraph according to the importance of the post.

An application of the electric light would be of the greatest use to fortified posts and night encampments.

10. Lastly, I have the satisfaction of saying the health of the troops is generally good, and reports of the wounded are favourable.

11. I continue to receive the greatest possible assistance from Rear-Admiral Sullivan, C.B., C.M.G., and all those under his command.

I have, &c.,
(Signed) CHELMSFORD, Lieut-Gen.

P.S. – I have endeavoured in my communication not to lessen the gravity of the situation in Natal and the Transvaal and their frontiers, but at a time when it is my sad duty to forward details of our losses, I would venture to add that I have received from many native and other sources information that the Zulus have been much disheartened by the severe losses they have experienced. Mr. Lloyd, Political Assistant to Colonel Wood, writes on February 1, 'They are said to be much disheartened with their losses in their attack on the Rorke's Drift Column (No. 3); the Undi Regiment, more especially the Tulwana division of it, suffered very heavily.'

No. 4 Column.
Enclosures from Colonel Wood.

Camp, Zungeni Nek,
23rd January, 1879.

D. A. GENERAL,
Lieut.-Col. Buller with Mr. Pict Uys reconnoitered the Tumguin Range on the 20th, but were unable to reach the eastern end, being opposed by about 1,000 Zulus.

That day No. 4 Column reached the Unwolosi; and Tinta, uncle of Seketwayo, came to me out of a cave to which I had gone, about six miles east of Unwolosi River.

In the evening I sent back Tinta's people with a convoy of wagons, about 70, escorted by one Company, 90th Light Infantry.

Later, hearing some Zulus had crossed the Unwolosi, I reinforced the escort.

On the 21st we built a stone laager fort, left all superfluous stores, over one week's supply, and crossing the river, pitched on the left bank, and at midnight 21st–22nd, leaving one Company, 13th Light Infantry, and the Company, 90th, which had just arrived from Blood River, marching 34 miles in 25 hours; at fort Tinta we started on patrol.

Colonel Buller, with the Dutchmen and two guns, marched up the right bank of the Unwolosi, while the 90th and 1st Battalion, Wood's Irregulars, marched direct for the range of the Zungeni, so as to strike it about three miles from the Unwolosi. Though until 3 a.m. it was very dark, and we passed over a difficult country, guided by some Dutchmen, the 90th arrived on the summit about 6 a.m., just as Colonel Buller ascended by the Yag Pad line.

After resting for two hours we moved on towards a few hundred Zulus who were on the south-eastern summit of the range. These retired hastily, leaving about 250 head of cattle and 400 sheep and goats, which were brought into camp, which had been formed by Colonel Gilbert, who marched at 3 a.m. on the 22nd from the Unwolosi River.

From the eastern extremity of the range we saw under the Iuhlobana Mountains, near Mabambas' Kraal, about 4,000 Zulus. They formed a circle, a triangle, and a square with a partition thus, ☐☐ They were moving later, so far as could be seen in the dusk, up the Iuhlobana Mountains.

The patrol reached camp at 7 p.m., having been under arms, the Infantry carrying 100 rounds, nineteen hours. One gun limber was broken in being let down by ropes, over a very steep hill, but we hope to repair it to-day.

(Signed) EVELYN WOOD,
Colonel.

P.S. – Our movements would not be possible without the aid of Mr. Pict Uys and his men, whose local knowledge is invaluable.

I propose to move on to-morrow, weather permitting, towards the Bagalusina Kraal, 18 miles about distant.

NOTE. – The Iuhlobana Mountain is part of the Ityenteka Range.

D. A. GENERAL,

Having yesterday seen the ground over which the reconnoitering party, under Colonel Buller, C.B., skirmished on the 20th, against a large body of Zulus, I deem it my duty to bring to the notice of His Excellency the Lieut.-General Commanding, that in my opinion, the presence of mind, tactical skill and determination which led Colonel Buller to advance at full speed, seize and hold a stony hill, accounts for the successful withdrawal of the party, with the insignificant damage it sustained.

(Signed) EVELYN WOQD,
Colonel.

D. A. GENERAL,

Report of a reconnoissance under Lieut.-Colonel R. Buller, C.B., Commanding Frontier Light Horse, is forwarded herewith for the information of his Excellency the Lieut.-General Commanding.

(Signed) EVELYN WOOD,
Colonel Commanding No. 4 Column.

22nd January, 1879. Camp Fort.

Camp White, Umfelosi River,
21st January, 1879.

SIR,

I have the honour to report that at 4 a.m. yesterday, Mr. Pict Uys kindly sent eight of his Dutch Burghers to reconnoitre the top of Zingan Mountain.

At 9 a.m., in accordance with instructions, I started on patrol, with the force detailed in the margin.* Crossing the Umfelosi River by an indifferent drift, about two miles above Mount Inseki, I moved towards Mabomba's Kraal, round the south-east spur of Zingan. About seven miles from the river Mr. Uys' men, who were reconnoitring the left, found about 50 armed Zulus in a kraal of Seketwayo, under the side of Zingan, leaving the kraal the Kafirs at once took to the rocks.

An engagement ensued, during which I reinforced the Burghers with 20 dismounted men under Captain Brunker.

Twelve Kafirs were I know killed, and I think a few more. One man, F.L.H., was wounded with an assegai thrown by a wounded Kafir, and another had a narrow escape. We found four guns and a good many assegais, all of which I had broken, but I did not search the ground thoroughly as I did not think the risk of getting men stabbed by wounded Kafirs worth the result.

About this time two of Mr. Uys' men came to us and reported a commando of Kafirs on the top of Zingan. Ascending the mountain by a difficult stony cattle track, we found the report was quite true, as the rocky ridges were lined with Kafirs.

I endeavoured to cross the upper plateau in order to get a view of Mabomba's Kraal from above, but the hill was too strongly held for us to force it. With the view of ascertaining the full strength of the enemy who were coming down to attack us in three columns, I seized a small stony koppie and commenced an engagement with the centre column. Our fire soon drove them to cover with a loss of about eight dead (seen a good many more reported), but meanwhile we were completely outflanked on our right by some 300 Kafirs who crept round among the stones and kraantzes of the ridge, and our left by some 400 men, boldly moved in tolerable order across the open ground about a mile off.

I accordingly decided to withdraw. In doing so one man F.L.H. was wounded and two men bit by spent balls, and the horse of Mr. Raymond, a bugler, was hit. The Kafirs pursued us to the Umfelosi River in force, and about 100 crossed the drifts; but having then secured my retreat I turned on the flats and drove them back. As far as I could see they all returned to the top of Zingan.

We reached camp about 9.30 p.m.

Throughout the day I received the greatest possible assistance from Mr. Uys, whose experience and courage are alike remarkable, and from his men, who shoot well and are excellent scouts.

I consider that we were engaged with about 1,000 Kafirs, the larger proportion of whom had guns, many very good ones; they appeared under regular command and in fixed bodies. The most noticeable part of their tactics is that every man after firing a shot or after being fired at drops as if dead, and remains motionless for nearly a minute. In case of a night attack an interval of time should be allowed before a return shot is fired at a flash.

I have, &c.,
(Signed) REDVERS BULLER,
Lieut.-Col. F.L. Horse.

* Frontier Light Horse: 7 Officers, 75 N.C.O. and men.
  Dutch Burghers: 22, under Mr. Pict Uys

Return of Wounded in the Action of the 20th January, 1879.

Frontier Light Horse, trooper J. Berrg, severely wounded, gunshot flesh wound of thigh; trooper J. Randell, slightly wounded, incised (assegai) wound of wall of chest. Both the wounded men are progressing favourably.

(Signed) T. O'REILLY, M.B.,
Surg. A.M.D. in Med. Charge.
The Officer Commanding Troops.

Camp W., 4 Column, Zululand,
26th January, 1879.

A. M. GENERAL,

Forwarded for your information. The story given by the Zulu woman evidently has reference to a skirmish which Colonel Buller had on the Zungeni Nek, which I reported through D. A. G.

(Signed) EVELYN WOOD,
Colonel.

From Commandant Schumbrucher to Colonel Wood, V.C., C.B.,
Commanding No. 4 Column, Zululand.

Luneburg, 23rd January, 1879.

1. At midnight last night I received news that Umbelini said to have a following of about 3,000 fighting men, was expected to move from Intombe

mountains during that night to gain the place called Umbelini's Caves, of which I gave you a description in my letter of 28th December last. There he would collect such additional forces as he could draw from this District, cross over in full force to the Pongolo Bush above Engelbrechts, and from there direct his attacks upon Luneburg and surrounding places. The information came through one of Umbelini's men, who had left the main force on Tuesday before day-light in order to warn a certain native family living on the Pombetrion, his particular friends, and it bore all the evidence of truth.

2. I immediately sent three men on horseback to the Pongolo Drift, where Umbelini would most likely cross, near the confluence of the Tombe of Pongolo, there to lay in wait; and hurry back should they observe any large party approaching.

I likewise despatched the natives attached to my command to watch the Tombe Drift, half-way between this and Umbelini's Caves, with similar instructions; and at daybreak I ordered a strong mounted patrol of German Burghers to patrol beyond the Pongolo towards Zungin's Neck.

3. All the patrols and scouts have returned now (5 p.m.) reporting everything apparently quiet, and no Zulu force to be seen nor any spoor to be found of a large number of men or cattle, but a Zulu woman was met by Nkosana (a fat native constable). She says that she came from Umbelini's Impi; that an engagement had taken place on Tuesday which prevented Umbelini from carrying out his march upon Luneburg; that Umbelini's and Magolosini's forces had been joined at Zungin's neck, and were attacked by a small white force; the white men fired and retired, stood again and fired and retired, and repeated this several times; that each time they killed many Zulus, whereas the Zulu bullets fell all short. She could not say how many, but she knew that very many Zulus were shot, and amongst the wounded she had seen with her own eyes a great Captain, Makukunesani, who belonged to Diligaan's people, and was the Captain of the whole Pongolo district; he was shot through the breast, and was still living on Tuesday night. His being mortally wounded had caused great consternation amongst the Zulus. The woman further states that she left Umbelini's force on Tuesday night, and that she heard all yesterday (Wednesday) heavy firing towards Zungin's Neck. The woman's statement seems to me very probably true, but under any circumstances I thought it well to give you a minute account. If true, it will give me all the more confidence in the sagacity and faithfulness of my own men in carrying out their reconnoitring patrol.

4. I have led the water close to the entrance of Fort Clery, and managed a sort of drawbridge, excavating the hitherto solid entrance to the depth of the ditch. All this, including wood for bridge and chains to draw up, involved an expenditure of five pounds, signature for which I request your authority of payment.

5. The laager here is now fully occupied, all the farmers having come in. I count amongst them 28 fighting men, armed with nine Winchesters, four breech-loaders of other pattern, and the rest muzzle-loaders, double barrels, all with adequate ammunition. They are very willing in doing patrol duty, and give me great assistance.

6. Seventy-eight (78) natives of the tame description have enrolled themselves to join here. I have placed them under command of Nkosana, and appointed their kraal to be above Mr. Filter's house, under the hill. They do also, cheerfully, duty as scouts and sentries all round, and cost nothing whatever neither pay nor rations. In case of attack, they will form a welcome addition, to my rather small force.

A supply of about 50 stand of arms with ammunition to be kept exclusively in the fort for use to repel an attack would be extremely useful in order to arm such defenders as I may be able to draw to the fort in cases of emergency.

8. Colonel Rowland, V.C., C.B., accompanied by Captains Harvey and Sherrard, and Commissary-General Phillips, paid a visit to Luneberg on the 20th, and returned to Derby on the 21st. I understood that Colonel Rowland, having received despatches from Head-quarters whilst here, authorising the formation of a column, No 5 will move as soon as possible to occupy Meyer's Station, and then move on to Makatee's Kop. I expect his advanced guard in a few days.

9. Yesterday's partial eclipse of the sun (between 3 and 4 p.m.) is looked upon by the natives as a sign of Umbelini's power, who is reported to have particular powers over that luminary. If he should have happened to get a thorough good thrashing on that day (which he most certainly did get, if it be true that he was engaged by you), it will have a most demoralizing effect upon all Zulu warriors, who looked to Umbelini's victory as certain whenever he should meet our forces.

The garrison here is well and in full fighting spirit. I have only had occasion to punish one man (Geo. Gibbs) for insubordination and inciting others to mutiny. I nipped the thing in the bud, by ignominiously dismissing Geo. Gibbs on the spot, and drumming him out of camp. Drink was, as usual, the cause. I have, however, succeeded in getting rid of the pest of liquor, by promising 50 lashes to any man, black or white, who would bring drink into the fort or laager.

Wishing glorious success to your arms,

I am,
Yours obediently,
SCHUMBRUCHER,
Commander.

LIST of Officers and Men killed in action at the Camp, Isandklwana Hill, Zululand, on the 22nd January, 1879.

'N' Battery, 5th Brigade R.A.

Captain and Brevet-Major		Stuart Smith
Brevet-Major		Russell, R.A., Rocket Battery
3483	Sergeant	Edwards William
1119	Corporal	Bailey, H.R.
2721		Cooper, William
1872		Langridge, John
746	Bombadier	Parker, John
1763		Nash, Thomas
3181	Acting Bombadier	Lequay, John
2196		McDonel, James
1882		Aylett, James
147		Boswell, Thomas
841	Farrier	Whenham, Robert
753	Collar Maker	Sheppard, Thomas
1462	Shoeing Smith	Elliott, Thomas
692	Gunner	Reede, John
1655		Meade, James
704		Woolacott, Alfred
1626		Wilson, William
2322		Page, Henry
1883		Beach, Frank
1773		James, Edward
2630		Miller, Thomas
1113		Lamb, James
2189		Byrne, James
2633		O'Neal, Daniel
1834		King, Charles

2652		Williams, Robert
2945		McGregor, Murdoch
1405		Smythe, Joseph
1885		Burk, James
2460		Regan, John
1412		Hicks, James
1311		Collins, Robert
655		Berry, Thomas
2183		Roscoe, William
1634		Davies, Isaac
1683		Marshall, William
1438		Redman, Alexander
2819		Wilson, Thomas
3484		Dickings, William
1833		Stevenson, Joseph
1082		Connelly, John
668		Harrison, Thomas
646		Cockrane, Samuel
707	Driver	Barren, William
723		Hutchings, James
1073		Bailey, George
1598		Clark, Thomas
2174		Brooks, James
2119		McKeown, George
751		Allen, Henry
2178		Jones, J. William
741		Marchant, John
2301		Cowley, Henry
1185		Dailey, John
2015		Murphy, Francis
727		Hiatt, William
1977		Joyce, Leonard
1471		Adams, William
648		Spread, Charles
1961		Bruce, Thomas
1524		Bishop, Charles

Royal Engineers.

Lieutenant-Colonel	Durnford
Lieutenant	McDowell
Corporal	Gamble

Sapper	Cuthbert
	Maclaren
	Wheatley
Captain	G. Shepstone, Political Assistant to Colonel Durnford

1st Battalion 24th Regiment.

Major and Lieutenant-Colonel	Pulleine, H.B.
Captain	Degacher, William
	Mostyn, W.E.
	Wardell, G.V.
	Younghusband, R.
Lieut. and Adjutant	Melville, T.
Lieutenant	Porteous, F.P.
	Cavaye, C.W.
	Anstey, E.D.
	Coghill, N.J.A.
	Daly, J.P.
	Hodson, G.F.J.
	Atkinson, C.J.
2nd Lieut.	Dyson, E.H.
Paymaster	White, F.F.
Qrt.-Master	Pullen, J.
Sergt.-Major	Gapp, F.
Qr.-Mst.-Srgt.	Leitch, T.
I.S. Msktry	Chambers, G.
Drm-Major	Taylor, R.
Ord.-R.-Sergt.	Fitzgerald, G.G.
P.-Mtr.-Sergt.	Mead, G.
Amry.-Sergt.	Hayward, H.
Sergt.-Cook	Field, A.
Tailor-Srgt.	Smedley, J.
Color-Sergt.	Brown, T.
	Whitfield, W.
	Edwards, W.
	Ballard, J.G.
	Wolfe, F.
Sergeant	Edwards, Jno.
	Heppenstal, C.
	Clarkson, Jno.
	Bradley, D.

	Fowden, J.
	Hornibrook, M.
	Piall, A.
	Fay, Thos,
	Bennet, G.
	Cooper, T.
	Upton, G.
	Gamble, D.
	Parsons, Wm.
	Cohalan, Wm.
	Giles, C.
	Ainsworth, P.
	Greatorex, J.
	Smith, Jno.
Lance-Sergeant	Milner, Jno.
	Reardon, Jno.
Corporal	Ball, N.
	Bell, P.
	Bellhouse, Jno.
	Board, A.
	Davis, R.S.
	Everett, E.
	Franks, Jno.
	Knight, Jno.
	Lawler, Jno.
	Markham, P.
	Miller, M.
	Rowden, Jno.
	Tarbuck, Jno.
	Williams, R.
	Richardson
Private	Abbot, R.
Drummer	Adams, W.H.
Private	Alingham, T.
	Amos, E.
Drummer	Andrews, C.
Private	Atkins, A.
	Bailey, Jno.
	Baker, E.
	Barry, Jno.
	Barry, Jno.

Bartles, J.
Bastard, C.
Beadon, R.
Beckett, Wm.
Benham, Jno.
Bennett, A.
Bennett, R.
Benson, R.
Betterton, N.
Birch, Jno.
Bishop, J.
Blackhurst, -
Blower, Jas.
Bodmin, F.
Boulton, S.
Boylan, Jno.
Bray, Jas.
Breese, Jno.
Brew J.W.
Brodrick, J.
Brown, J.
Brown, Wm
Bugby, F.W.
Bull, Jno.
Burke, T.
Burke, Wm.
Burns, Wm.
Busby, Thos.
Butler, W.
Bye, Jno.
Cahill, J.
Callanan, J.
Campbell, M.
Camp, Jas.
Canhillon, Jas.
Carpenter, W.H.
Carrol, P.
Casey, Jas.
Ceiley, E.

Lance-Corporal   Chadwick, Wm.
Private   Chalmers, W.

Chapman, Wm.
Chatterton, Jas.
Christian, D.
Clarke, A.
Clements, H.
Clutterbuck, Wm.
Cole, A.
Coleman, Jas.
Collins, D.
Collins, T.
Colston, J.
Lance-Corporal　Conboye, G.
Private　Conmelly, C.
Conmelly, Jno.
Cormers, S.
Cook, Jas.
Cooper, H.
Coughlin, R.
Cox, Jas.
Cox, T.
Clarke, M.
Cullen, M.
Davis, A.
Davis, E.
Davis, W.
Drummer　Dibden, G.
Private　Diggle, M.
Diggles, Jas.
Dobbin, Jno.
Dobbs, Wm.
Donohoe, C.
Dorman, Jno.
Doran, M.
Dowde, P.
Dredge, Wm.
Duck, T.
Duckworth, G.
Duffey, Jno.
Dugmore, E.
Dunn, F.
Dyer, Jno.

Edwards, Jno.
Edwards, W.G.
Egan, Wm.
Egan, Thos.
Elderton, G.
Eldrington, W.
Ellis, D.
Ellisan, H.
Evans, J. W.
Evans, D.
Ellsmone, J.

Lance-Corporal   Every, T.
Private   Faircloth, Jno.
Farmer, Wm.
Fay, G.H.
Ferris, M.
Fitzgerald, T.
Fortune, Jas.
Flint, E.
Freeman, W.
Gilder, T.
Gillan, Jno.
Gingle, C.
Glass, G.
Graham, A.
Goddard, C.
Goddchild, G.
Gass, T.
Green, W.
Greig, W.
Gregson, Wm.
Griffiths, G.
Hall, J.
Hadden, G.
Hall, Jno.
Hannaford, Jh.

Lance-Corporal   Hackin, T.
Private   Hannard, J.
Hamey, D.
Harris, T.
Harris, Wm.

	Hayden, Wm.
Drummer	Haynes, Jno.
Private	Hedges, Jas.
	Hemmings, C.
Lance-Corporal	Hewitt, Jno.
Private	Hibbard, Jas.
	Hickin, W.H.
	Hicks, T.
	Hitchin, Jno.
	Hines, T.
	Higgins, T.
	Holland, Jas.
	Holden, Wm.
Lance-Corporal	Horgan, Dd.
Private	Home, Jno.
	Hornbuckle, C.
	Horrigan, Wm., Rorke's Drift.
	Harrington, D.
	Harrington, T. J.
	Haugh, Wm.
	Hughes, E.
	Hughes, Jno.
	Hughes, John
	Hughes, Owen
	Hughes, S.
	Iggulden, A.
	Ilsley, F.
	Ivatts, E.
	Jenkins, Jas.
	Jenkins, Wm.
	Jenkins, Wl.
	Johnston, G.
	Johnson, H.
	Johnson, Job
	Johnson, Jno,
	Johnson, Jno.
Lance-Corporal	Johnson, Wm.
Private	Johnson, Jno.
	Johnson, Jas.
	Johnstan, A.
	Jones, E.

Jones, Jno.
Jones, Jno.
Jones, T.
Jones, Wm.
Jones, Wm.
Keene, J.
Keegan, Jas.
Kempsall, N.
Kempster, Jno.
Kelly, A.
Kelly, J.F.
Kelly, Jas.
Kelly, F.
Knight, Jas.
Lamb, Jas.
Lambert, Thos.
Leach, R. W.
Leaver, T.
Lee, Jno.
Lewis, H.
Lewis, R.
Lenain, Jno
Ling, Jas.
Lippet, S.
Lisbeck, G
Lloyde, G.
Lowe, C.
Lowe, R.
Lockett, W.
Lovell, C.
Lyons, Jno.
Lycett, Jas.
Lawrence, Jno.
Mack, H.A.
Maney, C.
Mann, Wm.
Martin, D.
McDonald, M.
McFarlame, M.
McHale, Jos.
McKenzie, G.J.

Mair, G.R.
Mahoney, C., Rocket Battery
Malarey, M.
Marley, L.
Meredith, J.H.
Millen, C.
Miller, P.
Moore, R.
Morgan, Jno.
Morgan, Wm.
Morris, Jno.
Morse, R.

Lance-Corporal,   Murphy, Jno.
Private   Murphy, Jno.
Murphy, P.
Murray, Jno.
Nash, P.
Newbery, A.
Newbery, T.
Nickolas, E., Rorke's Drift
Nickolas, Wm.
Nye, Wm.
Oakley, Wm.
Odey, G.
Ogden, Jas.

Drummer   Osmond, G.
Orlapp, J.F.

Private   Padmore, Jas.
Painter, T.
Parry, Jno.
Parry, R.
Patterson, G.H.

Drummer   Perkins, T.
Private   Petus, Jno.
Phillips, Jno.
Phillips, J.N.
Pickard, J.R.
Plant, S.
Plunkett, J.
Pallen, A.
Pope, W.

	Pottow, W.
	Powell, H.
	Procter, Jno.
	Prasser, G.
	Prasser, Jno.
	Pugh, Wm.
	Pugh, Wl.
	Quirk, Jas.
Drummer	Reardon, T.
Private	Remmington, E.
	Retford, W.
	Richards, G.
	Richardson, M.
	Rigney, Jno.
	Rettman, Jno.
	Roberts, Wm.
	Rowan, H.
	Rodgers, H.
	Rowbery, P.
	Rule, W.
	Rutter, T.
	Ryan, Jas.
	Salter, G.
	Sainey, F.
	Sears, H.
	Sellwood, W.
	Sharp, P.
	Shaw, R.
	Shea, D.
	Sheather, H.
	Shrimpton, Jno.
	Silcock, R.
	Skelton. W.
	Smith, C.
	Smith, C.
	Smith, E.
	Smith, Jas.
	Smith, G.
	Speed, T.
Drummer	Stansfield, S.
Private	Stevens, H.

Stevens, W.
Strange, E.
Sullivan, Jno.
Sullivan, P.
Sutton, P.
Swaffer, R.
Taylor, E.
Tate, R.
Terry, James
Theobold, W.
Thomas, J.B.
Thomas, Jno.

Drummer   Thompson, Jno.
Private   Thomett, Thos.
Lance-Corporal   Thrassell, C.
Private   Tillisard, H.

Tuneny, T.
Todd, G.
Townsend, J.
Trottmann, D.
Turner, E (Mounted Troop).
Trowell, W.
Tullett, Jas.
Vines, G.
Waller, E.
Walker, E.
Walsh, Thos.
Walsh, Thos.
Walham, W.
Wamer, J.
Watkins, H.W.
Watley, Jno.
Watts, H.

Lance-Corp.,   Wheatherhead, H.
Private   Webb, T.

Welsh, Wm.
Whealon, Jno.
Whelan, Tho.
Wilks, F.
Wilkinson, A.
Williams, Ellis

Williams, Jno.
Williams, E.
Williams, P.
Williams, M.
Williams, Thos.
Williams, Thos.
Williams, Jas.
Wilson, S.
Wolfendale, A.
Wolfendale, J.
Wood, Jas.
Wooley, Jno.
Worthington, E.
Wright, R.
Whybrow, E.

Lance-Corporal	Young, T.
Private	Desmond, P. Wounded at Rorke's Drift.
	Waters, Wounded at Rorke's Drift.

2nd Battalion 24th Regiment.

Lieutenant	Pope, C.D.A.
	Austen, F.
	Dyer, H.J.
Sub-Lieut.	Griffiths, T.L.G.
Quartermaster	Bloomfield, E.
Band Mstr.	Bullard, H.
Quartermaster-Sergt.	Davis, G.
Sergeant	Lines, J.
	Chew, C.
	Ross, J.
	Reeves, W.J.G.
	Carse, H.
	Shaw, W.
	Wilkins, G.
Lance-Sergt.	McCaffry, J.
	Haigh, H.
Corporal	Henshaw, J.
	Sims, G.
	Low, J.M.
	Thompson, T.
	Mortlock, H.

Corporal	Greenhill, W.
Drummer	Anderson, J.
	Holmes, J.
Private	Byrne, J.
	Quinn, J.
	McGuire, J.
	White, T.
	Mockler, M.
	Sherwood, S.
	Malley, E.
	Smith, J.
	Horrocks, G.
	Flynn, J.
	Hawkins, W.
	Jones, T.
	Broderick, M.
	Kelly, J.
	Kennedy, T.
	Phillips, D.
	Howells, R.
	Evans, J.
	Smith, P.
	Long, C.
	Jones, T.
	Emerson, R.
	Lynch, T.
	Edwards, E.
Boy	Gordan, D.
Private	Smith, R.
	Pritchard, D.
	Buerly, J.P.
	Jones, T.
	Jones, W.
	Sathand, B.
	Mack, J.
	Stevens, R.
	Pedler, T.
	Watkins, J.
	Woods, G.
	White, J.
	Bryant, J.

Lance-Corp.   Elvey, J.
Private   Carroll, J.
                               Cornish, T.
                               Davis, J.J.
                               Davis, J.
Boy   Gurney, J.
Private   Hacker, S.
                               Hall, C.
                               McCormack, J.
                               Hudson, J.
                               Hopkins, R.H.
                               Slade, H.
                               Thompson, G
                               Ball, T.
                               Hall, J.
                               Davis, J.
                               Fortune, M.
                               Lewis, E.
                               Williams, G.
Boy   McEwan, J.S.
Private   Montgomery, T.
                               Perkins, H.
                               McCaffry, P.
                               Waterhouse, W.
                               Bishop, H.
                               Byard, A.
                               Turner, E.
                               McCracken, S.
                               Fitzpatrick, M.
                               Watson, G.
                               Hill, J.E.
                               King, J.
                               Nobes, R.
                               Machin, J.
                               Neagle, T.
                               Quelford, T.
                               Fair, A.
                               Allen, J.
                               Bevan, S.
                               Bennett, T.
                               Byrne, J.

Buckley, R.
Bray, A.
Bridgewater, F.
Cleary, M.
Charles, T.
Davis, G.
Cherry, F.
Davis, D.
Dowle, J.
Donegan, M.
Edwards, J.
Earish, J.
Finn, T.
Fitton, G.
Flynn, D.
Fry, J.
Fox, T.
Gee, W.
Ghost, G.
Hall, W.
Griffiths, W. (V.C.)
Hughes, F.
Healy, J.
Hunt, J.
Johnstone, W.
Jenkins, W.
Jones, J.
Jones, E.
Jones, J.
Llewellyn, J.
Martingale, E.
Marsh, J.
Moore, F.
Morris, A.
Morrissey, J.
Morgan, J.
Murphy, J.
McDoon, G.
Poole, S.
Popple, S.
Price, H.

Price, J.
O'Keefe, T.
Rees, W.
Rice, W.
Roche, W.
Roche, M.
Sheane, W.
Smith, C.M.
Smith, H.
Smith, D.
Smith, F.
Ferrett, D.
Thomas, D.
Treverton, R.
Walker, S.
Williams, E.
Williams, E.
Williams, E.
Williams, E.
Williamson, J.
Wright, J.
Young, J.
Scott, J.
Waters, C.
Mulroy, J.
Hall, B.
Shuttleworth, W.
Barton, J.W.
Wightman, W.
Sanders, T.

Army Service Corps.

Corporal	Pritchard, Joseph.
Private	Cole, Jno,
	Jaques, Wm.

Army Hospital Corps.

Lieut, of Orderlies	Hall.
Corporal	Lee.
Private	Kremer.
	Lewis.

Dean.

Hughes.

Munn.

Gilman.

Hogan.

Keen.

Baker.

Army Medical Department.

Surgeon-Major	Shepherd
Boy	Green, servant to Surg.-Major Shepherd

Mounted Infantry.

80th Quartermaster Sergeant	Johnson, Wm.
9th Lancers Farrier	Sampson, Hy.
6th Dragoon Guards Private	McStravick, Jno.
2–3rd Private	Shaw, James
	Wheatley, Geo.
1–24th	Turner, Edwd.
80th	Chesterton, John
	Holman, Edwd.
	McDonald, Wm.
Shoeing-Sm.	Seymour, Wm.
Private	Whitehouse, Joseph
Civ. Servant	Popworth, Wm., servant to Capt. Gardner, special service.
	Turner, Robt., servant to Capt. Hallam Parr, 13th Reg.

Natal Mounted Police.

Corporal	Lally
Lance-Corporal	Campbell
Trooper	Banger, G.
	Berry
	Blakeman
	Clark, J.
	Capps
	Daniels
	Dorey
	Eason

Fletcher
Hunter
Lloyd
McRae
Meares, C.
Neil
Parsons
Pleydell
Pollard
Secretan, F.
Sidall
Stimson
Thicke
White, C.
Winkles
Pearce

Natal Carbineers.

Lieutenant	Scott, F.J.D.
Quartermaster	London, W.
Quartermaster-Sergt.	Bullock, J. C.
Trooper	Blakie, J.
	Borain, G.
	Christian
	Deane, J.
	Davis, H.
	Dickinson, H.
	Hawkins, W.
	Hayhow, C.
	Haldane
	Jackson, R.
	Jackson, F.
	Lumley, J.
	Macleroy, G.
	Mendenhall, W.
	Moodie, M.
	Ross, J.
	Swift, W.
	Tarboton, E.
	Whitelaw, J.

Newcastle Mounted Rifles.

Captain	Bradstreet
Quartermaster	Hitchcock
Sergeant	Swan
Trooper	Barnes
	Greenbank
	McAlister
	Dinkelman

Buffalo Border Guard.

Trooper	Eary.
	Guttridge.
	Wehr.

1st Battalion 3rd Regiment, N.N.C.

Captain	Krohn, Robert Lonsdale, Jas.
Lieutenant	Avery, Samuel
	Holcraft, Frank
	Jameson, Chas.
Acting-Surgeon	Bull, Frank
Quartermaster	McCormick, Jno.
Interpreter	Grant, Samuel
Sergeant	Connock, J.
	Cole, J.
	Church, H.
	Welsh, J.
	Patterson, C.
	Galling, W.
	Bryant, G.
	Atkins, H.
	Russell, W.
	Donnell
	Golding, W.
	McCarty, W.
	Humphries, W.
Corporal	Sibley, F.
	Anderson, W.
	Palmer, R.
	Balmore, J.
	Duprie, J.
	O'Connell, D.

	O'Neil, M.
	Davidson.
	Quinn, J.
	Willey, W.
	Pearson, J.
	Price, W.
Hospital-Sergeant	Cane.
Conductor	Doyle.
	Le Roue.
Cook	Neil, Geo.

2nd Bat. 3rd Regiment, N.N.C.

Captain	Erskine, Edwd.
	Barry, A.T.
	Murray, O.E.
Lieutenant	Pritchard, R.A.
	Young, L.D.
	Gibson, Arthur
	Standish
	Rivers, H.O.
Quartermaster	Chambers, A.
Quart.-Mr. Sergeant	Fair, A.
Sergeant	Schaap, D.
	Phillips, S.
	Brebner, W.
	Murray, W.
	Hamilton, W.
	Allen, J.
	Mowbray, G.
	Broderick, A.
	Broderick, M.
	Moore, G.
	Kemp, W.
	Elverson, G.
Corporal	Walker, J.
	Green, W.
	Delaharpe, D.
	Sturk, H.
	Harrington, T.
	Willis, J.
	Styles, R.

Caufield, J.

Welsh, E.

Allen, W.

Schneither, L.

De Villiers, D.

Stapleton, W.

Laughlin, W.

Pitzer, T.

W. BELLAIRS, Colonel,

6th February, 1879.   Deputy Adjutant-General.

From Lieutenant-General Commanding South Africa
to the Right Honorable the Secretary of State for War.

Durban, 9th February, 1879.

SIR,

I have the honour of forwarding certain documents which I was unable to attach to my letter of yesterday's date, sent by the 'Anglian,' viz:-

(1). Copies of statement of Lieutenant-Colonel Crealock, Assistant Military Secretary.

(2). Copies of statement of Captain Allan Gardner, 14th Hussars;

(3). Epitome of information given by natives to the Honorable W. Drummond and Mr. Longeast Head Quarter's Staff, which should be attached to the documents connected with the Court of Enquiry;

(4). A. copies of two letters received from Colonel Pearson; and

B. Précis of my answer;

(5). Copies of reports by Colonel Wood and Lieutenant-Colonel Buller regarding the destruction of Makulusini (pronounced Bagulucini) Kraal, which was referred to in my dispatch as an enclosure also.

I have, &c.,

(Signed) CHELMSFORD,

Lieutenant-General.

1.

Statement of Lieutenant-Colonel J. North Crealock, Acting Military Secretary.

1. Soon after 2 A.M. on the 2nd January I received instructions from the Lieutenant-General to send a written order to Lieutenant-Colonel Durnford,

R.E., commanding No. 2 Column, to the following effect (I copied it in my note-book which was afterwards lost): 'Move up to Sandhlwana Camp at once with all your mounted men and Rocket Battery – take command of it. I am accompanying Colonel Glyn, who is moving off at once to attack Matyana and a Zulu force said to be 12 or 14 miles off, and at present watched by Natal Police, Volunteers, and Natal Native Contingent. Colonel Glyn takes with him 2–24th Regiment, 4 guns R.A., and Mounted Infantry.'

2. I was not present during the conversation between Major Clery, Staff Officer to Colonel Glyn, and the Lieutenant-General, but the evening before, about 8.30 P.M., on this officer asking the Lieutenant-General if the 1–24th 'Were to reinforce Major Dartnell in the Magane Valley,' he said 'No.' The General received, I believe through Colonel Glyn, a subsequent representation which caused the fresh orders at 2 A.M. the 22nd, and the orders to Lieutenant-Colonel Durnford.

3. Lieutenant-Colonel Durnford, R.E., was not under Colonel Glyn's command at this time; he had been moved from his original position before Middle Drift, with some 250 Mounted Natives, 200 of Sikalis footmen, the Rocket Battery, and one battalion of the 1st Regiment Natal Native Contingent to the Umsinga District, on the Lieutenant-General's seeing the ease with which the Natal frontier could be passed in that part of the Buffalo River. The Lieutenant-General's order was therefore sent to him by me, being the only Head Quarter Staff Officer (except the Aide-de-Camps) with him. These details formed part of No. 2 Column under his command.

4. I sent the orders to him by Lieutenant Smith-Dorrien, of 95th Foot, with directions to leave as soon as he could see his way. I expected him to find Colonel Durnford at the Bashee Valley; it was delivered and acted upon.

5. Although I was not aware at that time of the Lieutenant-General's grounds for ordering the troops from camp, yet it was evident to me that he wished to close up to the camp all outlying troops, and thus strengthen it. He would naturally also consider that the presence of an officer of Colonel Durnford's rank and corps would prove of value in the defence of a camp, if it should be attacked.

6. The Lieutenant-General had himself noticed mounted men in one direction (our left front) on the 21st. A patrol of the Mounted Infantry had found another small body of the enemy in our front, and Major Dartnell, we knew, had a strong force before him on our right front. It was evident to me

that the Zulu forces were in our neighbourhood, and the General had decided, on the evening of the 21st, to make a reconnaisance to our left front.

7. It did not occur to me that the troops left in camp were insufficient for its defence. Six Companies British Infantry, 2 guns, 4 Companies Natal Contingent, 250 Mounted Natives, 200 Sikalis men, and details of Mounted Corps appeared to me – had I been asked – a proper force for the defence of the camp and its stores.

8. I subsequently heard Major Clery state that he had left precise instructions to Lieutenant-Lionel Pulleine 'to defend the camp.' Such instructions would, I consider, as a matter of course, be binding on Colonel Durnford on his assuming command of the camp.

9. The first intimation that reached me on the 22nd of there being a force of Zulus in the neighbourhood of the camp was between 9.30 and 10 A.M. We were then off-saddled on neck facing the Isipise range, distant some 12 miles from camp. During the three previous hours we had been advancing with Colonel Glyn's Column against a Zulu force that fell back from hill to hill as we advanced, giving up without a shot most commanding positions. Major Clery at this time received a half sheet of foolscap with a message from Lieutenant-Colonel Pulleine informing him (I think it ran) that a Zulu force had appeared on the hills on his left front. Our own attention was chiefly bent on the enemy's force retiring from the hills in our front, and a party being pursued by Lieutenant-Colonel Russell three miles off. This letter was not addressed to me, and I did not note on it the time of receipt, but one I received from Colonel Russell soon after is noted by me (I think, for it is at Pietermaritzburg) as received at 10.20.

10. Lieutenant Milne, R.N., A.D.C., shortly after this descended a hill on our left, whence he had been on the look-out with a telescope. All the news he gave regarding the camp was that the cattle had been driven into camp. I believe this to have been nearly 11 A.M.

11. In the meantime information reached the General that the right of our force was smartly engaged with the enemy's left. Two companies of 2–24th and the 2nd Battalion of the Natal Native Contingent climbed the hill to our right, and, striking across the flat hill, joined the Volunteers who were still engaged. Colonel Glyn accompanied them, having first ordered back the four guns and two Companies 2–24th to the wagon track, with instructions to join him near the Mangane Valley. He had also sent back instructions by Captain Alan Gardner, 14th Hussars, to Lieutenant-Colonel Pulleine. I was not informed of their nature. I took the opportunity of ordering our own

small camp to proceed and join us, as the General intended to move camp up to the Mangane Valley, as soon as arrangements could be made.

12. The 1st Battalion Natal Native Contingent had been ordered back to camp, and to skirmish through the ravines in case any Zulus were hanging about near the camp.

13. Not a sign of the enemy was now seen near us, and followed by the remaining two Companies 2–24th, we climbed the hill and followed the track taken by the others. Not a suspicion had crossed my mind that the camp was in any danger, neither did anything occur to make me think of such a thing until about 1–15, when Honourable Mr. Drummond said he fancied he had heard (and that natives were certain of it) two cannon shots. We were then moving back to choose a camp for the night, about 12 miles distant from Isandhlana. About 1.45 P.M., however, a native appeared on a hill above us, gesticulating and calling. He reported that heavy firing had been going on round the camp. We galloped up to a high spot, whence we could see the camp, perhaps 10 or 11 miles distant. None of us could detect anything amiss; all looked quiet. This must have been 2 P.M.

14. The General, however, probably thought it would be well to ascertain what had happened himself, but not thinking anything was wrong, ordered Colonel Glyn to bivouac for the night where we stood; and taking with him some forty Mounted Volunteers proceeded to ride into camp.

15. Lieutenant-Colonel Cecil Russell, 12th Lancers, now joined us, and informed me that an officer of the Natal Native Contingent had come to him (about 12 noon, I think) when he was off-saddled, and asked where the General was, as he had instructions to tell him that heavy firing had been going on close to the camp. Our whereabouts was not exactly known, but the 2–24th Companies were still in sight, and Colonel Russell pointed them out, and said we were probably not far from them. This officer, however, did not come to us.

16. This information from Colonel Russell was immediately followed by a message from Commandant Brown, commanding the 1st Battalion Natal Native Contingent, which had been ordered back to camp at 9.30 A.M. – (the Battalion was halted a mile from us, and probably eight miles from camp) – to the effect that large bodies of Zulus were between him and the camp, and that his men could not advance without support. The General ordered an immediate advance of the Battalion, the Mounted Volunteers and Mounted Infantry supporting it.

17. I am not aware what messages had been sent from the camp and received by Colonel Glyn, or his Staff; but I know that neither the General nor myself had up to this time received any information but that I have mentioned.

18. At 3.15 the Lieutenant-General appeared to think that he would be able to brush through any parties of Zulus that might be in his road to the camp without any force further than that referred to, viz.: – 1st Battalion Native Contingent and some 80 mounted white men.

19. At 4 P.M., however, the Native Battalion again halted, and I galloped on to order the advance to be resumed, when I met Commandant Lonsdale, who remarked to me as I accosted him, 'The Zulus have the camp.' 'How do you know?' I asked, incredulously. 'Because I have been into it,' was his answer.

20. The truth was now known, and every one drew his own conclusions; mine were unluckily true, that hardly a man could have escaped. With such an enemy and with only foot soldiers it appeared to me very improbable that our force could have given up the camp until they were surrounded.

21. The General at once sent back Major Gossett, A.D.C., 54th Regiment, to order Colonel Glyn to advance at once with everyone with him. He must have been five or six miles off. It was now 4 P.M. We advanced another two miles, perhaps. The 1st Battalion, 2 Regiment, Natal Native Contingent, deployed in three ranks, the first being formed of the white men and those natives who had firearms, the Mounted Volunteers and Mounted Infantry on the flanks, with scouts to the front.

22. About a quarter to five we halted at a distance, I should think, of two miles from camp, but two ridges lay between us and the camp, and with our glasses we could only observe those returning the way they had come. Colonel Russell went to the front to reconnoitre, and returned about 545 with a report that 'All was as bad as it could be;' that the Zulus were holding the camp. He estimated the number at 7,000.

23. The troops with Colonel Glyn had pushed on with all possible speed, though the time seemed long to us as we lay and watched the sun sinking. At 6 P.M. they arrived, and, having been formed into fighting order, were addressed by the General. We then advanced to strike the camp and attack any one we found in our path back to Rorke's Drift.

24. I consider it but just to the Natal Native Contingent to state that it was my belief that evening, and is still the same, that the two Battalions would have gone through any enemy we met, even as our own British troops were

prepared to do. I noticed no signs of wavering on their part up to sunset, when I ceased to be able to observe them.

(Signed) J.N. CREALOCK,
Lieutenant-Colonel, A. Mil. Sec.

2.

Statement by Captain Alan Gardner, 14th Hussars.

Camp, Rorke's Drift,
26th January, 1879.

I left the force with the General about 10.30 A.M. and rode back to Isandlana Camp, with the order to Lieutenant-Colonel Pulleine to send on the camp equipage and supplies of the troops camping out, and to remain himself at his present camp, and entrench it. Between twelve and one o'clock I reached Isandlana, and met Captain G. Shepstone, who told me he had been sent by Colonel Durnford for reinforcements; that his (Colonel D.'s) troops were heavily engaged to the left of our camp, beyond the hill, and were being driven back. We proceeded together to Colonel Pulleine. I delivered him my order; but the enemy were now in sight at the top of the hill, on our left. Lieutenant-Colonel Pulleine sent out two companies about half-way up the hill, and drew up the remainder, with the two guns in action, in line, on the extreme left of our camp, and facing towards the left, from which direction the enemy were advancing in great numbers. For a short time, perhaps fifteen minutes, the Zulus were checked, but soon commenced to throw forward their left, extending across the plain on our front. We had between 30 and 40 mounted men, and I asked permission to take them down in the plain, and check the enemy's turning movement. Lieutenant-Colonel Pulleine told me to do so, and I accordingly galloped them to the front, and lined the spruit running across the front of our camp. The Basutos who were previously retiring, formed line with us and the enemy halted and commenced firing from behind cover. Leaving the mounted men who were under Captain Bradstreet, I returned to Lieutenant-Colonel Pulleine who had previously told me to remain with him. Shortly afterwards, observing the mounted men retiring, I rode back to ascertain the cause. Captain Bradstreet told me he had been ordered to do so by Colonel Durnford, who soon afterwards told me himself that he considered our position too extended, and wished to collect all the troops together. But it was now too late. Large masses of the enemy were already in the camp and completely surrounded the men of the 24th Regiment. Numbers of these were also on the road to Rorke's Drift. The guns limbered up and attempted to retire to the left of that road, but were surrounded and overturned. The few mounted men remaining retreated up the small hill on the right rear of the camp, but were soon surrounded by the enemy advancing from the left and front. Many were killed. A few of us managed to escape by riding down the hill on the right, but many were shot riding along the narrow valley, and more drowned and shot in crossing the Buffalo. When I saw all was lost, I sent an order by a Basuto to the officer on Rorke's Drift, telling him to fortify and hold the house. I also sent a similar order to Helpmakaar. We reached Helpmakaar about five P.M., and near a laager round the Commissariat Stores I endeavoured to obtain a messenger to go to Colonel E. Wood, as 1 feared the General's force would be cut off, and hoped he, Colonel Wood, might be in time to lend his assistance. No one would go, the Basutos saying they did not know the way. So on the return of the two companies who had started for Rorke's Drift, I decided on going myself, and riding all night reached Utrecht about four o'clock the next day. I then got a messenger to go to Colonel Wood and returned myself to Helpmakaar. On the road, learning that Colonel Glyn's head-quarters were at Rorke's Drift, I proceeded thither. I trust I may not be thought, presumptous if I state my opinion, that had there been a regiment or even two squadrons of cavalry the disaster at Isandlana would not have occured. The enemy's advance across our front which was requisite in order to turn our right was in extremely loose order, the ground was an open plain and could easily have been cleared by a determined charge. The enemy's shooting was so indifferent that our loss would have been very small. The result moreover of a cavalry charge would have had a very different effect on the enemy's morale to the retreating fire of mounted skirmishers, and I feel confident we could have held our own till the return of the General's force.

(Signed) ALAN GARDNER,
Captain, 14th Hussars, Staff Officer,
3rd Column.

3.

Information received from Umtegolalo, a Zulu well known to Mr. Longeast, Interpreter to the Lieutenant-General, found wounded at Rorke's Drift on the 23rd January.

Statement made by Natives regarding the Action of the 22nd January, at the Sandhlivana Hill.

The Zulu army had, on the day of the 21st January, been bivouacked between the Upindo and Babmango Hills, from which position a portion of them were able to see our mounted men, viz., the Natal Carabineers and the Mounted Police, on the Ndhlaza Kazi Hill, and were seen by them.

The army consisted of the Undi Corps, the Nokenke and Umcityu Regiments, and the Nkobamakosi and Inbonambi Regiments, who were severally about 3000, 7000, and 10,000 strong, being the picked troops of the Zulu army.

During the night of the 21st January, they were ordered to move in small detached bodies to a position about a mile and a-half to the east of the camp at Sandhlwana, on a stony table-land about 1000 yards distant from and within view of the spot visited by Lord Chelmsford and Colonel Glyn on the afternoon of the 21st January.

On arriving at this position, they were ordered to remain quiet, not showing themselves or lighting fires. Their formation was as follows: – The centre was occupied by the Undi Corps; the right wing by the Nokenke and Umcityu; and the left by the Inbonambi and the Nkobama Kosi Regiments.

Their orders from the King were to attack Colonel Glyn and No. 3 Column, and to drive it back across the boundary river. They had, however, no intention whatever of making any attack on the 22nd January, owing to the state of the moon being unfavourable from a superstitious point of view. The usual sprinkling of the warriors with medicine previous to an engagement had not taken place, nor had the war song been sung, or the religious ceremonies accompanying been performed. They were going to make their attack either during the night of the 22nd or at daylight on the 23rd, and, trusting in their number, felt quite secure of victory.

When, on the morning of the 22nd January the mounted Basutos, under the command of Colonel Durnford, R.E., discovered their position and fired at a portion of the Umcityu Regiment, that regiment immediately sprung up without orders, and charged. It was at once followed by the Nokenke, Inbonambi, and Nkobamakosi Regiments, the Undi Corps holding its ground.

Up to this point in the day there had been no fighting. Early in the morning, soon after the departure of Colonel Glyn and the troops with him, a body (probably a company of the Natal Native Contingent) had been ordered to scout on the left, but do not seem to have come upon the enemy. About nine A.M. (approximately), Colonel Durnford arrived with 250 mounted men and 250 Native Infantry, who were at once divided into three bodies, one being sent to the left, east (who came in contact with the Umcityu Regiment), one to the left front, and one to the rear, along the wagon-road (which is supposed to have gone after the baggage wagons brought up by Colonel Durnford, R.E).

At this period of the day the position of the troops was as follows. They were drawn up to the left of the Native Contingent Camp, with the guns facing the left. A message was now brought by a Natal Native Contingent officer, probably one of Colonel Durnford's mounted men, that the Zulus were advancing in great force, and firing was heard towards the left (the firing of the mounted Basutos against the Umcityu Regiment).

It is stated by a wagon driver that a consultation now took place between Colonel Durnford and Colonel Pulleine, during which he imagined there was a difference of opinion, Colonel Pulleine ultimately, however, giving way to his superior officer.

A Company of the 1st Battalion 24th were then moved up to the neck between the Sandhlwana Hill and the position occupied by the Zulus, where they at once became engaged with the Umcityu Regiment whose advance they completely checked for the time. The distance of this neck is about a mile and a half from camp.

Meanwhile the Zulus had advanced in the following order. The Umcityu Regiment formed the right Centre, and was engaged with one company 1st Battalion 24th Regiment, and about 200 of Colonel Durnford's natives; the left centre was composed of the Nokenke Regiment who were being shelled by the two guns as they advanced. Next to them on the left, came the Inbonambi Regiment with the Nkobamakosi Regiment outside of it, both making a turning movement and threatening the front of the camp, while driving before them a body of Colonel Durnford's mounted men, supported by a patrol of Volunteers. The Undi Corps, on seeing that the other four regiments had commenced the attack, as above, marched off to their right, and, without fighting, made for the north side of the Sandhlwana Hill, being concealed by it until, their turning movement being completed, they made their appearance to the west of the Sandhlwana at the spot were the wagon road crosses the neck. Meanwhile the Nkobamakosi Regiment had become engaged on the left front of the camp with our infantry, and suffered very severely, being repulsed three times, until the arrival of the Inbonambi Regiment enabled them to push forward along the south front of the camp and complete their turning movement. This produced an alteration in the position held by those defending the camp. Two companies of the 24th Regiment and all the mounted Europeans being sent to the extreme right of the camp, at the spot where the road cuts through it. The guns were moved to the right of the Native Contingent camp, having the nullah below them to their left lined by the Native Contingent; three companies of the 1st Battalion 24th Regiment remained on the left of the camp, supported on their left by the body of Mounted Basutos, who had been driven back by the Umcityu Regiment. The one company of the 1st Battalion 24th Regiment which had been thrown out to the neck, was now retiring, fighting.

By this time the attack of the enemy extended along the whole front of the camp, a distance of not less than 800 yards, and along the whole left, a distance of about 600 yards, and although they were still held in check by our fire, they were advancing rapidly towards the gaps between the troops. Up to this point their advance had been steady, and made without noise, but now they began to double and to call to one another. The camp followers and the Native Contingent began to fly, making for the right, and in a few minutes more the troops were forced to retire upon the tents to avoid being cut off, as the Zulus had now burst through the gaps. So far, very few men had fallen on our side, the fire of the enemy being far from good, but as the men fell back the Zulus came with a rush, and in a very few minutes it became a hand to hand conflict. About this time also the Undi corps, made its appearance on the right rear of the camp, completely cutting off any retreat towards Rorke's Drift. Fortunately the Nkobamakosi, instead of attempting to completely surround the camp by making a junction with the Undi, followed the retreating natives, thus leaving a narrow passage open for escape, which was taken advantage of by such as were able to escape out of the camp. A few were met and killed by the Undi, but that corps, believing that the camp was already plundered, decided to make the best of their way to Rorke's Drift, and plunder it, never dreaming that any opposition could be offered by the few men they knew to be there.

The loss of the Zulus must have been exceedingly heavy. The Umcityu were frightfully cut up by the single company of the 1st Battalion 24th Regiment, which was sent out of camp, and never returned; the Nkobamakosi fell in heaps; the hill down which the Nokenke came was covered with slain; and the loss of the Undi at Rorke's Drift cannot be less than 500; they killed all their own wounded who were unable to get away. Much astonishment was expressed by the Zulus at the behaviour of our soldiers, firstly, regarding their death dealing powers considering their numbers; secondly, because they did not run away before the enormous numerical superiority of the enemy.

(Signed).
W. DRUMMOND,
Head-quarter Staff.

4B.

Précis of instructions contained in Lord Chelmsford's letters to Colonel Pearson.

Durban, 6th February, 1879.

Yours of 1st received.

Trust that the news that you are to be attacked and also Glyn may be true.

Having been attacked, and the enemy repulsed a decision as to your future movements absolutely necessary.

If you can reduce your garrison to one-half, it will give you a strong moveable column at Lower Tugela.

Should wish to see Naval Brigade garrisoning forts at Lower Tugela. Yourself and staff ought to be there also.

After a successful action, would be your best chance of withdrawing a portion of your garrison, otherwise a risk.

Endeavour to arrange for the holding an entrenchment requiring a lesser garrison.

Your best field officers should remain in command.

Bring back only what baggage, &c., is absolutely essential. The sick and wounded should come in empty wagons.

I trust that any attack made on our posts maybe simultaneous. We are ready for it.

400 men 88th Regiment, expected to-day; 200 remain here, 200 go to Stanger, thus releasing ninety-nine companies for Lower Tugela.

No news from Wood since 24th January.

No raids have, as yet, been made into Natal, but I expect one shortly.

Do all you can to hold out as long as possible with whole or part of your force, but let us know when the time has nearly arrived to fall back on account of want of supplies.

Native Contingent have disbanded themselves.

Durban, 8th February, 1879.

Contents of your letter, dated 6th February, received by telegraph.

My belief is, your garrison should be at once reduced to the minimum which you consider is necessary for its defence; this will give us more time for throwing in supplies.

There will not be a force at Lower Tugela for six weeks at least, sufficient to ensure a convoy to Ekowe, and unwise to attempt it, but if you withdraw surplus garrison, you will have troops enough for a very efficient flying column at that place.

Add 100 or 200 to the 400 you suggest for garrison, but cut down your defences to meet reduced garrison.

Your own presence is absolutely essential at Lower Tugela.

Mine is required all over Natal.

A Head Commander required to look after every post of your command.

Latest news, Zulus will not knock their heads against our posts, but will raid into Natal. All more necessary for a moveable force at Lower Tugela. Other columns are too weak for me to decrease them to increase yours, and each must hold on as best they can until reinforcements arrive, thus you must read my instructions.

Details I leave to you, only let us know when you propose to fall back.

A large force stated to be near Zuguin. 'It will not do to face too great odds, but you might, perhaps, manage to reach Umanidusi' (where be every available man from Lower Tugela should sent), without your move being discovered. Each man should carry 100 rounds, two days' food. Bring no wheeled carriage. Line of march to be most compact, and no delay on the march if a few shots are fired at you. The garrison left at Ekowe must be on the alert, as it will be imagined you have deserted the post altogether.

JOHN M. CREALOCK,
Lieut.-Col., Asst. Mil. Sec.

A second copy to be sent twenty-four hours after the first. Reported on 9th February that neither of these had passed through the lines.

Colonel Wood's Column,
Camp Kambulu Hill,
1st February, 1879.

SIR,

I have the honour to report that in accordance with orders I started with the force named in the margin* at four A.M. this morning for Makulisini Krall, at seven o'clock we off saddled for breakfast under the north side of Zingin Hill, starting again at 8.20 we shortly after hit the so-called wagon road from Potter's Store to the Makulisini. It is a very bad one, we found the country practicable for all arms up to a point about due north of the centre of Inhlobarm Interior, after that it was very difficult, and neither guns nor wagons could have traversed it, we saw a few Kafirs and cattle in the Inhlobarm.

When within four miles of this neck, from which I was told we should see the kraal, I increased our pace to a fast canter, we left thirty men in this neck and scrambled down the hillside into the basin in the centre of which the place is situated and then galloped up to it at 12.30 P.M.

The Kafirs in it fled in all directions, we took 270 head of cattle and entirely destroyed the kraal, which contained about 250 huts. About 6 Kafirs were killed. We had, I am happy to say, no casualty.

The Makulisini is about 30 miles east of this, it is in a basin entirely surrounded with precipitous hills which would be very difficult to take if held by any force. I do not think guns could be got there without men handling them. Throughout the day I received the greatest assistance from Mr. Pict Uys, indeed without his men I don't think we should ever have got to the place. As far as I could see I think that most of the Kafirs that were in this Inhlobarm have left it and gone to the south-east.

* F.L. Horse, Captain Barton, 8 officers, 106 non-commissioned officers and men; Dutch Burghers, Mr Pict Uys, 33 Burghers.

> I have, &c.,
> (Signed) REDVERS BULLER,
> Lieut.-Col., F.L. Horse.

> Kambula Hill, 10 P.M.,
> 1st February, 1879.

LT.-COL. CREALOCK.

On this, as on all occasions, Lieutenant-Colonel Buller, C.B. has done excellent service, and I am greatly indebted to him and to Mr. Pict Uys. The Bagalusini Kraal has been till now a rallying point for the most determined opponents of the British Government, and its destruction will have a good effect on all friendly or neutral natives, while the Zulus will see the spirit of the High Commissioner's message is fully carried out, for though this, a barrack, is destroyed, no dwelling places of the inhabitants have been wilfully damaged by the Troops of No. 4 Column.

> (Signed) EVELYN WOOD,
> Colonel.

> Ekowe, 2nd February, 1879, Sunday.

DEAR LORD CHELMSFORD,

Your letter of 27th January reached me this morning, also telegram of 30th, apparently to some one at Lower Drift, asking what ammunition I have got, and detailing position of Nos. 3 and 4 Column; also your telegram to me of 28th, informing me of 'Boadicea' men joining my column, asking what you can do for me, and telling me Wood has beaten 5,000 Zulus; also telegram of 23rd, detailing poor Durnford's defeat, and the losses sustained. It is all most sad; and no doubt the arms and ammunition taken will be used against us. The above is the plan of the entrenchment here. Of course it is not nearly finished, but it is a formidable place even now, and we work hard at it all day. I sent you a letter yesterday, describing our situation. As last night was rainy, I hope it will reach you all right. The messengers who brought yours came by the road we followed, and did not see any one, but no doubt they were all in the bush, as we believe there are numbers of Zulus between us and the Tugela. If you could send up the two companies Buffs now at Lower

Drift, and the three companies 99th, also at Drift, as well as the Stanger and Durban companies, we should be strong enough here, as I should then form an entrenched camp outside. But the difficulty would be to keep up the supplies, as convoys would be most likely molested, very likely in the neighbourhood of the Amatakula and Inyazane, where it is thick and bushy. This will be a difficult problem to solve, but now that we are here it would be a fatal mistake, in my opinion, to abandon the post, which, as I have already said, will be required as a forepost when you are ready to advance again. Indeed, if we retired to the Tugela, we should most likely have all the Zulu army at our back, and be obliged either to destroy all our ammunition and stores before we left Ekowe, or abandon them on the march if attacked, as in all probability we should be by overwhelming numbers.

We have 1,365 Europeans here all told, and about 100 Natives, including pioneers, but exclusive of leaders and drivers, the number of whom I don't quite know. We have in round numbers 1,200 rifles and 332 rounds of ammunition for that number, also 127,000 rounds Gatling, 37 Naval Rockets, 24-pounders (shot; not shell rockets), 46 Rockets, (shell) for 7-pounders, also for 7-pounders 200 Shrapnel, 254 common shell, 20 double shell, and 33 case. It is almost impossible to get an accurate return of food, but I think we must have over three weeks' supply, the cattle, however, may be swept away at any moment, as of course they have to be kept in the wagon laager outside. I am keeping a small reserve in the ditches, where we stable the horses also, although commanded, the ground is perfectly open round here, except one or two small patches of wood, which would give cover, but which are being cut down as fast as we can do it. The brushwood, however, is all destroyed, the road to Ekowe from the Tugela is a mere beaten track, and at this season of the year very bad in places, especially this side of the Inyazane, which is often very steep, narrow, and sloping towards the valley (where cut on the side of a hill) thus rendering a wagon liable to upset. The latter defect we remedied en route, but as there is no stone in the country I am afraid it will never be possible to do more than for each convoy to repair the road for itself. There is nothing to repair it with except logs and brushwood, which of course won't stand the traffic of a large number of wagons. I know of no place between this and the Lower Drift where a depôt could be advantageously formed, nor even fortified posts. The camping ground on the left bank of the Umsindusi is, however, nice and open, but it is commanded at one point toward the Amatikulu. Our camping ground at the Inyoni was on a knoll, but it is only nine miles from the Tugela. You ask if a Zulu can climb over our parapets here without assistance? I fear he can in some places, but we are working hard at deepening the ditches. We want medicines, and I have written to Tarrant about them, as I have told you what food and ammunition we have got, you will be able to judge of what we can do. I find it quite impossible to get information. Cur Kafirs won't do spy. They are afraid of being taken. Thanks for your good wishes. Has there been any raid made on Natal?

Sincerely and respectfully yours,
(Signed) C.K. PEARSON.

DEAR KINGSCOTE,

Send this letter to the General, by special mounted messenger if possible, to Durban, first telegraphing the pith of it to him. Send the enclosed small piece of paper to Dr. Tarrant. Tell Major Graves the following officers and non-commissioned officers Natal Native Contingent are here:- Captain Shervington; Lieutenants Orwin and Webb; Interpreter Grieg; Sergeants Swann, Behrends, Sherrer; Corporals Adams, Whiffler, Schulter, Schmidt, Meyer, Crossman, Phillipe, Fayard, Westphall, also twenty-six natives. Send us news whenever you can. Dark nights and rainy weather is the time.

Yours sincerely,
(Signed) C.K. PEARSON.

The position generally is weak, being slightly commanded on three sides by hills within musketry range, but the whole of the front has been traversed by wagons, cornsacks, &c.

The water (very good) is under the fire of the fort within 150 yards, and efforts (which show good results) are being made to obtain water by sinking on the site itself, the troops bivouac at the alarm posts shown.

Ekowe, 6th February, 1879.

DEAR LORD CHELMSFORD,

I received yesterday morning your letter of the 2nd instant and a Telegram from the Deputy-Adjutant-General of the 4th. In the latter I am reminded of the inadvisability of reinforcements being sent to me as they would only help eat our food. When I wrote upon this subject I was not quite clear as to the immediate future course of this column. I now quite recognize our position and I quite see, too, the mistake which would be made by reinforcing us. We are now very strongly intrenched. Good thick parapets, ditches no where less than seven feet deep and ten feet wide. In places they are both deeper and wider, the ditches are partly flanked as well, either by flanks, stockades, caponnieres or cuttings in the parapet. Enfilade and reverse fire have been well considered and traverses have been constructed to protect us from both.

The batteries are masked and spare sand bags provided to protect the gunners from fire upon any point from which the gun is not actually firing.

Trous-de-loups are being made on the glacis, and a zig-zag will be made to the watering-place about 60 yards from the fort, to ensure the safety of the watering party. We have three entrances, a main entrance over a drawbridge, over which carts or unloaded wagons can pass; this is drawn back at night; a small foot bridge to the watering place which is topped up on the alarm sounding, and a trestle bridge, also a footbridge, which is dismantled at retreat. Near the main entrance is a sally port leading into the ditch where at night we have some earth close's, as, of course the day latrines are some distance from the fort. In a hollow below this face are two cattle laagers built of wagons chained and reimed together. The circular one holds the slaughter cattle, and the other most of the trek oxen. These are protected by an L shaped work, nevertheless, the cattle are a constant source of anxiety to me, as they might be taken away during a dark night if the Zulus should be enterprising, at least so it seems to me. I trust I may be wrong. We are better off for food than I thought we were, and, if our cattle are left to us, we shall be able to get along for over three weeks from this day, and, with many essentials for some time longer. Heygate has sent a pretty accurate return to the Commissary General, which he must have received, as it went with my letter which you have acknowledged.

Our resources in the way of ammunition you also know. As regards dividing our entrenchments, so as to defend our stores efficiently in the event of the garrison being reduced, I am afraid it could not well be done without very, materially altering everything. Every building is now within the fort, and was preserved in the belief that all your columns were to have been fed from this line, and that, consequently, stores on a large scale would be required, also a fair-sized garrison. I mean some three hundred or four hundred men, for, of course, it was not then contemplated that the garrison would have to deal with any large bodies of Zulus.

As it is, it is highly probable, I suppose, that Cetywayo may make a supreme effort to drive us out and bring the bulk of his army this way. I trust he may do so and he will find it a very hard nut to crack indeed. We have got all the distances measured and this afternoon a table of ranges will be issued to the troops. If we have time the distances will all be cut on the hills which slope our way, and the cuttings filled in with white clay, which we get out of the ditches, so as to make the figures visible.

As regards our immediate future, I am of opinion, and I trust you will forgive me giving it frankly that, a convoy of wagons not exceeding 20 in number and all with good spans of 20 oxen, and none with larger loads than

4000 lbs. should be sent us, as soon as you can get an escort together, equal to a battalion of 600 or 700.

The wagons to contain nothing but food for men and a little more ammunition, especially for guns and rockets, which we want and would not be much good to the Zulus if it fell into their hands. The escort would not require tents, and could carry two days' provisions on their persons, which would save something. I would ask to have the two Companies Buffs, now at the Lower Drift, sent up, and with the return wagons I would send back the three companies and Head-quarters 99th, half the company Royal Engineers, the Native Pioneers, the odds and ends of Volunteers, Native Contingent, and drivers and leaders still here. In fact the latter have signified their intention to bolt the first opportunity. If the escort reported the road pretty clear, I would also suggest sending back the sick and wounded, who arc fit to travel, and some of the trek oxen which I should be very glad to get rid of. The drivers and leaders could take charge of them.

I most respectfully hope you will remember that I am only giving my opinion. I am ready to reduce the garrison to any limits you may choose to order, and to take my chance with the remainder, but having pretty well studied our position, I hope from every point of view, I do not think (unless we see no chance of being attacked by a very large body of the enemy) that it would be prudent just yet to reduce the garrison beyond the limits I have suggested.

In making the above suggestions, I have studied to reduce the number of mouths, and to retain, at the same time, all the fighting men I could. It will be better too, to keep units, *i.e.*, battalions together. The Natal Pioneers will be useful in repairing roads between this and the Tugela and the half company Royal Engineers will be necessary, should any intermediate station be fixed upon as a fortified post. I know of no place as I have already told you. The Inyone dries up in winter generally, and what water remains is brackish. Perhaps our camping ground on the left bank of the Umsindusi might do. The water is beautiful, but it is commanded, as I think I also told you, from the high ground towards the Amatakula, only in that direction, however, so perhaps the Engineers might manage to defilade it. The locality as regards the distance between Ekowe and the Tugela would be a very convenient one, I am speaking of places on the road, but I remember none adjacent to it. A few hundred men could cut down the bush along the road for several hundred yards on either side between the Inyone and Umsindusi, but I do not know whether it would not be too big a job to attempt to do so about the Amatakula and Inyazune. It would be a grand thing if it could be done. I think any escort coming up will have to look about them very carefully nearly everywhere between the Umsindusi and the high ground on this side of the Inyazune. On some places the bush is pretty thick; a few mounted scouts with the convoy would be of great use.

As regards the composition of a column, I have come to the conclusion that, although mounted men, if the horses could be fed in this country, would be of immense value, yet, considering that all their forage has to be carried, their utility is much lessened by the fact of the column being materially increased in length by the additional transport.

The Native Contingent, too, are of little or no use, unless all the men have firearms; when, perhaps, they would be as dangerous to friends as foes; and the officers and non-commissioned officers can speak Kaffir.

In the 2nd Regiment, scarcely one could do so, and I could never get anything done I wanted. The men were always grumbling at doing fatigue work, notwithstanding that they saw the soldiers working alongside them, and said they were enlisted to fight, and not to work. Yet, when they had the chance, they did not do over well.

We should be very glad of a newspaper or two giving an account of No. 3 Column. About what number of Zulus did poor Durnford's party kill before they were overpowered and slaughtered? Did the two guns fall into the hands of the Zulus?

Did the plucky company of the 2nd Battalion 24th at Rorke's Drift (I suppose it was guarding the Depôt) beat off the 2,500 Zulus whom they fought for twelve hours? How very foolish of poor Durnford's detachment to scatter about so far from the camps. Has any raid been made on Natal? The men here are very savage at the thoughts of so many of their wounded comrades being butchered, for, of course, as all were found dead, the wounded must have been murdered.

We are all still in very good health, and the work will not be so hard now I hope, as all the heavy work of the entrenchments is completed. 37 on the sick report to-day, two of the Buffs rather bad with the diarrhoea, one of them, Oakley, the married man whose name I sent the other day, is not so well, he had only fever then. Wounded doing very well.

We had some rain last night and the night before a very heavy thunderstorm. To-day it has been exceedingly hot.

I am going to send this letter off to-night. The messengers say the road is thoroughly watched, but I cannot hear of any large force of Zulus being between us and the Tugela.

Sincerely and respectfully yours,
(Signed) C.K. PEARSON.

CHELMSFORD'S DESPATCHES PUBLISHED ON 4 APRIL 1879

War Office, 4th April, 1879.
Despatches, of which the following are copies, have been received at the War Office from the Lieutenant-General Commanding the Forces in South Africa:-

From Lieutenant-General Lord Chelmsford, K.C.B.,
to the Adjutant-General to the Forces.

> Pietermaritzburg, Natal,
> 28th February, 1879.

SIR,

I have the honour to bring under the notice of His Royal Highness the Field-Marshal Commanding-in-Chief the accompanying report received from Colonel Glyn, C.B., commanding No. 3 Column, showing how the Queen's colour of the 1st Battalion 24th Foot, which had been lost on the 22nd January, has since been recovered, and giving an account of the gallant behaviour of Lieutenant and Adjutant Melville and Lieutenant Coghill, of that regiment, until they met their deaths in the endeavour to save this colour from falling into the enemy's hands.

> I have, &c.,
> CHELMSFORD,
> Lieutenant-General Commanding.

> Rorke's Drift, Buffalo River,
> 21st February, 1879.

SIR,

I have the honour to report that on the 22nd January last, when the camp of Isandlwanha was attacked by the enemy, the Queen's colour of the 1st Battalion 24th Regiment was in the camp, the head-quarters and five companies of the regiment being there also.

From all the information I have been since able to obtain, it would appear that when the enemy had got into the camp, and when there was no longer any hope left of saving it, the Adjutant of the 1st Battalion 24th Regiment, Lieutenant Teignmouth Melville, departed from the camp on horseback, carrying the colour with him in hope of being able save it.

The only road to Rorke's Drift being already in possession of the enemy, Lieutenant Melville, and the few others who still remained alive, struck across country for the Buffalo River, which it was necessary to cross to reach a point of safety. In taking this line, the only one possible, ground had to be gone over which from it ruggedness and precipitous nature would under ordinary circumstances, it is reported, be deemed almost utterly impassable for mounted men.

During a distance of about six miles Lieutenant Melville and his companions were closely pursued, or, more properly speaking, accompanied by a large number of the enemy, who from their well-known agility in getting over rough ground, were able to keep up with our people though the latter were mounted, so that the enemy kept up a constant fire on them, and sometimes even got close enough to assegai the men and horses. Lieutenant Melville reached the bank of the Buffalo, and at once plunged in, horse and all; but being encumbered with the colour, which is an awkward thing to carry even on foot, and the river being full and running rapidly, he appears to have got separated from his horse, when he was about half way across. He still however, held on resolutely to the colour, and was being carried down stream when he was washed against a large rock in the middle of the river. Lieutenant Higginson, of the Natal Native Contingent, who had also lost his horse in the river, was clinging to this rock, and Lieutenant Melville called to him to lay hold of the colour. This Lieutenant Higginson did, but the current was so strong that both officers with the colour were again washed away into still water. In the meantime, Lieutenant Coghill, 1st Battalion 24th Regiment, my orderly officer, who had been left in camp that morning when the main body of the force moved out on account of a severe injury to his knee, which rendered him unable to move without assistance, had also succeeded in gaining the river bank in company with Lieutenant Melville. He too had plunged at once, into the river, and his horse had carried him safely across, but on looking round for Lieutenant Melville and seeing him struggling to save the colour in the river, he at once turned his horse and rode back into the stream again to Lieutenant Melville's assistance.

It would appear that now the enemy had assembled in considerable force along their own bank and had opened a heavy fire on our people, directing it more especially on Lieutenant Melville, who wore a red patrol jacket. So that when Lieutenant Coghill got into the river again, his horse was almost immediately killed by a bullet. Lieutenant Coghill was thus cast loose in the stream also and notwithstanding the exertions of both these gallant officers, the colour was carried off from them, and they themselves gained the bank in a state of extreme exhaustion.

It would appear that they now attempted to move up the hill from the river bank towards Helpmakaar, but must have been too much exhausted to go on, as they were seen to sit down to rest again. This, I sorely regret to say, was the last time these two most gallant officers were seen alive.

It was not for some days after the 22nd that I could gather any information as to the probable fate of these officers. But immediately I discovered in what direction those who had escaped from Isandlwanha had crossed the Buffalo, I sent under Major Black, 2nd Battalion 24th Regiment, a mounted party who volunteered for this service, to search for any trace that could be found of them. This search was successful, and both bodies were found where they were last seen, as above indicated. Several dead bodies of the enemy were found about them, so that they must have sold their lives dearly at the last.

As it was considered that the dead weight of the colour would cause it to sink in the river, it was hoped that a diligent search in the locality where the bodies of these officers were found might lead to its recovery. So Major Black again, proceeded on the 4th instant to prosecute this search. His energetic efforts were, I am glad to say, crowned with success, and the colour, with the ornaments, case, &c., belonging to it, were found, though in different places in the river bed.

I cannot conclude this report without drawing the attention of His Excellency the Lieutenant-General Commanding, in the most impressive manner which words can command, to the noble and heroic conduct of Lieutenant and Adjutant Melville, who did not hesitate to encumber himself with the colour of the regiment, in his resolve to save it, at a time when the camp was in the hands of the enemy, and its gallant defenders killed to the last man in its defence, and when there appeared but little prospect that any exertions Lieutenant Melville could make would enable him to save even his own life. Also, later on, to the noble perseverance with which, when struggling between life and death in the river, his chief thoughts to the last were bent on the saving of the colour.

Similarly would I draw His Excellency's attention to the equally noble and gallant conduct of Lieutenant Coghill, who did not hesitate for an instant to return unsolicited, and ride again into the river under a heavy fire of the enemy, to the assistance of his friend, though at the time he was wholly incapacitated from walking, and but too well aware that any accident that might separate him from his horse must be fatal to him.

In conclusion, I would add that both these officers gave up their lives in the truly noble task of endeavouring to save from the enemy's hands the Queen's colour of their regiment; and, greatly though their sad end is to be deplored, their deaths could not have been more noble or more full of honour.

I have, &c.,
(Signed) R.T. GLYN,
Colonel, Commanding 3rd Column.

*From the Lieutenant-General Commanding in South Africa
to the Right Honourable the Secretary of State for War.*

Pietermaritzburg, Natal,
2nd March, 1879.

SIR,

1. During the past week no movements of the Zulu forces have been reported beyond that some regiments are said to be near Etshowe, watching Colonel Pearson's column; on the other hand, Captain Barrow, with a force of mounted infantry, patrolled by the lower or coast road as far as the Inyazane River without meeting any Zulu force.

2. It is reported that the Zulu King is anxious to attack Colonel Pearson's entrenchments.

3. H.M.S. 'Shah' left Simon's Bay yesterday, and I trust the reinforcements to the Naval Brigade may be at their posts within a week or ten days from now.

4. Admiral Sullivan informs me that Captain Bradshaw took upon himself the responsibility of coming to this station on hearing of the state of affairs, and apparently the Governor of St. Helena, in the same spirit, sent me all the available troops he had. In bringing this to your notice I wish to record my grateful appreciation of the manner in which these reinforcements have been diverted to South Africa. As I explained by last mail, their arrival will enable me at a critical moment to take the offensive on the Lower Tugela line, a course from which I am precluded, as at present situated, as long as Colonel Pearson finds it necessary or desirable to retain his whole force at Etshowe.

My last communication from him is dated the 24th.

5. From Colonel Wood, commanding No. 4 Column, I have received constant reports; he is holding an entrenched position at Kambula Hill (vide Durnford's map), and patrolling as far as his force of mounted men will permit.

6. Oham, Cetywayo's brother, has been for some time past in communication with Colonel Wood; he did not, however, surrender himself on the day he arranged to.

Colonel Wood believes he is sincere in his desire to do so, and I do not think it is likely he will be deceived by any subterfuge on his part.

7. The health of the troops has not changed since I last reported. I regret to say that Second Lieutenant Reg. Franklin died at Helpmakaar of Fever.

I enclose supplementary and corrected casualty reports.

8. I am informed by the Lieutenant-Governor that he has given directions for the additional force of natives to be sent to the frontier which I recommended.

9. The natives of the 1st and 2nd Regiments of the Natal Native Contingent are with their battalions, and the officers report that an excellent spirit exists in their ranks, and that they are anxious to cross the border; it is right I should add that the spirit of the 1st Regiment, has not yet been tested, and that of the 2nd Regiment when they were with Colonel Pearson's No. 1 Column a month or five weeks ago was not such as it is now stated to be.

10. By the Lieutenant-Governor's directions the natives constituting No. 3 Regiment (Commandant Lonsdale's) are not to return to the European cadre, on which they were grafted during Colonel Glyn's advance into Zululand, and I am not at present aware of the arrangements made for that regiment; in the meantime, the officers and non-commissioned officers of the cadre are doing useful service in patrolling that part of the frontier.

11. I am in communication with gentlemen in the Free State for the raising of 800 mounted men, and in a few days I shall be in a position to report the result.

12. From the Cape Colony very little material assistance has been received. The hopes I had been led to form on this head have not been realized, the reason of it would appear to be the anticipation of disturbances in the Cape Colony; indeed, from the last accounts it seems troubles have already arisen in Basutoland, and the colonial forces have been set in motion against the Chief Morosi.

13. I myself during the past week have visited Greytown and the frontier near Krautzkop, and was satisfied with the state in which I found the defences.

14. Since writing the foregoing I have received an express from Krautzkop, by which I learn of the arrival of messengers from Cetywayo suing for peace.

I have the honour of enclosing a copy of the report received from the Lieutenant-Governor, which is rather fuller than that received from the Officer Commanding.

I have, &c.,
(Signed) CHELMSFORD,
Lieutenant-General.

Special Border Agent, Umvoti, to the Honourable the Colonial Secretary.

1st March, 8 p.m., 1879.

The natives who have been expected from Entumeni for some days arrived about two hours ago, and I and Bishop Schröeder have had an interview with them.

They bring a message from Cetywayo, which they have delivered informally, two Zulus who accompany them being still on the other side of the Tugela. I have sent to have them brought up to the Bishop's house, and tomorrow morning we will receive the message in regular form in their presence.

I now proceed to give the substance of the message:-

Cetywayo begs that the Bishop will explain to the Government that he never desired this war; he has never refused the terms proposed at the Lower Tugela; he had already collected 1,000 head of cattle to pay the demand made on him. Sirayo's sons had escaped, and he was looking for them when he heard the English armies had crossed the Tugela; they attacked and killed many of Sirayo's people, but even then he did not despair of peace, for he then succeeded in arresting Sirayo's sons. He sent them bound with his army under Unvumengwana's charge to be delivered up to the General at Rorke's Drift; three men were sent on to try and obtain a hearing, but they were fired at and returned. The fighting at Sandhlwana was brought about accidentally; the English horse attacked outlying parties of Zulus who returned their fire, more came up and joined in the fray, until the battle became general. The King protests that he never ordered his army to attack the English column, and his Indema Unvumengwana is in disgrace for having permitted it.

As regards Inyezani, Cetywayo contends that Colonel Pearson provoked the attack made on him by burning kraals and committing other acts of hostility along the line of march.

He now asks that both sides should put aside their arms and resume the negociations with a view to a permanent settlement of all questions between himself and the Government.

The King also states he would have sent in a message some time since, but was afraid, because the last time when he sent eight messengers to Lower Tugela they were detained; and he now begs they may be sent back.

I only asked the Entumeni men one question, viz., whether the Zulu Army was assembled. They say it is not; the men are all at their kraals.

As soon as I get the formal message tomorrow morning, I will write more fully; in the meantime I send this on by special messenger.

(Signed) JNO. EUSTACE FANNIN,
Special Border Agent.

Return of such Casualties as have been officially reported up to date, from 20th January to 2nd March, 1879.

20th January, 1879, at Yungin's Nek.

WOUNDED.

Trooper J. Berry, Frontier Light Horse, severely.
Trooper J. Randall, Frontier Light Horse, slightly.

22nd January, 1879, at Rorke's Drift.

WOUNDED.

Private J. Waters, 1st Battalion 24th Regiment, severely.
Private Beckett, 1st Battalion 24th Regiment, dangerously.
Private Desmond, 1st Battalion 24th Regiment, slightly.
Sergeant T. Williams, 2nd Battalion 24th Regiment, dangerously.
Corporal Lyons, 2nd Battalion 24th Regiment, dangerously.
Corporal Allen, 2nd Battalion 24th Regiment, severely.
Private Hitch, 2nd Battalion 24th Regiment, dangerously.
Private Jones, 2nd Battalion 24th Regiment, slightly.
Private Tasker, 2nd Battalion 24th Regiment, slightly.
Corporal Scammell, Native Contingent, dangerously.
Private Scheiss, Native Contingent, slightly.
Storekeeper Dalton, Commissariat Department, severely.

15th February, at Laluka Hill.

WOUNDED.

Swazie Mlongene, Fairlie's Native Police, dangerously.
Swazie Ynyadi, Fairlie's Native Police, severely
Swazie Wilderman, Fairlie's Native Police,severely.
Swazie Luka, Fairlie's Native Police, severely.
Swazie unknown, Fairlie's Native Police, slightly.
Swazie unknown, Fairlie's Native Police, severely.

20th February, at Eloya Mountain.

WOUNDED.

Swazie Esaw, Fairlie's Native Police, slightly.
Swazie Kushlan, Fairlie's Native Police, slightly.

21st February, at Ekowe.

DIED.

Private W. Knee, 99th Regiment.
Private J. Shields, 99th Regiment.
Lance Corporal T. Taylor, 2nd Battalion, 3rd Regiment.

21st February, at Eloza.

WOUNDED.

Two Natives, Fairlie's Horse.

CHELMSFORD'S DESPATCHES PUBLISHED ON 7 MAY 1879

War Office, 7th May, 1879.

The following Despatch has been received by the Secretary of State for War from Colonel Bellairs, Deputy Adjutant-General to the Forces in South Africa.

Durban, Natal,
5th April, 1879.

SIR,

I have the honour in the absence of the Lieutenant-General Commanding to transmit for your information copies of despatches, with enclosures, which have reached me from Colonel Wood, V.C., C.B., referring to the affair of the 28th ultimo at the Inhlobane, and the action of the following day at Kambula Hill.

I have, &c.,
W. BELLAIRS, Col.,
D.A.G.

From Colonel Evelyn Wood, Commanding No, 4 Column, to the Deputy Adjutant-General.

Camp, Kambula, Zululand,
30th March, 1879.

SIR,

I have the honour to report that the Inhlobana Mountain was successfully assaulted and its summit cleared at daylight on the 28th by Lieuteuant-Colonel Buller, C.B., with the mounted riflemen and the 2nd Battalion Wood's Irregulars, under the command of 2nd Commandant Roberts, who worked under the general direction of Major Leet, commanding the corps. I append a copy of the orders I issued and the reports of the Commanding Officers. As I mentioned in my letter of 27th instant, addressed to His Excellency the Lieutenant-General Commanding, I had heard all Cetewayo's army was about to advance against this column, he having ordered that the local tribes only should remain about Ekowe to watch that line of advance. I considered that the great importance of creating a diversion of the Ekowe Relief Column justified me in making a reconnaissance in force, and moreover, the news which I received through Mr. Lloyd showed me that on account of the delay made by Masipula for doctoring his men, it was improbable that Cetewayo's army could leave Undi till the 27th instant. As will be seen, however, from my instructions, I took precautions against the events which actually happened.

I joined Colonel Russell's Column at dusk on the 27th instant, at his bivouac, about five miles west of the Inhlobana Mountain: I had with me Captain the Honourable R. Campbell, Chief Staff Officer to No. 4 Column, Mr. Lloyd, my Political Assistant, Lieutenant Lysons, 90th. Light Infantry, Orderly Officer, and my mounted personal escort, consisting of eight men 90th Light Infantry, and seven natives under Umtonga, one of Panda's sons.

Soon after 3 A.M. I rode eastward with these details, and at daylight got on Colonel Buller's track, which we followed. Colonel Weatherley met me coming westward, having lost his way the previous night, and I directed him to move on to the sound of the firing, which was now audible on the north-western face of the mountain, where we could see the rear of Colonel Buller's Column near the summit. I followed Colonel Weatherley and commenced the ascent of the mountain immediately behind the Border Horse, leading our horses. It is impossible to describe in adequate terms the difficulty of the ascent which Colonel Buller and his men had successfully made, not without loss however, for horses killed and wounded helped to keep us on his track where the rocks afforded no evidence of his advance. We soon came under fire from an unseen enemy on our right. Ascending more rapidly than most of the Border Horse, who had got off the track, with my staff and escort, I passed to the front, and with half a dozen of the Border Horse when within a hundred feet of the summit, came under a well directed fire from our front and both flanks, poured in from behind huge boulders of rocks. Mr. Lloyd fell mortally wounded at my side, and as Captain Campbell and one of the escort were carrying him on to a ledge rather lower, my horse was killed, falling on me. I directed Colonel Weatherley to dislodge one or two Zulus who were causing us most of the loss, but, as his men did not advance rapidly, Captain Campbell and Lieutenant Lysons and three men of the 90th, jumping over a low wall, ran forward and charged into a cave, when Captain Campbell, leading in the most determined and gallant manner, was shot dead: Lieutenant Lysons and Private Fowler followed closely on his footsteps, and one of them, for each fired, killed one Zulu and dislodged another, who crawled away by a subterranean passage, reappearing higher up the mountain. At this time we were assisted by the fire of some of Colonel Buller's men on the summit. Colonel Weatherley asked permission to move down the hill to regain Colonel Buller's track, which we had lost, and by which he later gained the summit without further casualties; by this time he had lost three men dead and about six or seven wounded.

Mr. Lloyd was now dead, and we brought his body, and that of Captain Campbell's, about half way down the hill, where we buried them, still being under fire, which, however, did us no damage.

I then rode slowly round under the Inhlobana Mountain to the westward, to see how Colonel Russell's force had progressed, bringing with the escort a wounded man of the Border Horse, and a herd of sheep and goats, driven by four of Umtonga's men. We stopped occasionally to give the wounded man stimulants, unconscious of the fact that a very large Zulu force was moving on our left, across our front. We were about half way under the centre of the mountain when Umtonga saw, and explained to me by signs, there was a large army close to us. From an adjacent hill I had a good view of the force, it was marching in five columns, with horns and dense chest, the normal Zulu attack formation. I sent Lieutenant Lysons to Colonel Russell who, as it appeared, had seen the army previously, with the following written order: '10.30 A.M., 28th March, 1879. Colonel Russell, there is a large army coming this way from the south, get into position on the Zunguin Neck. (Signed) E.W.' Colonel Russell reports that he moved from the Inhlobana to the Zunguin's Neck, but this is incorrect, on the contrary, he went away six miles to the west end of the range, misapprehending the position of the neck, which is at the eastern corner of the range, and for which Wood's Irregulars, the 1st battalion, and Oham's men were making, driving the captured cattle. Colonel Russell ordered all the cattle to be abandoned and moved off very rapidly under the western end of the range. He thus uncovered the retreat of Oham's people, about 80 of whom were killed by the Zulus running down from the Inhlobana, they being greatly encouraged by the sight of the large army now moving directly on the western end of that mountain. As Captain Potter, Lieutenant Williams, and Mr. Calverley were killed, and all Oham's men except one who deserted that night, I cannot be yet sure of the numbers. The Ulundi army being, as I believe, exhausted by its rapid march, did not close on Colonel Buller, who descended after Oham's people, at the westward point of the mountain: thus he was enabled, by his great personal exertions, and heroic conduct, not only to bring away all his men who had lost their horses, but also all his wounded who could make an effort to sit on their horses. Seeing from the Zunguin's Neck where I had gone with my escort and some of Oham's men, that although the Ulundi army did not come into action, yet some two or three hundred Zulus were pursuing our natives who still maintained possession of some hundred of cattle, I sent an order to Colonel Russell who was then ascending the western end of the range, to come eastward and cover the movement of our natives into camp; this he did, but, before he could arrive, some of the natives were killed. We reached camp at 7 P.M., and Colonel Buller, hearing some of Captain Barton's party were on foot some miles distant, at once started in heavy rain, and brought in seven men, as we believe, the sole survivors of the Border Horse and Captain Barton's party, who being cut off when on my track, retreated over the north end of the Itymtaka range.

While deploring the loss we have mentioned, it is my duty to bring to notice the conduct of the living and dead. In Mr. Lloyd, Political Assistant, I lose an officer whom I cannot replace. In writing to Sir Bartle Frere on the 12th instant explaining that the success I had hitherto obtained was in a great measure owing to my subordinates, I penned the following lines: 'I need not trouble you with the names of my military staff, but I am very anxious to bring under your notice the name of Mr. Lloyd who has been of the greatest assistance to me. To personal courage and energy he adds a knowledge of the Zulu language and character, and every attribute of a humane English, gentleman.' Yesterday he showed great courage and devotion. His Excellency knew Captain the Honourable R. Campbell, he was an excellent staff officer both in the field and as regards office work, and having showed the most brilliant courage, lost his life in performing a gallant feat; and, though he fell, success was gained by the courageous conduct of Lieutenant Lysons and Private Fowler, 90th Light Infantry.

Captain Barton, commanding the Frontier Light Horse, was always most forward in every fight, and was as humane as he was brave. On the 20th of January one of Umsabe's men, who Captain Barton wished to take prisoner instead of killing him, fired at Captain Barton within two yards, the powder marking his face. When last seen on the 28th he was carrying on his horse a wounded man.

Lieutenant Williams, 58th Regiment, came out for transport duties, I nominated him as Staff Officer to Wood's Irregulars, and he evinced on this as on other occasions marked courage.

Mr. Piet Uys gave, on the 28th, a fine example to his men, as he always did, remaining behind to see them safe down the mountain, was surrounded and assegaied. On the eve of the engagement I undertook, in the name of the Imperial Government, that, if Mr. Piet Uys fell, I would watch over the interests of his children. I trust that his Excellency the Lieutenant-General Commanding and the Resident in Zululand will thoroughly support my promise.

Colonel Buller naturally says nothing about his own conduct, but I hear from the men that it was by his grand courage and cool head that nearly all the dismounted men were saved. His services to this column are invaluable. I desire to bring to the notice of his Excellency the Lieutenant-General Commanding the names of those officers Colonel Buller mentions. I append a list of killed and wounded as far as I have been able to obtain particulars, and I will forward a corrected list later.

I have, &c.,
E.W. WOOD.

P.S. – I accidentally omitted the name of Major Leet, who showed the most distinguished courage in helping on a dismounted officer at the imminent risk of his own life. I should mention Major Leet sprained his knee six weeks ago and can walk only with great difficulty.

E.W.

From Colonel Evelyn Wood, Commanding No. 4 Column,
to the Deputy Adjutant General.

Camp Kambula,
30th March, 1879.

SIR,

I have the honour to report that this camp was vigorously attacked yesterday by 10 Zulu regiments from 1.30 p.m. to 5.30 p.m. The chief command was exercised by Myamana, who did not come under fire, and Tyingwayo. The Army left Ulundi on the 24th instant, with orders to repeat the operations of the 22nd January, near Rorke's Drift. On the 24th instant, 4 Regiments were left at Ulundi and 4 near Ekowe.

Early in the forenoon, Captain Raaf, who was out reconnoitering, sent in one of Uhamu's men: he told me that being behind with captured cattle he put his 'head badge' into his pouch, and being recognised by his friends who were ignorant that he had joined us, he marched with the Zulu army to the Umvelosi; at daylight he went out scouting, and giving his companions a message that they were recalled, he ran away to Raaf's men, and told us exactly how the attack would be made at 'dinner time.'

About 11 a.m. we saw dense masses approaching in five columns from the Zungin range and the Umvelosi. The two companies who were out wood cutting were recalled, the cattle were brought in and laagered with the exception of about 200, which had strayed away owing to the desertion the previous evening of the natives whose duty it was to herd them. At 1.30 p.m. the action commenced, the mounted riflemen under Colonels Buller and Russell, engaging an enormous crowd of men on the north side of our camp. Being unable to check them our mounted men retired inside the laager, and were followed by the Zulus until they came to within 300 yards, when their advance was checked by the accurate fire of the 90th Light Infantry, and the Zulus spread out in front and rear of our camp. The attack on our left had slackened, when at 2.15 p.m. heavy masses attacked our right front and right rear. The enemy, well supplied with Martini-Henry rifles and ammunition, occupied a hill not seen from the laager, and opened so accurate an enfilade fire, though at long range, that I was obliged to withdraw a company of the 1–13th Light Infantry posted at the right rear of the laager. The front of the cattle laager was strongly held by a company of the 1–13th; they could not, however, see the right rear, and the Zulus coming on boldly, I ordered Major Hackett, 90th Light Infantry, with two companies, to advance over the slope. The companies moved down to the rear of the cattle laager, guided by Captain Woodgate, and well led by Major Hackett, who with Captain Woodgate standing erect in the open under a heavy fire, showed a fine example to the men, as did Lieut. Strong, who, sword in hand, ran on well in front of his company. The Zulus retired from their immediate front, but the companies being heavily flanked I ordered them back. While bringing them in Major Hackett was dangerously, and I fear mortally wounded; in any case I doubt his being able to serve again, and he will be a heavy loss to the regiment. The two mule guns were admirably worked by Lieut. Nicholson, R.A., in the redoubt, until he was mortally wounded, since dead: when Major Vaughan, R.A., director of transport, replaced him and did good service. The horses of the other four guns, under Lieuts. Bigge and Slade, were sent inside the laager when the Zulus came within 100 yards of them, but these officers with their men and Major Tremlett, R.A., to all of whom great credit is due, remained in the open the whole of the engagement.

In Major Hackett's counter attack, Lieutenant Bright, 90th Light Infantry, an accomplished draughtsman and a most promising young officer, was wounded, and he died during the night. At 5.30 p.m., seeing the attack slackening, I ordered out a company of the 1–13th to the right rear of the cattle laager to attack some Zulus who had crept into the laager, but who had been unable to remove the cattle; and I took Captain Laye's company of the 90th Light Infantry forward to the edge of the Krantz on the right front of the cattle laager, whence they did great execution amongst a mass of retreating Zulus. Commandant Raaf at the same time ran forward with some of his men at the right rear of the camp, and did similar execution. I ordered out the mounted men who, under Colonel Buller, pursued for seven miles the flying Zulus, retreating on our left front, chiefly composed of the Makulosini Kafirs under Umfonga, killing great numbers, the enemy being too exhausted to fire in their own defence.

From prisoners we have taken, it appears that the column which attacked our left, and then, being repulsed, moved round to our front rear and right rear, was composed of the Nokenki, the Umbonamba, Ukandampemva regiments; the Makulosini, under Umfonga, attacked the front; the Undi the right front, and the Nkobamakosi the right. I append the list of our casualties, and we are still burying Zulus, of whom there are 500 lying close to the camp, and I cannot yet estimate their entire loss, which is, however, very heavy. 300 fire-arms have already been picked up close to camp, several Martini rifles being among them. I received every assistance from the officers commanding, Lieut.-Colonel Gilbert, Lieut-Colonel Buller, Major Tremlett, and Major Rogers, V.C., and from the following officers of my staff:-

Captain Woodgate, who evinced the same cool courage for which I in vain recommended him for promotion after the Ashantee expedition.

Captain Maude, who, replacing temporarily the late Captain the Honourable E. Campbell, rendered me very great assistance.

Lieutenants Smith and Lysons, Orderly Officers, who with Captain Woodgate carried in a wounded soldier of the 13th who was lying under fire, in doing which Lieutenant Smith was himself wounded. The wounded were cared for most promptly by Surgeons O'Reilly, Brown, and Staff generally under fire.

I have. &c.,
EVELYN WOOD, Colonel,
Commanding No. 4 Column.

Number of Officers, Non-commissioned Officers, and Men Wounded in the Action of 28th March admitted into the 1st Field Hospital, No. 4 Column, Kambula Hill, Zululand.

Non-commissioned Officers and Men (Irregulars). – Frontier Light Horse, 1 severe; 1 slight. Baker's Horse, 1 severe. Transvaal Rangers, 1 severe. Weatherley's Horse, 1 severe. Total 5.

Number of Officers, Non-commissioned Officers, and Men Wounded in the Action of 29th March admitted into the 1st Field Hospital, Kambula Hill, Zululand.

Officers (Regular Troops). – Royal Artillery, 1 dangerously (since dead). 1–13th Light Infantry, 2 slightly. 90th Light Infantry, 2 dangerously (one since dead); 1 slightly. Total 6.

Non-commissioned Officers and Men (Regular Troops). – Royal Artillery, 1 dangerously, 1 severe. 1–13th Light Infantry, 8 dangerously (2 since dead), 7 severely, 5 slightly. 90th Light Infantry, 7 dangerously (3 since dead), 6 severely, 4 slightly. Mounted Infantry, 1 severely, 1 slightly. Total 41.

Irregular Troops, Officers. – Transvaal Rangers, 1 dangerously.

Non-commissioned Officers and Men. – Frontier Light Horse, 1 dangerously; 1 severely. Kaffrarian Rifles, 1 dangerously. Baker's Horse 1 slightly. Transvaal

Rangers, 1 severely. Burghers (Dutch), 1 severely. Basutos (mounted) 2 slightly. Total 8.

Staff, 14th Hussars. – 1 officer severely.

T. O'REILLY, M.B.,
Surgeon A.M.D. in Med. Charge of Troops.

Camp, Kambula Hill, 30th March, 1879.

Return of Wounded in Regiments in the Action at Inyenzana.

April 2, 1879.

Nominal Return.

Staff – Colonel Crealock, slightly.

3rd Battalion 60th Rifles – Colonel Northey, dangerously.

19th Hussars – Captain Barrow, slightly.

57th Regiment – Captain Hinxman, slightly.

99th Regiment – Lieutenant Johnson, dangerously (since dead).

Royal Navy – Surgeon Longfield, dangerously.

2nd Battalion 3rd Regiment – Private Flannery, dangerously.

57th Regiment – Private T. Perkins, dangerously.

57th Regiment – Private Deacon, slightly.

57th Regiment – Private Harris, slightly.

3rd Battalion 60th Foot – Colour-Sergeant E. Dallard, slightly.

3rd Battalion 60th Foot – Private F. Aylett, slightly.

3rd Battalion 60th Foot – Private W. Poplett, dangerously.

3rd Battalion 60th Foot – Private E. France, slightly.

3rd Battalion 60th Foot—Private M. Lahiff, dangerously.

91st Regiment – Private H. Richards, severely.

91st Regiment – Private Standye, slightly.

91st Regiment – Private Bryan, dangerously.

91st Regiment – Private Malley, dangerously.

91st Regiments – Private Hanlon, dangerously.

91st Regiment – Private McIntyre, dangerously.

91st Regiment – Private Sutton, severely.

91st Regiment – Private Gillespie, severely.

99th Regiment – Private J. Blackwall, slightly.

99th Regiment – Private J. Drew, dangerously.

99th Regiment – Private P. Armstrong, dangerously.

99th Regiment – Private G. Baker, severely.

Mounted Infantry (90th Regiment) – Private A. Hartley, severely.

Mounted Infantry (88th Regiment) – Private P. Bryan, dangerously.

'Shah,' Royal Navy – A.B.S. J. Bird, severely.
'Shah,' Royal Navy – A.B.S. J. Bulger, severely.
'Boadicea,' Royal Navy – Boy, J. Hinchley, dangerously.
'Boadicea,' Royal Navy – Carpenter's Mate, P. Condy, slightly.
'Boadicea,' Royal Marine Artillery – Acting Bombardier J. Parfitt, dangerously.
Nettleton's Contingent – Natives, 2 dangerously, 8 severely; 2 since dead.
'Tenedos,' Royal Navy – Petty Officer Porteous, slightly.

THOMAS TARRENT,
Surgeon-Major.

The following Return of Casualties at the Inhlobane on the 28th ultimo has been made by Colonel Wood, V.C., C.B.

KILLED.
Frontier Light Horse.

	Captain	Barton, Coldstream Guards.
	Lieutenant	Von Shetencron.
	Lieutenant	Williams.
83	Corporal	George Dodwell.
57	Corporal	H. Plante.
16	Lance-Corporal	H. Runchman.
251	Trooper	Alfred James Burton.
228	Trooper	K. Dobson.
184	Trooper	W. Gordon.
24	Trooper	J. Hasseldine.
37	Trooper	John Kirwien.
248	Trooper	William A. Rogan.
279	Trooper	George Seymour.
266	Trooper	James May.
288	Trooper	Peter William Caffin.
325	Trooper	Archibald L. Stewart.
112	Trooper	Thomas Halliday.
113	Trooper	George Horn.
200	Trooper	Henry Hillwig.
178	Trooper	James Grills.
314	Trooper	Londsary Shearer.
227	Trooper	Julius Gebser.
236	Trooper	William Tirrill.
20	Trooper	August Shermer.
	Trooper	John Livingstone.

Trooper	D.A. Robson.
Trooper	Charles Lynden.
Trooper	Martin Pendergast.
Trooper	Edward Higgins.

Total, 3 Officers and 26 Men.

Burgher Force.

Mr. Piet Uys.

Total, 1 Officer.

Transvaal Rangers.

Captain T. Rice Hamilton.
Sergeant-Major Thomas Brophy.
Sergeant-Major J.F. Cummings.
Sergeant Thomas Beiley.
Sergeant Wm. H. Martin.
Colour-Sergeant Charles Stanley.
Trooper J. Benkes.

Total, 1 Officer and 6 Men.

Border Horse.

Lieutenant-Colonel Weatherley.
Adjutant Lys.
Lieutenant Poole.
Sub-Lieutenant Weatherley.
Sub-Lieutenant Parminter.
Regimental Sergeant-Major Brown.
Sergeant-Major Fisher.
Quartermaster-Sergeant Russell.
Orderly-Sergeant Brissenden.
Sergeant Stewart.
Corporal Porter.
Corporal Ford.
Corporal Blackmore.
Corporal Coctzee.
Paymaster-Sergeant Johnson.
Farrier-Major Freize.
Trooper Wynan.
Trooper Shepherd.

Trooper Mann.
Trumpet-Major Meredith.
Trooper Underwood.
Trooper Reed.
Trooper Evans.
Trooper Craig.
Trooper Jeffries.
Trooper Brooks.
Trooper Bart.
Trooper Bourdoin.
Trooper Mulot.
Trooper Jacob Muller.
Trooper Millna.
Trooper John Muller.
Trooper G. Westhusen.
Trooper Hartman.
Trooper Cameron.
Trooper Grandeur.
Trooper B.J. Crany.
Trooper Martin.
Trooper Thompson.
Trooper King.
Trooper Darcy.
Trooper Farquharson.
Lance-Corporal Burnhard.
Trumpeter Reilly.
Trooper Williams.

Total 5 Officers and 40 Men.

Baker's Horse.

Trooper W. Walters.
Trooper C. Ward.
Trooper W. Dunbar.
Trooper J. Campbell.
Trooper J. Robinson.
Trooper J. Darwin.
Trooper M. Christian.
Trooper R. Davis.

Total 8 Men.

Mr. L. Lloyd, Political Agent.

Totals – Frontier Light Horse 3 Officers, 26 Men; Burgher Force 1 Officer; Transvaal Rangers 1 Officer, 6 Men; Border Horse 5 Officers, 40 Men; Baker's Horse 1 Officer, 8 Men.

Total 11 Officers, 80 Men.

W. BELLAIRS,
Deputy-Adjutant General.

Durban, April 5, 1879.

The following Despatch has been received by the Secretary of State for War from Lieutenant-General Lord Chelmsford, K.C.B., Commanding the Forces in South Africa:-

From the Lieutenant-General Commanding in South Africa
to the Right Honourable the Secretary of State for War.

Durban, Natal,
10th April, 1879.

SIR,

In accordance with the intention expressed in my last despatch, I took personal command, on the 23rd March, of the column in course of formation at the Lower Tugela, which was destined for the relief of the force under Colonel Pearson at Etshowe.

For some weeks Lieutenant-Colonel Law, R.A., had been hard at work arranging details connected with this column; in this arduous duty he was most ably assisted by his staff officer, Captain Hart, 31st Regiment (special service), and Assistant Commissary Walton, and I wish to record my appreciation of the exertions of these officers.

For some little time we had been in daily communication with Colonel Pearson by means of flashing signals: for this very great assistance to our operations I am indebted to Lieutenant Haines, R.E., who, despite some failure and discouragement at first, persevered until complete success was attained.

By the 28th March the whole force (*vide* enclosure A) was assembled on the left bank of the Tugela and organized in two Brigades. The labor of transferring the force and the necessary transport and stores was very great, and the success attained was due to the energy displayed by the detachments of the Naval Brigade under Lieutenant Abbott, R.N.

Those troops who were bivouacking experienced constant rain during the two or three days previous to the advance.

Sketch of Lord Chelmsford
May 1827 to 9 April 1905)
de by an officer shortly
ore the battle of Ulundi,
ist unknown.

Cetshwayo ka Mpande, photographed by Alex Bassano.

e Battle of Isandlwana from 'Zulu War pictures from the *Illustrated London News* and *The Graphic*', '9.

The defence of Rorke's Drift 1879, by Alphonse-Marie-Adolphe de Neuville.

The battlefield at Rorke's Drift. The burning and badly damaged building in the background is the hospital. (*HMP*)

e Relief Column arriving at Rorke's Drift. Lieutenant-Colonel Russell can be seen leading the
rsemen, whilst a flag is being waved from the roof of the Reverend Mr Witt's house. In front of it
he cattle kraal. Tyana Mountain forms the backdrop. (*HMP*)

esent day view of the battle site at Rorke's Drift. The buildings are modern, and their positions do
t reflect the positions of the storehouse and hospital that were there during the battle.

Anthony William Durnford (24 May 1830 to 22 January, 1879), a photograph by MacKinnon and Shadbold.

A contemporary illustration showing soldiers being attacked during an attempt by the Relief Column to reach Rorke's Drift. (*HMP*)

The burning of Ulundi, artist unknown.

eld-Marshal Sir Evelyn Wood, VC.

The Battle of Kambula.

Lieutenant-Colonel John Rouse Merriott Chard VC (1847–1897), photographer unknown.

The Battle of Intombe, artist unknown.

Field-Marshal Viscount Garnet Wolseley.

A Zulu *Impi* on the march. The word *Impi* is used as a description for any armed body of men. However, in English it is often used to refer to a Zulu regiment, and is usually described as such in the despatches, which is called an *ibutho* in Zulu. Its beginnings lie far back in historic tribal warfare customs, when groups of armed men called *impis* battled. (*HMP*)

I decided on advancing to the relief of Etshowe by the lower or coast road, and thus avoid the tract of bushy country around the Amatakulu until the last march, when it was my intention to move on Etshowe with the lightest possible train, in fact with only what was barely necessary for the relief of the garrison, and three days' biscuit and preserved meat for my own force.

On the 29th March the column marched at six a.m., reached Inyone and formed a wagon laager which was entrenched.

On the 30th it reached the Amatakulu River, and did the same.

Up to this time nothing had been actually seen of the enemy by my scouts, but reports reached me from the Border Agents that bodies of Zulus had been seen moving in an easterly direction from the Indulinda range. I fully anticipated I should not reach Etshowe without an engagement, and I was only anxious that the long train of wagons should be kept together, so that at any time on the march we might be able to fight without the chance of the camp followers and transport animals suffering. I therefore found it necessary on the 31st March to content myself with only crossing the Amatakulu River, and forming a wagon laager one mile and a half beyond. The river was very high, and the transfer of the train across the stream took from 6 a.m. to 3 p.m., each wagon requiring 32 instead of 16 oxen.

During this day (31st) the scouts noticed small bodies of Zulus in the vicinity of the Amatakulu bush. Captain Barrow, 19th Hussars, with a portion of his command, pushed on some 12 miles towards the Engoya forest, and burnt the kraal of Magwendo, a brother of the Zulu king.

The 1st April the column marched six miles to the Gingilovo stream: about one mile from the Inyazane River, a laager was formed in a favourable position. From this point the road to Etshowe, after crossing swampy ground, winds through a bushy and difficult country for some 15 miles, the last eight or nine being a steady ascent. The whole country is covered with very high grass, and even what appears to be open plain is really sufficiently undulating to afford easy cover to considerable bodies of natives.

Etshowe could be plainly seen from the laager, and flash signalling was at once established. Before the laager was completed a heavy thunder storm came on; rain came on again at nightfall, and lasted during the night. The laager defences were, however, satisfactorily completed after dark.

The north or front face was held by the 60th Rifles; the right flank face by the 57th Regiment; left flank face by the 99th Regiment and 'The Buffs'; the rear face by the 91st Regiment; and each angle was manned by the Naval Brigade, Blue Jackets, and Marines, the Gatling of the 'Boadicea' being on the north-east corner; two rocket tubes on the north-west, under Lieutenant Kerr; two 9-pounder guns under Lieutenant Kingscote on the south-west;

and one Gatling and two rocket tubes, on the south-east, under Commander Brackenbury. The night passed without any alarm.

On the 2nd April, according to our invariable rule, the troops stood to their arms at 4 A.M. A heavy mist shrouded the country; the sun rose about 6.15 A.M.: our mounted men, as usual, were at earliest dawn scouting around. At 5.45 reports came in from them simultaneously with the picquets of the 60th and 99th Regiments, that the enemy were advancing to the attack: no preparation was necessary and no orders had to be given beyond the saddling up of the horses of the officers of the staff: the troops were already at their posts and the cattle had not been let out to graze. At 6 A.M. the attack commenced on the north front; the Zulus advanced with great rapidity and courage, taking advantage of the cover afforded by the undulations of the ground and the long grass: the enemy, however, did not succeed in approaching nearer than 20 yards: several casualties took place here at this time, among them Lieutenant-Colonel Northey 3–60th who, I regret to say, received a bullet wound from which he eventually died two days ago. Lieutenant Courtenay's horse was shot as he stood beside him, Captain Barrow and Lieutenant-Colonel Crealock being slightly wounded at the same time, and Captain Molyneux's horse was shot under him. The Gatling gun was of considerable value at this period of the defence.

The attack, checked here, rolled round to the West, or left face: here Lieutenant G.C.J. Johnson, 99th Regiment, was killed. Whilst this was being developed, a fresh force came round to the rear, probably, from the Umisi Hill, anticipating (so prisoners state) that our force would prove insufficient to defend, at the same time, all the faces of the laager: here they obstinately held their ground; finding cover in long grass and undulations. The Mounted Infantry and Volunteers meantime having left the laager had been engaged in clearing its front face, I now directed Captain Barrow to advance across the right or East face and attack the enemy's right flank. It was now 7.30 A.M. and during one hour and a half the Zulus had obstinately attacked three sides of the laager.

Even previous to the mounted men appearing on their flank, the Zulus had, I believe, realised the hopelessness of attempting to pass through the zone of heavy rifle fire which met them on their attempting to charge up against the rear face; but on their appearance, the Zulu retreat commenced. On seeing this the Natal Native Contingent, who were formed within the entrenchment on the rear face, clearing the ditch, rushed forward with loud cheers in pursuit. Led by Captain Barrow's horsemen, the pursuit was carried on several miles. This officer reports the sabres of the Mounted Infantry to have proved of the greatest service, some fifty or sixty men having been sabred.

At 8 A.M. Colonel Pearson, who, through a glass, had witnessed the fight from Etshowe, telegraphed his congratulations to us.

Bodies of Zulus were to be seen hurrying away towards the Indulinda, making a stand nowhere, and throwing away their arms to assist their flight.

Within a short time I directed officers and burying parties to count the enemy's loss within one thousand yards of the entrenchment: 471 were buried, 200 have been since found near the scene; but from the chance wounded men we have found five miles away, and the execution done at long ranges by the artillery, I have no hesitation in estimating the enemy's loss at one thousand men.

It appears from the statements of the prisoners taken that about 180 companies were engaged either in the attack or in reserve, which, estimated at sixty men per company (less than half their strength) would give about 11,000 men. This I am inclined to think may be the number of the force that was ordered to attack us, but this is far less than that given by the prisoners taken.

Our casualties are small considering the easy mark the laager afforded the assailants, and, had it not been for the cover afforded the troops by the broad shelter trench, I should have had to a much heavier loss.

It appears from the statements of the prisoners that the Zulus were unaware of the march of my force until thirty-six hours before we were attacked; neither were they aware of its strength

I attribute this ignorance, on the enemy's part, of our movements in a great measure to the excellent manner in which the scouting duties of my force were carried out, under the personal arrangements of Captain Barrow, 19th Hussars, who, with his small mounted force, assisted by some 150 Zulus belonging to Mr. John Dunn's people, completely shrouded our movements.

Mr. John Dunn, at my request, accompanied me, and I am greatly indebted to him for the assistance he afforded me by his knowledge of the country and sound advice.

The following day, 3rd April, I left Major Walker, 99th Regiment, with two companies of the Buffs, two of the 91st, and five of the 99th, and 400 Naval Brigade, together with the Natal Native Contingent, as a garrison for the laager, which was altered in size to meet the reduced strength. The remainder of the column, carrying three days' biscuit and meat, with a ground sheet between every two men, and escorting eight carts of stores for the Etshowe garrison, moved off in compact order for Etshowe. The distance to be traversed was only some fifteen miles, but the streams were deep and the swamps heavy, and for the last eight or nine miles of the road the ascents steep; in two places the road had been partly destroyed by the Zulus. It was 11.30 p.m. before the whole relief column reached Etshowe. Colonel Pearson and a portion of the garrison came out to meet me, which would have been of great assistance had the enemy opposed our advance, but none were to be seen that day.

I have the honour to enclose the account furnished by Brigadier-General Pearson, C.B. (enclosure C) of his ten weeks' stay at Etshowe, together with a state of the garrison on 3rd April (enclosure D). See P.S.

The 4th April, next day, Colonel Pearson evacuated the fort, taking with him the whole of his stores, &c.

I accompanied a patrol under Captain Barrow, who, with his mounted force, Dunn's scouts and a company of Natal Pioneers of the Etshowe garrison, proceeded to destroy a kraal of Dabulamanzi's, some eight or nine miles off, on the Entumeni Hill: two of the enemy were killed, and one prisoner taken. A small body of some 40 Zulus kept up a well directed fire from a neighbouring hill, but no casualty occurred on our side. The 5th April, the relieving column left Etshowe, covering the movement of Colonel Pearson, who encamped near the Inyezane the same evening, while my force bivouacked near the Imfuchini mission station.

I regret to report that at 3.30 p.m., the following morning (6th April), a sentry of the 91st fired a shot at what he took to be a party of the enemy who did not answer his challenge. On hearing this shot the picquet of the 60th Rifles, on the opposite flank of the entrenchment, retired without orders from its officer, together with Mr. Dunn's scouts, who had been occupying some mealie fields beyond. It was bright moonlight, and I can offer no excuse or explanation of what occurred, beyond the youth of the men of the 60th, for it was perfectly well known to officers and men that these scouts were in their front. It appears that some of the 60th, lining the entrenchment, seeing the picquets running in fired, probably at the native scouts, but five of the 3–60th were wounded by their own comrades, and I deeply regret to say that some nine of our native allies were bayonetted as they attempted to gain, as they thought, the shelter of the laager: one man was killed, and two natives have since died of their wounds.

In the interests of discipline I assembled a General Court-Martial the same day to try the sergeant who had retired the picquet without the orders of the officer, and confirmed the sentence passed of reduction to the ranks and five years penal servitude.

On the 6th April the force marched by the Gingilovo laager, and formed a new one on fresh ground one mile beyond.

On the 7th Major Walker, 99th Regiment, was to move from the old laager to the new ground, the atmosphere of the old laager being tainted by the results of the engagement of the 2nd April.

My reasons for ordering Colonel Pearson to evacuate Etshowe were that I found the last fifteen miles of the road of a most difficult nature, far more so than I had been led to believe by the reports furnished me before Colonel Pearson crossed the frontier in January.

Every advantage from a military point of view, in our present intention of destroying the Mangwane and old Undine kraals, can be equally gained by occupying a strong post upon the coast road: this will be done, and the future operations on this line will be entrusted to Major-General Crealock, C.B., who will receive special instructions from, me regarding the future operations of what is now the 1st Division of the South African Field Force.

I am much indebted to Colonel Pearson for so tenaciously holding on to Etshowe after the bad news of the Insandhlwana affair had reached him. The occupation of that post, and of that one held by Colonel Evelyn Wood during a time of considerable anxiety, had no doubt a very powerful moral effect through South Africa, and diminished the effect of what would otherwise have been considered as a complete collapse of our invasion of Zululand.

I cannot close this despatch without acknowledging the assistance I received from Commodore Richards with regard to all arrangements connected with the Naval Brigade, which, under its respective commanders, did good and useful service.

I am much indebted to Lieutenant-Colonel Pemberton, 60th Rifles, and to Lieutenant-Colonel Law, Royal Artillery, who were in charge of brigades, and to the several commanding officers serving under their command.

The 57th Regiment under Lieutenant-Colonel Clarke, was conspicuous for its steadiness and for the manner in which the men controlled their fire.

Dr. Tarrant, Senior Medical Officer with the column, gave me every satisfaction with regard to the medical arrangements; and Assistant-Commissary Walton deserves great credit for the successful exertions he made in overcoming the difficulties of supply and transport.

I have already mentioned Capt. Barrow's name as having performed very excellent service, and the Commanders of the several mounted detachments under his command ably assisted him.

I have, as usual, to acknowledge the services of my personal staff. Lieut.-Colonel Crealock, in the absence of Colonel Bellairs, whom I was reluctantly compelled to leave behind at Durban to perform the duties of Deputy-Quartermaster General, acted as Senior Staff Officer to the column, and was slightly wounded.

Captain Buller, A.D.C., at my request acted as Brigade Major to Colonel Pemberton.

Captain Molyneux, A.D.C., who had his horse shot under him, and Lieutenant Milner R.N., were indefatigable in their efforts to carry out my orders and give every assistance in the defence of the laager.

The Honorable W. Drummond, head of my Intelligence Department, has worked indefatigably to obtain information, and I am much indebted to him for his assistance.

I have, &c.,

CHELMSFORD, Lieutenant-General.

P.S. – Owing to an extra steamer having been ordered to leave to-day, I take the opportunity of forwarding this dispatch – but I regret I am unable to transmit, until next mail, enclosures referred to, from Lieut-General Pearson and Capt. Barrow.

Owing to the press of time since I returned here, 36 hours ago, the various returns of wounded and numbers engaged are hardly written out in the manner I should have wished, but the matter therein contained is correct.

C.

Return of Wounded in the Action at Gingilovo.
Column under Personal Command of Lieutenant-General Commanding.

2nd April, 1879.

WOUNDED.

Staff. – Lt.-Col. North Crealock, slightly.
3rd Batt. 60th Reg. – Lt.-Col. F.V. Northey, dangerously.
19th Hussars, Mounted Infantry. – Major P.H.S. Barrow, slightly.
57th Reg. – Capt. H.C. Hinxman, slightly.
99th Reg. – Lieut. G.C.J. Johnson, dangerously.
Royal Navy. – Staff Surg. Longfield, dangerously.
2nd Batt. 3rd Reg. – Private Flannery, dangerously.
57th Reg. – Private J. Perkins, dangerously.
57th Reg. – Private Deacon, slightly.
57th Reg. – Private Harris, slightly.
3rd Batt. 60th Reg. – Col.-Serj. E. Dallard, slightly.
3rd Batt. 60th Reg. – Private Aylett, slightly.
3rd Batt. 60th Reg. – Private W. Poplett, dangerously.
3rd Batt. 60th Reg. – Private E. Traney, slightly.
3rd Batt. 60th Reg. – Private W. Lahiff, dangerously.
91st Reg. – Private H. Richards, severely.
91st Reg. – Private Standye, slightly.
91st Reg. – Private Bryan, dangerously.
91st Reg. – Private Malley, dangerously.
91st Reg. – Hanlow, dangerously.

91st Reg. – Serg. McIntyre, dangerously.
91st Reg. – Private Sutton, severely.
91st Reg. – Private Gillespie, severely.
99th Reg – Private J. Blackwell, slightly.
99th Reg – Private Drew, dangerously,
99th Reg – Private P. Armstrong, dangerously.
99th Reg – Private G. Baker, slightly.
Mounted Infantry, 88th Reg. – Private P. Bryan, dangerously.
Mounted Infantry, 9th Reg. – Private A. Hartley, severely.
Royal Navy, 'Shah'. – A.B. Seaman J. Bird severely.
Royal Navy, 'Shah.' – A.B. Seaman J. Bulger, severely.
Royal Navy, 'Boadicea.' – Carpenter's Mate P. Cowdy, slightly.
Royal Navy, 'Boadicea.' – Boy J. Hinchley, dangerously.
Royal Marine Artillery, 'Boadicea.' – Bombardier J. Parfitt, dangerously.
Royal Navy, 'Tenedos.' – Petty Officer J. Porteus, slightly.
Nettleton's Contingent. – Natives, 2 dangerously, 8 severely.

Total: 18 dangerously, 14 severely, 13 slightly.

J.A. WOOLFRYES,
Surgeon-General, P.M.O.
D.A.G. Durban.

Return of Casualties which, have occurred in 5th Battalion N.N.C.,
in action of 2nd April, 1879, at Ginhalovo.
A 2. Private (Native). Killed.
B 4. Private (Native). Severely wounded.
C 7. Private (Native). Severely wounded.
D 5, 8. Two Privates (Native). Slightly wounded.
E 9. Private (Native). Severely wounded.
F 10. Private (Native). Killed.
G 13, 11. Privates (Native). 1 Slightly wounded. 1 Killed.
H 15, 18, 19. Privates (Native). 2 Severely wounded. 1 Killed.
J 12, 30, 31. Privates (Native). 3 Severely wounded. 1 Slightly wounded.
Captain Gunning's horse killed.
Lieutenant Jay's horse killed.
Lieutenant Thompson's horse badly wounded.

W.J. NETTLETON, Commandant.

Barton's N.N.C., Battalion.
1 Killed. 5 Wounded (2 severely).

Nominal Roll of Killed.

Gingilovo, 2nd April, 1879.

91st Regiment, Private R. Marshall.
99th Regiment, Lieutenant G.C.J. Johnson.
99th Regiment, Private John Smith.
99th Regiment, Private John Lawrence.
3rd Battalion, 60th Regiment, Private J. Pratt.
3rd Battalion, 60th Regiment, Lieutenant-Colonel Northey died of his wounds, 6th April.
Natal Native Contingent, 5 killed.
Dangerously wounded 18 ; severely wounded 24; slightly wounded 20: total 62 wounded, 11 killed.

J. NORTH CREALOCK, Lieut.-Col.,
Assistant Military Secretary, Staff Officer.

Near Imfuchini Mission House.
Report Gun-shot Wounds.

6th April, 1879.

3rd Battalion, 60th Regiment.
1982 Private F. Lambert, compound comminuted fracture left elbow.
1939 Private W. Burton, severe flesh wound, penetrating left thigh and inside right leg.
 783 Private J. Barker, penetrating flesh wound, left thigh.
3279 Private T. Crowdson, wound left shoulder.
2033 Private R. Winter, penetrating bullet around glatial region.

EDWD. BOULTON, Surgeon-Major.

To Officer Commanding 3rd Battalion, 60th Regiment.
Forwarded for information of Lieutenant-General Commanding.

A. TUFNELL, Captain,
3rd Battalion, 60th Regiment.

April 6, 1879.

Dunn's Men (natives), 8 men wounded; 2 dangerously; 1 since dead.

J. NORTH CREALOCK, Lieut.-Col.,
Staff Officer.

Detail of the force engaged at Ginginhlovo, April 2nd, 1879.

Lieut-General Lord Chelmsford, K.C.B., Commanding.

Lieut.-Colonel North Crealock, A.M.S., Staff Officer.

Captain W.F. Molyneux, 22nd Regt., Lieut. A. Milne. R.N., A.D.C.

Surgeon-Major Tarrant, Senior Medical Officer.

Assistant Commissary Walton, Senior Commissariat Officer.

The Hon. W. Drummond, Mr. John Dunn, Intelligence Department.

1st Brigade.

Lieutenant-Colonel Law, R.A., commanding.

Captain Hart, 31st Regiment, Staff Officer.

Naval Brigade of H.M.S. Shah and Tenedos (except Marines of Shah), 350 fighting men; 91st Highlanders, Major Bruce commanding, 850 fighting men; 2 Companies the Buffs, 140 fighting men, 5 Companies 99th Regiment, 430 fighting men, Major Walker, 99th Regiment, commanding; 4th Battalion Natal Native Contingent, 800 fighting men, Captain Barton, 7th Regiment, commanding.

Artillery.

2 9-pounder guns; 2 24-pouuder Rocket tubes; 1 Gatling gun.

Commissariat Department; Transport Department; Medical Department.

Total fighting men 1st Brigade. British troops and Naval Brigade, 1,770; Native Contingent, 800. Total, 2,570.

2nd Brigade.

Lieutenant-Colonel Pemberton, 60th Rifles, commanding.

Captain Buller, Rifle Brigade, Staff Officer.

Naval Brigade of H.M.S. Boadicea, 190 fighting men; Royal Marines of Shah and Boadicea, 100 fighting men; 57th Foot, Lieutenant-Colonel Clarke commanding, 640 fighting men; 6 companies 60th Rifles, Lieutenant-Colonel Northey commanding, 540 fighting men; 5th Battalion of Natal Native Contingent, Commandant Nettleton, commanding, 1,200 fighting men.

Artillery.

2 24-pounder rocket-tubes; 1 Gatling gun.

Commissariat and Transport Department; Medical Department.

Total fighting men, 2nd Brigade, British troops and Naval Brigade and Marines, 1,470; Natal Native Contingent, 1,200. Total 2,670.

Divisional Troops.

Major Barrow, 19th Hussars, Commanding.
Captain Courtenay, 20th Hussars, Staff Officer.

Mounted infantry, 70 fighting men; volunteers, 50 fighting men; mounted natives, 130 fighting men; Captain Cook's non-commissioned officers, 30 fighting men; native foot scouts, 150 fighting men. Total fighting men, British troops, volunteers, and non-commissioned officers, 150; mounted natives, 130; foot scouts, 150. Total, 430.

Grand total fighting men of force engaged at Ginginhlovo, April 2nd, 1879.
1st Brigade, 1,770 white men, 800 natives; 2nd brigade, 1,470 white men, 1,200 natives; divisional troops, 150 white men, 280 natives. Total, 3,390 white men, 2,280 natives. Grand total, 5,670.

J. NORTH CREALOCK, Lt.-Col.,
Staff Officer.

From Colonel Bellairs, Deputy Adjutant-General,
to the Secretary of State for War, London.

5th Durban, April, 1879.

SIR,
The disembarkations have been progressing very satisfactorily, men and horses having come ashore without accident, and in good health and condition. The large quantities of stores which arrived at the same time with the troops have been also safely landed. The difficulties attending disembarking troops and horses, with such quantities of supplies and war material, on the South African coast, are of course considerable, especially as the landing wharves at this port are confined in space and the railway rolling stock small; but, though taxing the powers of the staff and departments, have been successfully over-come – a good result, largely contributed to by the cordial co-operation of the Naval Department with the Military.

The two companies of the 3rd Battalion 60th Rifles, and the draft for the 57th Foot, have been sent forward to the Lower Tugela.

The 2nd Battalion 21st Foot has proceeded, and the 58th Foot is about to leave, for the Doornberg, viâ Botha's Hill (half-way to Pietermaritzburg, as far as the railway works at present), Pietermaritzburg, Ladysmith, and Dundee, leaving two companies of the former to garrison Pietermaritzburg, and one of the latter at Durban.

The 94th Foot has proceeded to the same destination, viâ Greytown, Helpmakaar, and Dundee. These three battalions will form the First Brigade of No. 4 Column, under Major-General Newdigate, who, as soon as he lands will be directed to accompany the troops now on the march. The two companies of the 2nd Battalion 4th Foot, now at Pietermaritzburg, and two at Greytown will, on being relieved as above, march to join the head-quarters of their battalion at Utrecht; and head-quarters and one company of the 88th Foot, now at Pietermaritzburg, to join the remainder of the battalion on the Lower Tugela.

M and N Batteries, 6th Brigade, and the Gatling battery, Royal Artillery, are at present encamped at Cato Manor, on the Berea Hill, about three miles out. The horses are greatly improved in appearance.

The Lieutenant-General Commanding does not consider it desirable to move a battery to the Lower Tugela line until horse sickness has disappeared from that district, which, with cooler weather, in about a fortnight may be expected to be the case.

Colonel Reilly, C.B., arrived on the 4th, and assumed command of the Royal Artillery in South Africa.

The 30th Company Royal Engineers, per s.s. 'Palmyra,' will proceed immediately to the Doornberg. Lieutenant-Colonel Steward is attached to head-quarters as Commanding Royal Engineer in the field, Colonel Hassard, C.B., Commanding Royal Engineers, having some time since been invalided to Cape Town.

Of the three companies, Army Service Corps, two will be employed on the Lower Tugela line, and the third in the Utrecht district.

The remaining reinforcements to arrive are the 1st Dragoon Guards and 17th Lancers, and the draft for the 1st Battalion 24th Foot.

Telegraphic information has been received that the s.s. 'Clyde,' carrying the 1st Battalion 24th Foot, has run ashore between the Cape and Mossel Bay, and has been obliged to land the troops, which appears to have been effected without loss of life, on the beach. H.M.S. 'Tamar' had gone to the spot and will bring on the troops.

I have, &c.,
W. BELLAIRS, Colonel.
Deputy Adjutant-General.

The following Despatch and Enclosures have been received from Major-General Crealock:-

s.s. 'Egypt' Simon's Bay,
5th April (1 o'clock), 1879.

SIR,

I have the honour to enclose for the information of H.R.H. the Field Marshal Commanding-in-Chief an account of the wreck of the transport

'Clyde' furnished me by Colonel Davies, Grenadier Guards, who was in command.

You will have received the general details of the accident telegraphed to the Secretary of State for War.

I have received a verbal account of the accident from Colonel Davies, and also from Captain Liddell, R.N., commanding the 'Tamar.'

Nothing could have been more judicious than the arrangements made by Colonel Davies, and he states that the conduct of all on board was admirable, whether officers or men.

He mentions certain officers names especially deserving of notice.

Captain Liddell has expressed himself in very strong terms of approval of the manner in which Colonel Davies and all under his orders behaved under very trying circumstances.

The accident occurred not far from where the 'Birkenhead' was wrecked. As I am now leaving Simon's Bay for Durban. I will not add more, as Colonel Davies has given full particulars in his enclosed despatch.

Telegrams to the Secretary of State, to General Clifford, and to Adjutant-General at head-quarters, Natal, have been despatched, so that all requisite stores, clothing. &c., may be ready for the drafts on arrival. It is probable they will proceed next Monday in the 'Tamar.'

I have, &c.,
H. HOPE CREALOCK, Major-General,
The Quartermaster-General of the Forces, Horse Guards.

From Colonel A.F. Davies, Grenadier Guards, Commanding Drafts,
24th Regiment, to Major-General Crealock, C.B., Commanding Troops, Simons Bay.

H.M.S.S. 'Tamar,' 5th April, 1879.

I regret to have to report to you, for the information of H.R.H. the Field Marshal Commanding-in-Chief, that the hired transport 'Clyde' was totally lost near Dier's Island, on April 3rd, 1879; but I am glad to report that no lives were lost.

1. About 4.35, A.M., I was called by the officer of the watch, who informed me that the ship was aground. I immediately ordered the officers to be called, and went on deck.

As soon as it was light, we saw Dier Island about two miles on the starboard beam.

2. At 4.50, A.M., Captain Luckhurst informed me that the ship was aground fore and aft. I ordered the assembly to be sounded.

The men fell in with the greatest order and regularity. Sentries were at once posted over the boats and the spirit room.

3. At 5.25 A.M., two life boats were ready.

4. 5.30, A.M. – Ordered breakfast to be prepared for troops at once.

5. 5.40, A.M. – Ordered sick and A and D Companies to get arms and accoutrements, and all they could put into valises, and be ready to land. Ordered preserved meat cases, tea and biscuits, to be got ready on deck, also water in the barricoes.

6. 6 A.M. – Ordered remaining companies to be got ready.

7. 6.20 AM. Sick under Surgeon-Major E. Ward and as many men of D Company as the boats would hold left for the shore under Captain Brander, 24th regiment, and Lieutenant Carey, 98th regiment having previously had breakfast, and having filled their water bottles with tea or water, and biscuits in their haversacks.

8. I ordered each boat to take preserved meat and water with them, which was carried out.

9. 7.10 A.M. Asked Captain Luckhurst to get horse boat ready. He said it was not possible to get it off under half a day's work.

10. Two to three feet of water in the hold at 7.10.

11. At 7.35 A.M. 8 feet of water in hold, closed ports.

12. 7.45 A.M. Boats began to return having landed first men who embarked in the boats for shore, continued sending boats to and fro between ship and shore until 11.10 A.M. when all the troops were landed except 4 officers and 84 men left as a working party. Arms and accoutrements of these men I had sent on shore.

13. 7.52 A.M. The chief officer (Mr. Abbott) left in the smallest boat for Simon's Bay, to report to senior naval officer, leaving us five boats only, distance about seventy miles.

14. 8.30 A.M. Bumping heavily aft. Began to make a raft.

15. 9.23 A.M. A small boat with 2 men came from Dier Island.
Sent a non-commissioned officer and 5 men to Dier Island to get larger boat.

16. 9.45 A.M. Received note from Captain Glennie, 24th Regiment, to say that Mr. Albert Van der Byl had come down to beach, and marked with flags the safest place to land.

17. 10.10 A.M. Destroyed rum and porter in forehold and afterhold, and nailed down hatches over wine.

18. 10.20 A.M. E Company dined.

19. 10.50. Raft ready, and Dutch boat came along side from Dier Island.

The latter was most useful to us, both disembarking and embarking on the following day; and we are much indebted to the boatman, Francis Anthony for his assistance.

20. 10.55 A.M. Received letter from Captain Glennie, 24th Regiment, from shore, to say that he had, by my directions, arranged to relieve crews as they landed.

21. Received letter from Lieutenant Carey, 98th, on shore, reporting he had found good camping ground and water about two miles from landing place; that he had sent off telegram to Simon's Bay, viâ Caledon, forty-five miles distant; and that Mr. Albert Van der Byl could supply us with fresh meat, etc.

22. 11.30A.M. Sent away raft, towed by one loaded boat, which was joined by another half-way to the shore. The raft was loaded with preserved meat and biscuit.

Unfortunately, before the raft could be got to the shore, the ship was sinking so fast that the boats were obliged to cast it off and come to our assistance, consequently nearly all our biscuits were lost.

23. All the men but the working party having landed, I now considered it my duty to save some of the officers' baggage and the horses.

Two of the latter were thrown overboard and safely landed.

24. 12.10 P.M. Received letter from Captain Brander, 24th Regiment, saying he had plenty of water and wood.

25. 12.15 P.M. About 12 feet of water in the hold, the tide having risen the ship now slipped off into deep water.

26. 12.35 P.M. 20 feet of water in the hold, and as the ship seemed to be sinking fast in 43 feet of water, I considered it my duty to send off as many men as possible in the boats then along side. I remained on board with Captain Cotton, and 27 non-commissioned officers and men besides some of the crew.

27. 12.45 P.M. Captain Luckhurst let go the anchor.

28. Threw overboard sheep pens, hen coops, hatches and ladders, and secured them alongside. Made a small raft with assistance of Captain Cotton and a few soldiers.

29. Captain Luckhurst now informed me that, the ship might sink at any moment. Sent off raft with four men and gave out the life buoys to the soldiers as far as they would go, ordered all men into the rigging.

30. We now passed a most trying 45 minutes; we knew the ship was sinking fast, and we had no boat within two miles of us; the officers in charge of the boats not knowing we were in the slightest danger, our position having so entirely altered since they left the ship. Notwithstanding the imminent danger we appeared to be in, most perfect discipline and regularity was maintained, and the men were as calm as if on parade on shore.

Three boats were away with the horses. We shouted, fired pistols, and waved to them, and after some time they became aware of our danger, and then rowed to our assistance as fast as possible.

31. 1.30 P.M. Having seen the last soldier into the boats, Captain Cotton and myself also left the ship.

32. Having a boat full, I rowed to the shore. Captain Cotton's boat having very few men in it, he remained alongside and afterwards again went on board and threw overboard the other horses (who were safely towed ashore), and with the assistance of Lieutenant Colville, Grenadier Guards, saved two more boats of baggage.

33. At 2.10 P.M. I landed and formed working parties at the landing place. I left orders that the boats were to keep going to and from the ship and try to rescue as much baggage as possible.

34. I then walked to the bivouac ground, where I found that Captain Brander, 24th Regiment, and Lieutenant Carey, 98th Regiment had made kitchens and were preparing huts for all the men.

They had chosen an admirable spot – plenty of wood and water, and a certain amount of brushwood and grass, which prevented it from being dusty, all the ground round being sand hills. The bivouac was well sheltered.

35. When I returned to the landing place I found the other two horses and 2,400 rounds of Martini-Henry ammunition, and other things, including tea, just landing.

36. I sent the boats back to the ship, but on their arrival Captain Luckhurst told Lieutenant Colville, Grenadier Guards, who was in charge, that it was not safe to go on board. He then very properly returned to shore.

37. Every man had dined before 3 P.M., either on fresh beef or preserved meat, biscuits and tea.

38. 5.45 P.M. We hauled up our boats beyond high-water mark, and I sent the men to the bivouac, waiting myself to meet Captain Luckhurst, who landed at dusk. He informed me that he expected the ship to go down immediately.

39. I gave the men a supper of preserved meat and tea. Before 8.30 P.M. every man was under cover for the night, rifles and valises having been put into the huts.

40. At 7.45 P.M. a bullock wagon, kindly lent us by Mr. Albert Van der Byl, arrived, and brought most of our baggage up from the landing place by 9 P.M.

41. At daylight next day (Friday, April 4th) we found that the ship had sunk during the night, the water being about half-way up the lower masts.

42. Gave the men breakfast of preserved meat and tea.

43. Mr. Van der Byl's wagon brought up most of the baggage, &c.

44. Having no biscuit, I determined to ride to Mr. Van der Byl's farm to see whether I could procure flour and vegetables, but when I was on the point of starting Her Majesty's steam ship 'Tamar' hove in sight.

45. About 10.10 A.M., Her Majesty's steam ship 'Tamar's' boats came ashore.

46. At 10.20 A.M., sounded assembly.

47. At 8.30 P.M., every man and all baggage and stores saved (except the preserved meat and tea left on shore with Captain Luckhurst, who had to remain), were safely embarked on board Her Majesty's steam ship 'Tamar,' and not only am I happy to report without loss of life, but even without anyone sustaining any injury.

48. There being a difficulty about re-embarking the four horses they were sent by land to Simon's Town, under charge of the two batmen.

49. I am glad to be able to report that not only no lives were lost, but that not a single casualty occurred, and although the landing-place was three miles from the ship, we landed about 450 men in under five hours, and through a surf. It was most fortunate that the weather was favourable, or in all probability not a man would have been saved.

50. I regret to say that we lost nearly all the regimental documents, the whole of the stores on board, practically the whole of the men's clothing and necessaries, but all the arms, accoutrements, helmets, and great coats, with the exception of those belonging to about 20 men are saved.

51. It affords me very great pleasure to report how admirably both officers and men behaved, how hard and cheerfully they worked, and how steady, and calm they were under most trying circumstances, where all behaved so well it seems invidious to mention any in particular, but I cannot conclude my letter without bringing to the notice of H.R.H. the Field-Marshal Commanding-in-Chief the very great assistance I received from my Adjutant, Captain the Honourable R. Cotton, Scots Guards, who worked with his usual zeal, also how much I owe to Lieutenant the Honourable C. Colville, Grenadier Guards, for the admirable way in which he took charge of the boats, and to Captain Brander, 24th Regiment, and Lieutenant Carey, 95th Regiment, for the great judgment they showed in selecting a landing-place and camping-ground, and to the latter officer for the excellent huts which he so quickly constructed for the troops. The boats were all rowed by men belonging to the draft of the regiment, with the exception of the first two.

52. I have the greatest pleasure in bringing to your notice the very great assistance and kindness which we received from Mr. Albert Van der Byl. He marked out the best landing-place; he placed a waggon with sixteen bullocks at our disposal for moving baggage; offered to provide us with fresh meat, corn, and cheese; he also invited the officers to his house, but it is needless to add that this offer was declined, the officers bivouacking with the men. He also took charge of our horses and grooms, finding them with forage, &c. He further sent a telegram to Caledon by special messenger, a distance of forty-five miles, and a guide with the horses on their way to Simon's Bay. He refused all remuneration, although he must be very considerably out of pocket by it. I trust I am not wrong in expressing a hope that some public recognition will be made of Mr. Albert Van der Byl's great kindness and attention.

53. The night was bitterly cold, and the men being wet felt this more.

54. Annexed are reports from Captain Brander, 24th Regiment, and Lieutenant Carey, 98th Regiment.

55. It might appear that more of the stores could have been saved, but I must point out that the landing-place opposite Dier's Island, which was three miles distant, is a very bad one, and if the wind had freshened or veered to the west, within half an hour nobody would have been able to land. I watched the

appearance of the weather most anxiously; the sea is also infested by sharks, as is known from the great loss of life at the wreck, of the 'Birkenhead,' which occurred within a few miles. For these reasons it was most necessary to land the men as soon as possible. If Lieutenant Colville, Grenadier Guards, had been able to go on board the last time all the men's kits would have been saved; but as the ship was sinking, and it was expected momentarily that the decks would burst up, it would have been most unsafe for anybody to go below.

I have, &c.,
H.F. DAVIES, Colonel Grenadier Guards,
Commanding Draft for 24th Regiment.

From Captain Brander, 24th Regiment,
to Colonel H. F. Davies, Grenadier Guards.

SIR,

I have the honour to report for your information that, in accordance with your orders, I left the s.s. 'Clyde,' then aground, in the first boat, containing about 30 men of the 24th draft and 4 seamen, with a view to discover a landing-place as near the ship as possible.

We made a good landing at a place sheltered by a long reef of rocks about three miles directly abreast of the wreck, and immediately sent back the boat to the ship.

I then posted sentries on the rocks with full instructions how to signal the proper channel to succeeding boats, and leaving Dr. Ward with the water and provisions, walked into the bush to find a road or track to some dwelling.

I came upon wheel tracks in a few minutes and following them for a couple of hours, arrived at the house of a farmer named Swartz from whom I hired a cart and two horses, and drove to Mr. Van der Byl's house to get a man sent on horseback to Caledon with a telegraphic message. On arriving there found Mr. Van der Byl already gone to the beach, so took the horses out of the cart and, guided by Swartz, rode after him, met his man about half way with a message from Mr. Cary, to be telegraphed on, read, approved it, and hastened the man on his way, then returned to the beach, found the landing progressing excellently, inspected the two water supplies, and made arrangements for the night's bivouac.

I have, &c.,
W.M. BRANDER, Captain,
1st Battalion 24th Regiment.

H.M.S. 'Tamar,' 5th April, 1879.

From Lieutenant J. Brenton-Carey, 98th Regiment,
to Colonel Davies, Grenadier Guards:-

> H.M.S. 'Tamar,' Simon's Bay,
> 5th April, 1879.

SIR,

I have the honour to report, for your information, as follows:- about 6.30 A.M. on the 3rd instant I quitted the 'Clyde' with the last boat of my company, and on arrival at the landing place found about half of my Company in charge of Lieutenant Fairer, Grenadier Guards, then on the sick list. He reported to me that Captain Brander had landed at a point about three-quarters of a mile further south, and that the remainder of my company was there. On landing I found a good deal of surf on shore, so I ordered my men to take off boots and tuck up trousers in order to haul the boats up as they reached the shore. I then proceeded to the spot where the remainder of my company had landed, and found them busily engaged in helping boats ashore, under the direction of Surgeon-Major Ward, A.M.D. I remained here for a few moments, until Captain Glennie had reached the shore, when I removed the remainder of my company to the place where I had landed, in order to assist the boats ashore, some of which were moving in that direction. Surgeon-Major Ward had reported to me on arrival that Captain Brander had proceeded inland in search of a mounted messenger to despatch to Simon's Bay. As soon as I had got my company together I set them to work to erect bivouacs, in order to obtain some shelter from the sun. This the men did with a good will, and thanks to the assistance rendered by Doctor Ward and Lieutenant Farrer, who, notwithstanding his sprained ankle, walked about continually, they were soon under shelter. I then despatched a sergeant and 10 men in search of water, and proceeded myself on the same duty. A Dutch farmer whom I met pointed out a hole in the sand close to Captain Brander's landing place, and I got the men to scrape with their hands for water. On returning to my bivouac I found a Dutch gentlemen, Mr. Van der Byl, of whom I enquired the resources of the country. He informed me he had a large farm two or three miles inland, with a good road along the river leading to it; that he had ample cattle, corn, cheese, &c., with which he was willing to feed the troops, and that he had good camping ground in the shape of a meadow adjoining the river. He also offered to supply bullock waggons as required, and to send a mounted messenger inland to Caledon, 45 miles distant, from whence a telegram would be dispatched to Simon's Bay. As Captain Brander had not returned, and had proceeded, so I heard, in a direction where there were no farms. I assumed the responsibility of telegraphing as follows:-

'From Lieut. Carey, 98th.
'For O.C. Troops, on board Clyde.
'To Commodore, Simon's Bay.
'Transport Clyde ashore off Dyer's Island. Ship making water. Troops landing on beach.'

This telegram I despatched by mounted messenger at 10 A.M., and by the next boat I sent you all the information I could gather about the country. Shortly after Captain Brander appeared, approved of what I had done, and took me with him to examine a small pond pointed out to him by the natives about two miles off. After we had reconnoitered it he gave me orders to examine again the water supply at his landing-place, and then to use my judgment as regards the number of companies to be sent to the new camping ground. I was to issue orders in his name. The result of my examination was, that I ordered three companies at once to proceed to the pond, two only remaining at Captain Brander's landing-place to disembark stores, I then marched my own company to the pond in compliance with this order, and about 2 P.M. the men lit fires and had their tins of meat issued to them. Throughout the day the company under my command worked incessantly under a hot sun with the greatest good will, and Surgeon-Major Ward and Lieutenant Farrer rendered me the greatest assistance in controlling the men who were necessarily very much scattered.

I regret to report, that with the exception of the defaulter's book, I lost the whole of my company's books and accounts, but I have secured the men's small books as far as possible, and their credits and debts may be ascertained. My men are nearly complete in arms, equipment, great coats, and helmets, but have nothing in the way of clothing but their sea kits, and one pair of socks and boots.

I have, &c.,
J. BRENTON CAREY, Lieutenant,
98th (The Prince of Wales's) Regiment.

Lord Chelmsford reports the death of the following Officers since last report- Lieutenant Mason, 3rd Foot; Captain Sandham, 90th Foot; Captain Wynne, Engineers; Commissary Phillimore; Commissary Alderton; Captain Gough, late Coldstream Guards; Captain Stourton, 63rd Foot; Lieutenant Evelyn, 3rd Foot.

Sub-Enclosures of Colonel Bellair' Despatch.

Camp, Kambula,
29th March, 1879.

SIR,

I have the honour to report that in accordance with instructions I left camp with the force named in the margin* on the 27th March, at 8 A.M.

At the old camp, south of Zugin's Nek, we were joined by the Second Battalion Wood's Irregulars, who had come from Potter's store.

Here for some reason, of which I am ignorant, Colonel Weatherley remained behind with the Border Horse, and did not rejoin us, he bivouacked on the flats south of the Ityenteka Nek.

At 3.30 A.M. on the 28th, we left our bivouac and ascended the Hlobana Mountain. It was luckily a misty morning and our attack was practically a surprise. This was fortunate as the position was an extremely strong one, and had the Zulus had time to prepare we could not have got up without very heavy loss.

The men led by Mr. Piet Uys, Commandant Raaff, and Captain Barton, carried the position with a rush, our loss being two officers. The Baron von Stietencen and Lieutenant Williams, Frontier Light Horse, who were killed in the assault, and while occupying the krantz which was the key of the position, and one man, Trooper Stewart, Frontier Light Horse, mortally wounded.

Directly we gained the table land which forms the summit of the Hlobana Mountain, and which is an irregular rectangle deeply indented by the Kloofs of this side, of about three miles long by one and a half wide, the natives who occupied it, disappeared into the rocks and caves of the side krantzes. These, the 2nd Battalion Wood's Irregulars, worked through splendidly, collecting many cattle. To assist them, I placed men all round the edge of the plateau to fire into the rocks below, and then proceeded to the western edge, beneath which I found Lieutenant-Colonel Russell with a few of his men, the rest being about one mile off, having apparently just ascended the lower Hlobana Mountain.

I waited until he had sent the Kafirs with him to assist my Kafirs collecting cattle, and then returned to the east end of the plateau to bury the bodies of Lieutenant Williams and the Baron Von Stietencen. On arrival then, I found that the Zulus had been largely reinforced, and were pressing us hard, and that, owing to the great size of the mountain, and the great difficulty of the path by which we had to retire, there was every probability of the enemy being able to assemble at one end out of fire, and then rush upon us as we retired.

I accordingly sent Captain Barton down the hill with 30 men to bury Lieutenant Williams at once and return to camp direct.

Just after we had seen Captain Barton and his men safely off, we observed a very large number of Zulus advancing in order across the flats on the southeast, and I at once sent two more men after Captain Barton, directing him to drop Lieutenant Williams' body and retreat at once to camp by the right side of the mountain, down which there was I knew a decent footpath, fairly practical for horses in single file, and offering no serious obstacle for his small force.

Just at this time I received a despatch from Lieutenant-Colonel Russell informing me of the advent of the Zulu force. Hastening back to the west end of the plateau I collected the scattered detachment on my way, and commenced a retreat.

Our line of retreat was most difficult, descending on to the plateau of the Lower Hlobana Mountain, which had earlier in the day been occupied by Colonel Russell, but which he had now left, by a narrow – almost perpendicular – cattle track down a krantz some 120 feet deep, with scarcely room for three horses abreast, by rocky steps, in many cases only a few inches broad, and with jumps of three, four, and even five feet between them; and having crossed that plateau, we had then the mountain itself, very steep, rocky, and precipitous to descend. But there are only three ways down, the one at the east end, by which we came up, I considered to be closed by the advancing Zulu force, and the other one is worse than the one I adopted.

In such a descent a certain amount of confusion was unavoidable, and this was increased by the Zulus crowding on our rear and flanks, and commencing a heavy fire, which killed a large number of the horses.

We should though, I think, have got down with little loss, had not some one called out to the rear guard to cease firing, as a party of natives advancing towards us across the plateau were our own Kafirs, and not Zulus.

They did cease firing, and in a moment the Zulus were among us. In the struggle that ensued we suffered heavily, losing 1 officer, 15 men, and Mr. Piet Uys who had got down safely but returned to assist his son and was assegaied.

The Zulus pursued us in force, and with so many dismounted men we experienced great difficulty in descending the mountain, and, but for the exertions of a few our retreat would have been a route, as it was we got down with a loss of those men only who were too badly wounded to be kept on horses.

As specially distinguishing themselves in the retreat I wish to mention Commandant Raaff, Transvaal Rangers, and Captain Gardner, my Staff

Officer, both of whom were also conspicuous in the assault in the morning. Major Leet, 13th Light Infantry, and Captain Darcy, Frontier Light Horse, who, although himself dismounted, rallied the men, saving the lives of many footmen, Lieutenants Blaine and Smith, Frontier Light Horse, Lieutenant Wilson, Baker's Horse, Captain Loraine White and Adjutant Brecher, Wood's Irregulars, Serjeants Crampton and Ellis, Troopers Landsill, Whitecross, Duffy, Pietersen, Hewitt, and Vinnicombe, Frontier Light Horse.

On reaching camp I found that most of the cattle we captured, some 2,000 head, and which had been sent out before we left the mountain, had been abandoned by order of Lieutenant-Colonel Russell, only about 300 being brought in.

I found also that Captain Barton's party and Commandant Weatherley's Border Horse, who had joined him, had been almost destroyed. Captain Barton and 18 out of his 32 men, and Commandant Weatherley, with 44 of the 54 Border Horse, being killed.

I annex Captain Dennison's report, and have only to remark on it that I never knew where Colonel Weatherley was on the 28th, and never sent him any order whatever. His orders on the 27th were to conform to the general movements of the leading troop in the column, but to march independently. He was fully aware of what we were going to do, and I cannot understand why he waited for individual orders, and did not saddle up when he heard the trumpet sound 'horses in.'

I annex a return of the killed and missing, that of the wounded has been sent to you by the Senior Medical Officer. Our loss was very heavy, among them Mr. Piet Uys, whose death is a misfortune to South Africa. One so courageous and so sagacious I shall never see again, we had better spared 100 men. Captain Barton is also a great loss, active, energetic, and intrepid, he was an excellent officer, and devoted to his profession.

I have, &c.,

REDVERS BULLER, Lieutenant-Colonel,

Commanding Mounted Troops.

*4 Royal Artillery Rocket Party, Major Tremlett, 7 Non-commissioned Officers and Men. Dutch Burghers, Mr. Piet Uys, 32 men. Frontier Light Horse, Captain Barton, 156 officers and men. Transvaal Rangers, Commandant Raaff, 71 officers and men. Border Horse, Commandant Weatherley, 53 officers and men. Baker's Horse, Lieutenant Wilson, 79 officers and men. Second Battalion Wood's Irregulars, Major Leet, 13th Light Infantry, 277 officers and men. Staff Captain Gardner, 14th Hussars. Total, Europeans 404 officers and men. Natives, 278 officers and men.

Information required by Corps Commandant concerning the Retreat at Hlobana, 27th March, 1879.

When I was at the bottom of the last hill, a Kafir from the 2nd Battalion Wood's Irregulars, told me that the Zulus were taking the cattle away from them (the 2nd Battalion), as they had no more ammunition. I sent Lieutenant Darcy to Colonel Russell, who was then on the first rise on the road to the camp, to ask if I might remain and help them. Lieutenant Darcy returned to me, and said 'The Colonel says you are to leave the cattle, and push on as fast as you can.'

J. LORRAINE WHITE, Commandant,
1st Battalion Wood's Irregulars.
Camp, Kambula Hill, 29th March, 1879.

I went to Colonel Russell with the above order. He interrupted me before I finished speaking, and said 'Tell Commandant White to leave the cattle, and push on as fast as he can.'

P.F. DARCY, Lieutenant, Wood's Irregulars 1st Battalion.
Camp, Kambula Hill, 29th March, 1879.

Camp Kambula Hill,
29th March, 1879.

SIR,
In compliance with your instructions, I have the honour to report on the occurrences of yesterday:

I marched from my bivouac about 4 A.M., with force as per margin,* and arrived at the foot of the westernmost portion of the Hlobana Mountain about daybreak.

I directed the battalion Wood's Irregulars and Oham's people to move up the hill, following them closely with the Mounted Infantry, Rocket Trough, Basutos, and Schermbrucker's Corps.

I did not take the time of arriving on the plateau, but I think it was about 6.30 to 7 A.M.

It was reported to me by Mr. Williams, 58th Regiment, that Colonel Buller's force was already in possession of the upper plateau, and that he and others could be seen upon it.

I at once moved with a small party of the first formed men to try to communicate with Colonel Buller, while the rear of my column was still coming up the hill.

I was fired at and my escort returned the fire. I heard Colonel Buller shout 'Bring your men up to fire,' or words to that effect. I sent back to bring up the rest of the force which quickly arrived.

In the meantime, it had been pointed out that there were large quantities of cattle on the sides of the Hlobana Hill, within easy reach, I therefore directed Commandant White's battalion to go and collect the cattle on the south of the Nek, and Oham's people, those on the north of the Nek.

The Mounted Infantry, Basutos, and Schermbrucker's Corps were ready to cover them with fire.

Commandant White brought back a considerable number of cattle to the plateau, but Oham's people drove what they found in a westerly direction towards the Zunguin. I did not again see them during the day.

Captain Browne, M.I., had been directed to cross the Nek, and to get to the top of the second plateau, to find out, if possible, if assistance was required from me by Colonel Buller, and generally what was the situation. Everything appeared to be nearly quiet and the whole object of the reconnaissance to have been gained.

Captain Browne remained on the top of the second plateau for some time. He was unable to see Colonel Buller, but he spoke to Major Tremlett and Major Leet; and he reported to me when he rejoined me that their force had had a success, that they had come to see if they could get home by that way, *i.e.* down the steep path leading from the second plateau to the Nek, but they thought it impracticable for horses, and that Colonel Buller had gone back along the hill to look for Colonel Wood, as they believed that they were apparently perfectly easy about the state of affairs and that they had had no orders.

A considerable number of cattle commenced to come down from the second plateau.

Shortly before 9 A.M. it was reported to me that a Zulu army was seen on the range of hills to the south of the Hlobana.

At 9 A.M. I sent a message addressed to Colonel Wood to that effect, and I collected my force together.

I thought that there would be time to get away the cattle.

The Zulu army assumed such very large proportions and moved with such extreme rapidity that at about 10 A.M. I thought it necessary to abandon the cattle, as I did not see how I was to protect the large number of natives who were driving them. I moved all my force down the hill, I told Commandant White to move his men at once to the Zunguin (as they were in very small numbers and would have only impeded the action of mounted men with whom I intended to remain near the Hlobana Hill, and join Colonel Buller if necessary.)

At this time I received a memorandum from Colonel Wood, dated 10.30 A.M. desiring me to 'get into position on Zunguin Nek.'

I moved to that point, therefore, and remained there till the last of Colonel Buller's force passed towards camp, and I received further orders to move east to cover the natives who were retiring on camp.

I returned to camp between 4 and 5 P.M.

I append list of casualties.

I have, &c.,

J.C RUSSELL, Lieut.-Col.

* Royal Artillery Rocket Trough, Mounted Infantry, Basutos, Schermbrucker's Corps, Battalion Irregulars, Oham's People.

List of Casualties.

Royal Artillery, Rocket Trough, nil.

Mounted Infantry, 1 man wounded, 2 horses knocked up and left.

Basutos, nil.

Schermbrucker's Corps, 7 horses knocked up and left.

Battalion Irregulars, nil.

Oham's People, Lieutenant Williams, Captain Potter, missing.

Total. – 2 officers missing, 1 man wounded, 9 horses lost.

P.S. – I know of Captain Potter, Lieutenant Williams, 58th Regiment, and I believe of 80 of Uhamn's people, being killed.

EVELYN WOOD, Colonel.

From Captain Dennison to Colonel Buller,

Frontier Light Horse.

Kambula Hill, 29th March, 1879.

SIR,

In compliance with your order, I beg to give you the following statement of facts of the disaster at Thlabana on the 28th of March, 1879.

On the morning of the 28th, after having missed the main column the previous night, we marched towards the eastern point of Thlabana. We met Colonel Wood and staff on the tracks of the main column. He ordered Colonel Weatherley to push on to the point of attack, which was done. We reached the top of Thlabana about ten o'clock, after having been on the point for about an hour. Colonel Weatherley received an order through a messenger (one of the Frontier Light Horse) to the effect that we were to return at once by the same path that we had gone up shortly after reaching the foot of the mountain. Captain Barton, with about 40 or 50 of the Light Horse, came up to us and told Colonel Weatherley that he had received orders to push round the southern side of Thlabana, as a large impi of the enemy had been seen on that side, and that our Colonel was also to push on with his corps. We immediately did so, and on getting to the turn of the mountain, we saw great numbers of the enemy, which I estimated to be at least 10,000. When we reached within about a mile and a half of the western point of the mountain, we were obliged to make a hurried retreat, as we found our way completely blocked up by the enemy. We retreated under a very heavy cross fire to the Nek on the eastern point of the mountain. The enemy following us within a short distance. On getting over the Nek we found the mountain extremely steep with a succession of precepitous ledges, in getting down the enemy rushed down and assegaied our men. Myself, and about 26 of our men, and the Light Horse reached the bottom of the Nek; several of us kept up a fire for a short time but finding the enemy outflanking us we had to race for our lives across country in the direction of Makateese Kop, we were followed by some of the enemy to within three miles of Potter's stores, many of the men were killed on the retreat.

I beg to add further, that the reasons of our men not being camped on the night of the 27th with the main column arose through our Colonel not having received orders to march from our first camping ground.

C.G. DENNISON, Capt.,
Border Horse.

CHELMSFORD'S DESPATCHES PUBLISHED ON 16 MAY 1879

War Office, 16th May, 1879.

A despatch and its enclosures, of which the following are copies, have been received from the Lieut.-General Commanding in South Africa, by the Secretary of State for War:-

From the Lieut.-General Commanding in South Africa to the Right Hon. the Secretary of State for War.

Durban, 14th April, 1879.

SIR,

I have the honour, in continuance of my despatch, No. 13, forwarded by last mail, to forward the enclosures therein referred to, viz.:-

(a) The report of Brigadier-General Pearson, giving an account of his proceedings from the 24th January to 9th April.

(b) The report of Major Barrow, commanding the mounted portion of the relieving column on the 2nd April; together

(c) With some enclosures connected with number of horses killed or wounded, and arms taken from the enemy.

I am informed by my Deputy-Adjutant General that copies of every document received by him from Brigadier-General Wood connected with the events of 28th and 29th March have been forwarded to you; likewise that full particulars of all events since I crossed the border have been sent by telegraph, *viâ* Madeira.

I had no opportunity of perusing these documents until my return to Durban on the 9th April, but I refrain from making any remarks on the events of those two days, as the reports will have been in your hands for some considerable time when this reaches you. I can, however, most fully endorse the terms in which Brigadier-General Wood has spoken of several officers under his command, knowing, as I do personally, the character of almost every officer referred to; but in the case of Mr. P. Uys, I had only known him from the letters, public and private, of those with whom he had been associated when serving Her Majesty. Colonel Wood and Colonel Buller had invariably spoken of him in the warmest terms, and his loss at such a time must, I consider, be considered a national one.

I trust that the brilliant success of the 29th March may be some consolation for the sad loss of life on the 28th. The full value of this success and that of the 2nd April in the south-east of Zululand, is yet to be known, and I cannot but think these successes will most materially affect the whole course of politics in South Africa.

I have not observed in Colonel Wood's despatch any reference to the reason why he considered it desirable to attack on the 28th, I desire, therefore, to state that previous to advancing on Etshowe, I had given instructions along the whole line to make demonstrations against the enemy, for I had reason to believe at that time that I should find the whole Zulu army between my force and Etshowe.

I left Colonel Wood completely unfettered as to what action he should take in furthering this common object, but it is evident that the affair of the 28th was the result of his carrying out my wishes.

I have, &c.,
CHELMSFORD,
Lieutenant-General.

(A.)

From Colonel Pearson, Commanding No, 1 Column,
to the Military Secretary, &c., &c., Durban.

Fort Tenedos, Lower Tugela Drift, Zululand,
9th April, 1879.

SIR,

Circumstances, as you are aware, have prevented my continuing to acquaint you periodically with the proceedings of the column under my command, as directed by His Excellency the Lieutenant-General, Commanding. Since my despatch of the 23rd January, ultimo, when I reported my arrival at Ekowe and the action near the Inyazana River, in continuation of this correspondence, it will be remembered that my original orders were to entrench Ekowe, which was eventually to become an important Commissariat Depôt, and to assist that department in every way in my power to equip it as speedily as possible.

I, accordingly, at once placed the question of the defences in the hands of Captain Wynne, R.E., the Senior Engineer officer, and on the morning of the 24th January I despatched 2 Companies 2nd Battalion, the Buffs, and 2 Companies Native Contingent, with a few mounted men, to meet a large convoy of commissariat wagons, under the orders of Brevet Lieutenant-Colonel Ely, 99th Regiment, which had started from the Lower Tugela on the 22nd en route for Ekowe.

I also, on the morning of the 25th, sent back to the Tugela 48 empty wagons for further supplies under escort of 2 Companies 2nd Battalion, the Buffs, 2 Companies 99th Regiment, 2 Companies Native Contingent, and a few mounted men, the whole under command of Major Coates, 99th Regiment.

By the 27th January, the day on which we first heard of the disaster at Isandhlana by a telegram from Sir Bartle Frere (no details however being given), the entrenchments had made considerable progress, all available men having been employed on them.

Major Barrow with his mounted men had also reconnoitred towards the Umhlatoosi River and Intumeni, the Norwegian Mission Station, some 12 miles N.W. of us, which was to be the immediate destination of the 2nd Column.

About 9 A.M. on the 28th January, I received by special messenger a telegram from Lord Chelmsford, confirming the news sent me by Sir Bartle Frere. His Lordship was pleased to give me full liberty to act as I thought best in the interests of my column under the circumstances, and sanctioned my retiring, if I thought fit, either to some position nearer the Tugela, or even to the left bank of that river. I was to be prepared, however, if I held my position at Ekowe, to have the whole Zulu army down on me.

I at once assembled all my Staff and Company Officers and laid the position of affairs before them, and requested them to give me their opinions unreservedly. Some were for retiring, whilst others most strongly opposed any retrograde movement.

Personally I was in favour of retiring at first, as I believed, until further reinforcements could arrive from home, that the presence of every available soldier would be necessary in Natal to protect the colony from wholesale raids by the Zulus; but, on further reflection, I judged that if we continued to hold our forward position in the country – nearly 40 miles from the frontier – it might have a good moral effect and even afford protection to that part of the colony immediately behind us; at any rate we should be keeping a certain force of the enemy watching us, which could not therefore be available elsewhere.

Having satisfied myself that we were sufficiently supplied with ammunition for our present wants, it was finally decided to remain at Ekowe, and to fortify ourselves as strongly as possible.

The question of our food supply had of course been duly considered. The troops had started with 15 days' provisions, and most fortunately Colonel Ely's Column was now in sight, about 7 miles distant. I lost no time in acquainting that officer with the state of affairs, and I sent him several extra spans of oxen to help his wagons over the hilly road before him. Such was the state of the roads, however, after the constant rain which had fallen during many weeks past, that, notwithstanding the additional assistance, the last of Colonel Ely's wagons did not arrive until 12 o'clock that night, and he had to abandon eight. I sent oxen to bring them on the following morning, but meantime the contents had been looted by the Zulus.

In order still further to increase our food supply, and to add to the defensive power of the colony, I had already decided on sending back the whole of the mounted troops attached to my column, together with the remaining companies of the 2 Battalions Native Contingent. These troops left Ekowe about noon on the 28th, with wagons of course, and, as we afterwards learnt, reached the Lower Tugela that night by cross country paths.

Our next care was to laager some of the wagons along the parapets in such a manner as to protect the men from the reverse and infilade fire to which in many places they would be exposed; all the other wagons were afterwards formed into a laager for the oxen under the fire of the Fort.

Pending the result of the stock taking of our food supply, which I had ordered, I now placed the garrison upon a reduced bread and grocery ration; but as a large number of slaughter cattle had been driven up with Colonel Ely's convoy, I increased the meat ration by ¼ lb.

Having reason to believe that the troops whom I had sent away had brought a certain quantity of private supplies with them, I had their wagons officially searched, and a quantity of food, medicines, and medical comforts were thus added to our stock, the two latter subsequently proving of the utmost value to us.

All articles of luxury, tobacco, matches, &c., I caused to be handed over to the Commissariat Department to be dealt with as I might afterwards determine; they were eventually sold by auction and fetched fabulous prices – matches were sold for 4*s.* a box, bottles of pickles for 15*s.*, tobacco for 30*s.* per lb., In fact about £7 worth of things realized upwards of £100.

When I received the Commissariat report about our food, I found that we could not safely calculate upon our supplies lasting beyond the latter end of March, it having been found advisable, owing to the discovery of a large quantity of rotten biscuit and flour, to make a large deduction – 10 per cent – in anticipation.

Fortunately the loss of these articles never reached this amount, and not only, as time went on, did we find our supplies holding out far better than we ever expected, but I felt enabled for a time to comply with the recommendation of my Senior Medical Officer to increase the bread ration if only temporarily. I did so for about ten days, and yet, nevertheless, such was the care exercised by the Commissariat Department to avoid waste, that with the reduced ration on which the troops were again placed, we should have been able to hold out till 10th April; a few things only, sugar, pepper, and preserved vegetables having run out.

With medicines we were not so fortunate, and long before we were relieved many of those most required were exhausted.

Our defences meantime were being perfected and long before the end of February we were quite secure, and I feel sure could have repelled an attack by any number of Zulus.

For the description of Fort Ekowe I beg to refer to the paper by Captain Courtney, R.E., attached to this letter. Our sanitary arrangements were placed in the hands of the Quartermaster of the Buffs, and 99th Regiment. The former looked after the interior and the latter the exterior of the Fort and its immediate surroundings.

The water supply was fortunately excellent both in quality and quantity. The upper part of the stream gave us an abundant supply of drinking and cooking water, and along the lower portion of it Quartermaster Bateman, 99th Regiment, constructed excellent bathing places both for officers and men, which I am convinced contributed in no small degree to the preservation of our health.

The horses and cattle were watered in a separate stream.

An Infantry water picquet, assisted by a mounted patrol, was posted daily between reveille and retreat, when everyone had to retire within the Fort to prevent any evasion of the orders relative to our water supply, no cattle, horses or cooking (which was all done outside the Port), being permitted near the stream upon any pretence.

Each Quartermaster had a large fatigue party placed at his disposal daily, and the following routine was invariably adopted.

At reveille the urine barrels which had been provided for the use of the men during the night were carried out of the Fort and emptied into trenches dug the night before at some distance off, and which were filled in at once as soon as this duty was performed.

The places where those barrels had stood in the Fort were then sprinkled with ashes from the kitchens, and afterwards with clean sand, the ashes having been first removed.

The fatigue parties next proceeded to clean up all dirt and litter both inside and outside the fort, and cart it away to the offal pits, the contents of which were buried as far as possible before they were filled up.

The hospital patients were removed daily – those, at least, who could bear removal to a shelter constructed of boughs of trees, on an eminence near the fort. This arrangement gave them abundance of fresh air, the hospital itself got purified, and the cleaning could be done more effectually.

I have purposely entered into detail in this matter, as I am naturally anxious to prove that no precautions were neglected to keep the fort and its vicinity in as sanitary a condition as possible.

At first the health of the troops was extremely good, but before the end of February the percentage of sick had largely increased, and when we were relieved on the 4th April there were 9 officers and nearly 100 men on the sick list. Some of them are still seriously ill, and 4 deaths have occurred since we left Ekowe. We buried there 4 officers and 21 C. K. P. men.

The chief disorders were diarrhoea, dysentry, common, continued and typhoid fever; no doubt much of the sickness was attributable to the constant wet weather, and the overcrowding in the fort, the work having been constructed for a much smaller garrison.

The large percentage of deaths were probably due to the want of proper medicines and medical comforts. A state showing the strength of the garrison is herewith attached.

As regards shelter, there was only room in the fort for a very few tents in addition to those required for hospital purposes, and both officers and men lived under the wagons, over which the wagon sails were spread, propped up with tent poles: thus the wagons being all round the parapets, as I have already described, the troops actually lived at their alarm posts, and could be on the banquettes in a few seconds.

The buildings of the Mission Station were handed over to the Commissariat, and just sufficed to store our supply of food.

The church was used as the hospital. By day the picquet duties were performed by a small vedette corps, formed by a few men of the Mounted Infantry and Natal Volunteers, and organized by Lieut. Rowdon, 99th Regiment, and Captain Sherrington, Native Contingent.

I cannot speak too highly of the careful and zealous way in which this responsible duty was done, and which I consider reflects much credit on the officers above named, as well as those under their command. These vedettes were constantly under fire; one was killed at his post; another, Private Carson, 99th Regiment, was attacked by about a dozen Zulus, who crept up near him in the long grass. They shot off two fingers of his right hand; he had a bullet through each thigh, and another in his right arm. His horse was also assegaied. He nevertheless got away, retained his rifle, and rode back to the Fort. At night or in foggy weather the outposts were withdrawn, and each company furnished a guard with two or more sentries. Natives were also distributed along the parapets, their eyesight being so good.

As regards the oxen, we had several hundred head, besides a number of mules and horses. On our first arrival at Ekowe, there was an abundance of grass close to the Fort, but it soon got eaten down, and the cattle had to be driven further off, till at last there was nothing for them to eat nearer than between 2 and 3 miles distant.

This, of course, necessitated strong guards, and the greatest care and vigilance had to be exercised by the Transport Officer to prevent their straying and getting captured.

The cattle was my chief source of anxiety, more especially latterly, when they had to go so far for their grass. No attack, however, was ever made upon them by the Zulus, who contented themselves with firing upon them from long distances, much too far generally to cause any damage.

Very soon after our arrival at Ekowe we found ourselves being gradually cut off from all communication with Natal, though occasionally a native messenger was persuaded to run the gauntlet through the enemy.

Between 11th February and 2nd March we had no communication whatever with the Lower Tugela, but on the morning of that day we had the happiness to see signals flashed to us from that neighbourhood.

At first we were unable to reply, but Captain Macgregor, Deputy Assistant Quartermaster-General, whom I placed in charge of the signalling arrangements, soon got an improvised heliograph constructed, and when the weather permitted we were able to communicate with Natal daily.

Our information regarding the movements of the Zulus was absolutely nil, and so many men being daily employed on the entrenchments and cattle guards, besides having but a very few mounted men and scarcely any natives, I consider it only prudent to remain on the defensive, and therefore, with the exception of burning all the kraals in our immediate neighbourhood, and sometimes sending foraging parties to the nearest mealie and pumpkin gardens, we confined our attention almost entirely to strengthening the fort and guarding our numerous cattle.

The Chief Dabulamanzi – a half-brother to Cetawayo – had a military kraal near Ekowe, which I thought it would be desirable to destroy, but it being 7 miles distant and unapproachable, except over country more or less covered with bush, I considered it would not be right to attempt it, except with a comparatively large force. Accordingly, on the 1st March, I started at 2 A.M. with 450 men and 1 gun Royal Artillery, and reached the vicinity of the kraal a little before daylight. The Zulus were completely surprised, and if we had only possessed a good body of horsemen we would no doubt have killed or taken prisoners a great number. As it was, they ran off to the neighbouring hills, and I fear we did them but little damage. The military kraal consisting of upwards of 50 huts were, however, completely destroyed, besides 3 others which we burnt on our way back. Returning, we were followed by the enemy, but at a long distance and in no great numbers, which satisfied me that at any rate in that immediate neighbourhood the Zulus were not at that time in any force. Our casualties were nil, but, as far as I could observe, we killed or wounded about a dozen of the enemy. We knew from the messages flashed to us, that a force was being collected for our relief, and it was evident that the Zulus had either got news of it or that they imagined our food could not hold out much longer, for we could see numerous fires – daily increasing – in the Inyazane Valley; evidence of the presence of a large force in that neighbourhood. The vedettes, too, were constantly seeing large bodies of Zulus filing down the distant hills towards the Inyazane, where they were evidently collecting either to intercept our relief or retreat.

To make a new road from Ekowe to the nearest point of the regular road from the Inyazane, so as to avoid a long detour of over 7 miles, had long been contemplated. It was surveyed early in March and commenced on the 7th. The road was made practicable within a week, but owing to the heavy rains which fell in March, it became too soft in places for heavy traffic. In winter, however, it would have been an excellent road.

Either the working or covering parties were nearly always under fire, though fortunately we had only one casualty; Lieutenant Lewis, the Buffs, wounded in the head. This new road is fully described by Captain Courtney.

Most unaccountably no attempt was ever made at night to capture the cattle or to annoy us inside the Fort. Had it been otherwise, the men would have been so harassed from want of sleep that the works would have been very materially delayed, and no doubt, our sick list would have been largely increased. We had a few 'scares' during the night, as might be expected, but in every instance they proved to be false alarms.

The alacrity, however, with which the parapets were invariably manned satisfied me that the garrison was already fully on the alert. On the 3rd April we were still hard at work improving the defences when we received intelligence that Lord Chelmsford intended to evacuate Ekowe, and to establish a fortified post on the coast road instead. The works still in contemplation were described in a paper, prepared for the new garrison (had we been replaced as at first intended), by Captain Courtney, so there would have been no check or interruption in going on with them.

Captain Macgregor had also made a ground plan [*not enclosed*] of the Fort and its immediate vicinity for the information and guidance of our successors.

On evacuating Ekowe, I am happy to be able to report that, with the assistance of some spans of oxen sent me by His Excellency the Lieut-General from his camp (we had lost many by death, and had long since commenced to eat the trek oxen), I brought away every wagon and all stores which were of the slightest use. My march to the Tugela was performed without any interruption from the enemy. At one of my camps on the way down, between the Inyazane and Amatakulu Rivers, and about 5 miles from the Head Quarters laager, several dead bodies of Zulus were found, showing, I think, that the number killed in the attack on Lord Chelmsford was under estimated in the official accounts, as no doubt many other bodies were lying about in other directions equally distant from the laager.

It now only remains for me to bring to the favourable notice of His Excellency the Lieut.-General the names of those officers who, from the positions they held, came under my personal observation; and this I find a task of some difficulty, for I am proud to state, that without exception, no officer, non-commissioned officer or private behaved otherwise than with credit to the British Army. From first to last, the men showed an excellent spirit, the highest discipline was maintained, and the reduction of the food was never grumbled at or regarded in any other light than a necessity and a privation to be borne, and which they were determined to bear cheerfully. The Officers of my Staff, Colonel Walker, C.B., Scots Guards, Captain Macgregor, 29th Regiment, and Lieutenant Knight, the 'Buffs,' my orderly officer, were indefatigable, and gave me every support, and much valuable advice, Captain Macgregor's position perhaps, as Deputy Adjutant Quartermaster-General, was the most prominent, and I have to thank him for the deep interest he took in all sanitary questions and reconnoissance duty. A sketch by him of the Fort and its neighbourhood is enclosed, but I trust the intelligence department in which he has served will ere long have the benefit of the report which he is compiling from his official journal.

The several Commanding Officers, Commander Campbell, Royal Navy, Lieutenant Lloyd, Royal Artillery, Captain Wynne, Royal Engineers, Lieut.-Colonel Parnell, the 'Buffs,' and Colonel Welman, 99th Regiment, with their officers, are entitled to full credit for the good discipline and cheerful spirit of their men.

The Royal Engineers, of course, took a very prominent part in the construction at Fort Ekowe. Captain Courtney's paper will show all that was accomplished under their able guidance. Captain Wynne's illness is much to be deplored. I consider him a most valuable officer, and his illness is entirely due to over exertion at a time when he was in very indifferent health. I much fear he is dying. Of Captain Courtney, his successor, I entertain a very high opinion, and it gives me much pleasure to endorse the favourable, opinion expressed by him of his subalterns, Lieutenants Main and Willock, attached to the Royal Engineers. I had a small corps of Native Pioneers who, and their excellent officers Captain Beddoes and Lieutenant Paringdon, did much valuable service. These two officers managed their men extremely well, and gave proof that, properly officered, the Natal Kafirs are capable of being made into excellent soldiers.

The Medical Department was under the orders of Staff Surgeon Morbury, Royal Navy, and though he had many and great difficulties to contend with, he did his utmost to mitigate the discomforts to which the sick were exposed, and most carefully watched over the sanitary condition of the Fort.

The Medical Officer acting under Dr. Morbury gave him every support. The Transport Branch of the Commissariat Department was superintended by Captain Pelley Clark and Lieutenant Thirkill, 88th Regiment. Both are able and hard working officers, and assisted by their conductors did their utmost to look after the valuable property in their charge. I am very sorry to say that both these officers have returned in very indifferent health.

The Commissariat Department was most satisfactorily worked by Assistant Commissary Heygate, until he became too ill to continue at his duty, a short time before the evacuation of the Fort. Attached to the Commissariat Department as issueer was Sergeant-Major Wishart 90th Light Infantry, one of the hardest working and most deserving non-commissioned officers I have ever met with.

Connected with the vedette duties, I wish to mention a circumstance which I think reflects great credit upon Captain Sherrington, Native Contingent, and the undermentioned men, viz.:- Corporal Adams, Native Contingent, Privates Whale, Robson, Higley and Keys, 99th Regiment, and Trooper Garlands, Victoria Mounted Rifles.

The vedettes, shortly after our arrival at Ekowe, were daily annoyed when they patrolled in the morning, before finally taking up their posts, by the fire of a party of Zulus from a high hill. It was believed that this party took up their position very early in the morning, and Captain Sherrington and the above party volunteered to go out at night and lie in wait for them behind some rocks near the top of the hill, being utterly ignorant, however, of the number of the Zulus.

I consented, and this little expedition resulted in 3 Zulus being wounded (though not so seriously as to prevent them making good their escape), and the vedettes never being annoyed from this hill again.

In fact, no Zulu was ever afterwards seen there. I must not conclude this letter without publicly acknowledging the devotion to their duties of the Reverends R. Robertson and A. Walsh, Church of England and Roman Catholic Chaplains, respectively. The former was also my political assistant, and I owe him many thanks for his valuable advice and information upon all subjects connected with Zululand.

I have, &c.
C.K. PEARSON, Colonel,
Commanding No. 1 Column.

Report on Fort Ekowe.

The following report is drawn up from the diary of Captain Wynne, R.E., commanding 2nd Company Royal Engineers. This diary closes on the 11th March, 1879, since which date Captain Wynne has been on the sick list; from the 11th March to the 4th April Captain Courtney, R.E., continued the diary:-

No. 1 Column, under command of Colonel Pearson, reached Ekowe about noon on the 23rd January, 1879.

Ekowe lies about 1½ miles off the main road from Tugela to Ulundi. It is a Norwegian Mission Station, but has been abandoned for several months. There are three thatched buildings, built of brick and plastered, one a dwelling-house with verandah and several small rooms (on plan X).

One a school-room (marked Y on plan), and a third containing a workshop and stores (Z on plan).

There is also a church built of the same materials but with a corrugated iron roof with a vestry at the east end (Q on plan). An open shed lay to the north of these buildings but was destroyed during the construction of the fort; a small outhouse to the north of the dwelling-house (W on plan) was worked into the parapet at the northeast angle of the fort (on plan). These buildings lie within a space 120 yards by 80 yards, on ground sloping from west to east, the church being on the higher ground, and the dwelling-house, with a good garden of orange trees on the lower part of the slope, at the bottom of which was a stream of good water well supplied by springs from all sides.

This stream runs in a south-east direction, and is met by another small watercourse on the south side of the station.

On the rising ground beyond the junction of these two streams stood a dwelling-house with a garden of orange trees, &c., and on the south side of the watercourse stood another smaller house.

There was also a dwelling-house on the high ground to the south-west of the fort and about 250 yards distant; these three last-mentioned houses were all demolished and the materials utilized in the construction of the fort.

The valleys of the streams and the neighbouring kloofs were wooded and thickly grown with underwood.

The station stands high as regards the neighbouring country generally (about 2,000 feet above the sea) but is commanded by hills from 400 to 1,200 yards distant on the north and south sides.

To the west of the church at a distance of 70 yards, the ground falls suddenly and forms a deep kloof, the sides of which were covered with bush. The approach by the branch from the Tugela road is along a narrow ridge running a short distance from north-west to south-east, past the station; otherwise the ground falls away from the station on all sides.

This station was selected as a depôt for stores for the supply of No. 1 Column, and also of the others after concentration on Ulundi. It was chosen (from description only) on account of its position as regards distance from the Lower Tugela, the ample supply of water and the healthiness of the site, but chiefly because of the existence of buildings ready for occupation as storehouses.

When the position was examined after the arrival of the Column, it was pointed out that in itself it was weak and subject to great disadvantages in a military point of view, and that had materials been brought for the erection of a store, it would have been far preferable to have selected the more open and commanding ground to the north of the station.

As, however, shelter for the stores was required without delay, and there was no good material immediately available for building, it was decided to include the station buildings within the area of the fort, and minimise the defects by constructing traverses and parados.

The work of clearing the ground was commenced on the afternoon of the 23rd instant, and continued for a considerable time afterwards, as it was not possible to burn the bush, and all had therefore to be cut down.

It was proposed to leave a garrison of 400 men with two guns. The trace decided on had a peremeter of 450 yards, which was undoubtedly too great, but it was impossible to reduce it, and at the same time include the buildings, without entirely neglecting military considerations. As it was, the west face was too retired to command the nearest slope of the deep kloof on that side, and the valley of the stream on the north side was not thoroughly exposed to fire.

The plan accompanying this report shows the trace adopted, also the profiles of the parapets and ditches. The general relief of the work was 6 feet, but at the re-entering angle on the north face it was increased to 8 feet 6 inches, running to 7 feet at the north-east angle and to 6 feet at the north-west angle. At the south-east angle a stockade was contructed 17 feet high, with a double tie of loopholes, so that the undefended ground on the valley to the south could be searched by a few marksmen.

Work was commenced on the 25th January 1879, the Engineers and Natal Pioneers working eight hours, the Infantry and Naval Brigade six hours, and the Native Contingent eight hours; the latter were only employed in clearing the ground.

The strength of the parties were – Royal Engineers, 50; Pioneers, 40; Infantry, 140; and Natives, 250.

On Sunday, the 26th instant, the working hours were reduced for the day, excavation of ditches and hurdle revetting being the work in hand.

Similar work was continued till mid-day on the 28th instant, when, in consequence of the receipt of adverse news from the Lieutenant-General Commanding, it was decided to occupy the fort at once, and withdraw the troops from their encampments into the fort. The work was pressed on as much as possible, but the immediate occupation of course delayed the completion of the revetments, slopes, &c.; and as several alarms occurred during the following days, involving cessation of work, and the use of temporary expedients, such as tents, blankets, &c., for completing the parapets for immediate use, the time taken in constructing the work was necessarily much greater than it would otherwise have been. Wagons loaded with provisions and other stores were used to form (*sic*), and as soon as possible the provisions were removed to store, and the sacks filled with earth and replaced on the wagons. Nearly all these wagons remained in their positions till the evacuation of the fort, and do not appear to have been injured in any way. Shelter for the troops was formed under and in front of the wagons, by stretching out the tarpaulins, and also by throwing spare tarpaulins over frameworks of poles, &c.

The church was loopholed, and a gallery formed for the defenders so as to interfere as little as possible with the use of the floor space for hospital patients. Platforms were made for four guns and one Gatling gun, as shown on the plan; blindages of sand bags resting on frames of timber being provided for the protection of the gunners.

The greatest difficulty lay in providing for the permanent protection of the large number of wagons and oxen which the severed communication with Tugela left on our hands. At first the oxen were driven into the ditches and into a laager of wagons formed in the shape of a ravelin on the south face; they escaped, however, from the ditches unless constantly watched, and the wagon laager screened so much of the direct fire of the south face that it was subsequently abandoned and reformed in the deep kloof at the west side of the fort, so that the fire from that face was not marked. Here, however, the slopes were too steep to allow good standing ground for all the oxen, and after a few days' experience about half the cattle were removed from the laager and tethered at night on the south glacis. In the middle of March the laager in the kloof was abandoned, and two circular laagers formed on the reverse slopes of the valley on the south side of the fort. It will thus be seen that the presence of so many cattle, which was not contemplated when the fort was traced, was really the chief difficulty to be considered in arranging for the defence of the fort. The horses were picketed in the ditch of the north face.

Three bridges were provided. One at the main gate was a rolling bridge with a wagon roadway. This bridge was run in every night, and though subject to very heavy traffic, no difficulty ever occurred in working it. It was designed and erected by Lieutenant Main, R.E.

A drawbridge for foot passengers was provided at the north-east angle, as this was the shortest way from the fort to the water. It was called the water gate. A temporary bridge was constructed near the stockade to facilitate access to the cookhouses, &c.; on the glacis the parapet was crossed by steps, and no opening made here.

The flank defence of the south and west faces was effected by constructing the caponiers shown on the plan, that of the north face by constructing indents near the re-entering angle where the prolongation of the escarp cut the crest of the adjoining parapet.

The stockade flanked the south-east ditch, and the north-east ditch was left unflanked, also parts of the stockade ditch; the greater portion of these undefended ditches was staked, so as to render a rush more difficult.

Trou de loups were formed on the east faces and wire entanglements on parts of the south and north faces.

The drainage from the fort was carried into the ditch by openings left at the eastern salient and stockade, these being the two lowest points; from the ditch the water was carried into the stream on the south side by a large drain, eleven feet deep at the counterscarp; the glacis was made good over the upper portion of this drain.

There was a great deal of heavy rain, and the main openings were amply large enough for carrying off all the water, but there was room for a great deal of improvement in the many small drains which existed in the fort.

There was no foul drainage to provide for, as urine tubs and metal earth-closets were used by night, and by day the latrines, &c., outside the fort were alone allowed to be used.

All refuse within the fort was removed every morning and buried outside.

The nature of the surface soil (about four feet of vegetable mould) rendered communications and paths about the fort very disagreeable in wet weather. A gravel pathway was made near the water gate, and the road through the centre of the fort to the main gate was in course of being macadamized. The stone could only be obtained in large blocks, and a good deal of labour was required in breaking it.

The question of hutting the troops was considered as soon as the defences were considered complete, and at the end of February a hut 33 feet long and 20 feet wide was commenced near the south-east angle; this hut was only just finished in the beginning of April, when it was decided to use it only for stores. The design at first provided for a traverse in the centre constructed of wattles filled in with earth, but this was found impracticable and abandoned. The slow progress of this work was due to the difficulty experienced in getting straight timber for the frame work and roof, to the wet weather and to the pressure of other works; the walls and roof were formed of timber with hurdles between the uprights, and a hurdle roof, the whole plastered with a mixture of cow-dung, clay, and grass. Later on, a hut of simpler construction was erected near the main gate, omitting the earth traverse; the roof was formed by stretching a tarpaulin over the rafters, and the sides were not daubed. This hut was occupied for a few days and appeared to answer well. The difficulty experienced in obtaining suitable timber showed that huts could not be constructed in a reasonable time, and it was decided to use tents, and to construct parados of timber in short lengths, the waggons being removed as the parados were finished.

This work was commenced, but the evacuation of the fort put a stop to it. As the hurdle revetments decayed, sod revetments were substituted for them, and sod traverses for the traverses of sacks and wagons; this work was nearly completed when the evacuation was ordered.

The supply of water was obtained entirely by carrying water from the stream; a constant reserve supply was kept up by filling all the available vessels in the fort, and the water in them was constantly changed. Wagons lined with tarpaulins were also used at first for keeping water in, but the supply was not maintained, as the oil in the tarpaulins gave the water an unpleasant taste; they would however, have been most valuable if filled immediately before any emergency arose. Gutters were provided to catch the rain water from the church roof; the water from the roofs of the other buildings (which were plastered with mud to reduce the risk of fire) was not collected. During the excavation of the ditch several springs were found, and a well 25 feet deep was sunk on the glacis of the north face, but the supply was found insufficient to be of much use, and the risk of surface contamination was considered too great, so the work was abandoned and the well closed in. There was also a good spring in the south ditch, and had there been any necessity for it this supply could have been utilized.

Captain Wynne, R.E., commenced a regular trigonometrical survey of the whole position. The triangulation was completed and plotted and the contouring commenced when his illness put a stop to the work.

A range table was prepared by Captain Wynne, and the positions marked on the ground; the triangulation also served as the basis for the military sketch of the ground made by the Assistant Quartermaster-General.

On the 5th March it was determined to reconnoitre the country between the fort and a point on the existing Tugela road, about 6 miles from the fort, with a view of constructing a more direct road. The route was considered practicable; it involved the construction of three drifts or fords and several side cuttings on the hills. Strong working parties were employed on this work, and it was considered fit for use on the 13th March when the surplus garrison was to have retired to Tugela. After that date further improvements were made, and this road would have proved most useful, as it saved 3 miles in distance; but the heavy rains at the end of March and on the 1st April damaged parts of it so much that it was not considered advisable to use it when the garrison evacuated the fort on the 4th April. It was used, however, by the relieving force, both in advancing and retiring, on the 3rd and 5th April. The execution of the work was several times opposed by the enemy, and the working parties were under fire.

On the 2nd March flashing signals were observed at the Tugela, and endeavours, which ultimately proved successful, were made to open communication. Captain Wynne constructed a large screen, working on horizontal pivots, and erected it on the high ground to the north of the fort. The signalmen at Tugela, however, failed to see it, and a looking-glass on a horizontal hinge with a vertical pivot was successfully used.

The signalling was entirely under the direction of the Assistant Quartermaster-General at Ekowe, Lieutenant Haynes, R.E., initiated the signalling at Tugela, the valuable results of which cannot be over estimated. The fort was evacuated but not destroyed on the 4th April. All useful tools, materials, &c., were removed as far as possible, and unserviceable tools and metal work buried.

In conclusion, although the fort at Ekowe was open to many objections, both as regards position and some points of construction and trace, there can be no doubt that it would have been sufficiently strong to check any force brought against it by the enemy, so long as the supply of ammunition lasted. Had there, however, been any activity shown by him in annoying the garrison by occasional firing into the fort at night, it would have been impossible to have avoided sending out picquets and constructing outworks and rifle pits in advance; the disadvantages of the site would then have been keenly felt, and the troops would have been much harassed. It is therefore to be hoped that in future operations full latitude in the selection of the site may be left to those charged with the construction of the work.

It is very much to be regretted that Captain Wynne's illness has prevented him from writing this report, which in his hands would have been much more complete, but there can be no doubt that he would have wished to bring to your notice the services of Lieutenant Main, R.E., who joined the company at Tugela, and took charge of the Natal Pioneers on the road to Ekowe, when he executed many useful repairs to the road in advance of the column. His previous experience of South African wars, and knowledge of the materials available for use, has been most invaluable at Ekowe, where many of the works involving extra care and skill were designed and carried out by him.

Lieutenant Willock, R.E., has also rendered valuable service; it is to be regretted that he also is on the sick list, having fallen ill on the 19th March. The sketch annexed to this report is copied chiefly from his drawings and those of Lieutenant Main's, and his sketch of the new road has, I think, been incorporated in the Assistant Quartermaster-General's sketch of the ground near Ekowe.

D. C. COURTNEY, Capt. R.E.
9th April, 1879.

(B)

Staff Office, Head Quarters.

I have the honour to furnish the following report relative to the part taken by the mounted troops in the action at the Gingindhlovo on the 2nd instant. At 6 a.m. Captain Nourse reported that some of Thausie's mounted scouts had seen the Zulus crossing the Inyezana, and almost immediately afterwards the attack commenced. I directed the mounted troops to saddle up and stand to their horses for dismounted duty, one man holding four horses, leaving three-quarters in reserve for use in the trenches if required. At 6.40 a.m. I advanced out of the laager by the front face with the Volunteers and mounted Infantry, and opened fire on the enemy who had retired into the long grass out of fire from the laager.

At 7 a.m. the rear face of the laager was attacked in force, and I took half squadron of mounted Infantry to observe the movement.

Captain Cook's troop of Natal Horse, also two squadrons of mounted Natives then advanced out of the laager by the right face.

The enemy then retired to the low ground below the rear face, and the Natal Horse brought an effective flank fire on them, assisting in causing the Zulus to break.

The dispositions of the mounted troops at this period were as follows:-

Inyezana.

1. Half squadron mounted Infantry, Lieutenant Sugden.
2. Volunteer squadron.

3. Half squadron mounted Infantry, Lieutenant Rawlins.

4. Natal Horse Troop.

5. Mafunzi's Natal Horse.

6. Thausie's Natal Horse.

At about 7.15 a.m. the Zulus retired from the rear face and the Natal Native Contingent advanced out of the laager. At the same time, accompanied by Lieut. Courtnay, I succeeded in making a flank attack on the retreating Zulus with half a squadron mounted Infantry under Lieut. Rawlins who led his squadron with considerable dash and to my entire satisfaction.

The half squadron drew swords and charged the Zulus, who were in large numbers, but utterly demoralized. The actual number of men killed with the sword were probably few, but the moral effect on the retreating Zulus as the swordsmen closed in on them was very great. In most cases they threw themselves down and showed no fight, and were assegaied by the Natal Native Contingent who were following up. A few Zulus showed fight and assegaied one or two horses, but the majority did not do so.

The half squadron then rallied and followed up again up to a distance of 1¼ miles from camp, when it was at last checked by a spruit.

The Natal Horse followed up in support, but were unfortunately unable to charge owing to having no arm blanche or revolver. They fired however with effect.

I have no hesitation in saying, that had a regiment of English Cavalry been on the field on this occasion scarcely a Zulu would have escaped to the Umisi Hill.

The half squadron mounted Infantry, under Lieut. Sugden, and the Volunteer squadron endeavoured to follow up on the front face, but were unable to close on enemy on account of the boggy ground and the fire of the Natal Native Contingent.

The mounted Natives followed the enemy for some miles towards the Gingindhlovo Kraal and Amatakulu, and Thausie's squadron succeeded in recapturing some 15 head of cattle, which the Zulus had found outside the laager.

I think that credit is due to these Native mounted squadrons for advancing out of the laager by the right face when the main attack of the Zulus was being made.

The loss of the mounted troops was as follows:- Mounted Infantry, 2 men wounded severely; 1 man wounded slightly; 2 horses killed; 5 horses wounded. Volunteer Squadron, nil; Natal Horse, nil; Thausie's Native Horse, 1 man killed; Mafunzi's Native Horse, 1 man wounded severely.

The few casualties amongst the horses of the mounted troops, half of whom were outside the laager during the whole action, except the first half-hour, does not say much for the accuracy of the Zulu fire.

P.H.S. BARROW, Major,
Commanding Mounted Troops,
No. 1 Column.

Camp Gingindhlovo,
6th April, 1879.

About two hours after the action all the mounted troops made a reconnaissance for some six miles, but did not succeed in cutting off any of the enemy, who had fled in all directions.

Supplementary Return of Wounded in the Action at Zhlobana Hill (Col. Wood's Column) 28th March, 1879.

Frontier Light Horse – Sergeant J. Dews, severely.

JAMES L. HOLLOWAY,
Deputy Surgeon-General,
for Surg.-General absent on duty.

The Deputy-Adjutant General,
&c., &c., &c.,
Durban.

Supplementary Return of Wounded in the Action at Kambula Hill (Col. Wood's Column), 29th March, 1879.

1st Battalion 13th foot – Private J. Cogan, slightly.

JAMES L. HOLLOWAY,
Deputy Surgeon-General,
for Surg.-General absent on duty.

The Deputy Adjutant-General,
&c., &c., &c,,
Durban.

(C.)

Return of Arms Captured at Gingilovo, 2nd April, 1879, by Relieving Column.

Martini-Henry Rifles, 5: 3 of 24th, 1 of 32nd, 1 unmarked; double fowling pieces, 4; revolvers, 1; guns and rifles (various), 425, mostly 'Tower' and Prussian. Total, 435.

Return of Arms Captured at Kambula, 29th March, 1879, *by No. 4 Column.*

Martini-Henry rifles, 15: 9 of 1–24th, 2 of 2–24th, 4 of 80th; Enfield rifles, 19; 1 Snider carbine, R.A.; rifles and guns (various), 292, mostly 'Tower' or Prussian. Total, 326.

Return of Horses Killed and Wounded in Action at Gingilovo, 2nd April, 1879.

Staff, 2 killed, private horse, Lieut.-Colonel Crealock; public do., Capt. Molyneux; Mounted Infantry, 2 killed, 5 wounded, private horse, Lieut. Courtenay, 20th Hussars; Transport Department, 1 killed; 5th Battalion Natal Native Contingent, 2 killed, 1 wounded, Capt. Gurney, Lieut. Jay, and Lieut. Thompson. Total, 7 killed, 6 wounded.

J. NORTH CREALOCK, Lieut.-Colonel,
Staff Officer.

No. 1 Column.
State of Column, Ekowe, 1st April, 1879.

Effective.

Staff – 4 Officers, 2 Non-commissioned Officers and Men. Naval Brigade – 6 Officers, 143 Non-commissioned Officers and Men. 11 / 7 Royal Artillery – 1 Officer, 25 Non-commissioned Officers and Men. No. 2 Company Royal Engineers – 2 Officers, 77 Non-commissioned Officers and Men. The Buffs – 16 Officers, 548 Non-commissioned Officers and Men. 99th Regiment – 7 Officers, 317 Non-commissioned Officers and Men. Mounted Infantry – 1 Officer, 18 Non-commissioned Officers and Men. Commissariat Department – 3 Non-commissioned Officers and Men. Transport Department – 3 Officers, 5 Non-commissioned Officers and Men. Army Hospital Corps – 5 Officers, 12 Non-commissioned Officers and Men. Mounted Volunteers – 8 Non-commissioned Officers And Men. Native Pioneers – 4 Officers, 98 Non-commissioned Officers and Men. Native Contingent – 3 Officers, 11 Non-commissioned Officers and Men. Her Majesty's Troops – 25 Natives, 45 Officers, 1,150 Non-commissioned Officers and Men. Colonial Troops – 8 Non-commissioned Officers and Men. Native Service – 7 European Officers, 11 European Non-commissioned Officers and 123 Natives.

Sick in Hospital and Quarters.

Naval Brigade – 1 Officer, 5 Non-commissioned Officers and Men. No. 2 Company Royal Engineers – 2 Officers, 3 Non-commissioned Officers and Men. The Buffs – 1 Officer, 15 Non-commissioned Officers and Men. 99th Regiment – 3 Officers, 10 Non-commissioned Officers and Men, Mounted Infantry – 3 Non-commissioned Officers and Men. Commissariat Department – 1 Officer. Army Hospital Corps – 1 Non-commissioned Officer. Her Majesty's Troops – 8 Officers, 37 Non-commissioned Officers and Men.

Attending Hospital.

Staff – 1 Non-commissioned Officer. Naval Brigade – 6 Non-commissioned Officers and Men. No. 2 Company Royal Engineers – 12 Non-commissioned Officers and Men. The Buffs – 20 Non-commissioned Officers and Men. 99th Regiment – 29 Non-commissioned Officers and Men. Mounted Infantry – 4 Non-commissioned Officers and Men. Transport Department – 1 Non-commissioned Officer. Army Hospital Corps – 1 Non-commissioned Officer. Mounted Volunteers – 3 Non-commissioned Officers and Men. Her Majesty's Troops – 74 Non-commissioned Officers and Men. Colonial Troops – 3 Non-commissioned Officers.

Present Strength.

Staff – 4 Officers, 3 Non-commissioned Officers and Men. Naval Brigade – 7 Officers, 154 Non-commissioned Officers and Men. 11/7 Royal Artillery – 1 Officer, 25 Non-commissioned Officers and Men. No. 2 Company Royal Engineers – 4 Officers, 92 Non-commissioned Officers and Men. The Buffs – 17 Officers, 583 Non-commissioned Officers and Men. 99th Regiment – 10 Officers, 356 Non-commissioned Officers and Men. Mounted Infantry – 1 Officer, 25 Non-commissioned Officers and Men. Commissariat Department – 1 Officer, 3 Non-commissioned Officers and Men. Transport Department – 3 Officers, 6 Non-commissioned Officers and Men. Army Hospital Corps – 5 Officers, 14 Non-commissioned Officers and Men. Mounted Volunteers – 11 Non-commissioned Officers and Men. Native Pioneers – 4 Officers, 98 Non-commissioned Officers and Men. Native Contingent – 3 Officers, 11 Non-commissioned Officers and Men. Her Majesty's Troops – 25 Natives, 53 Officers, 1,261 Non-commissioned Officers and Men. Colonial Troops – 11 Non-commissioned Officers and Men. Native Service – 7 European Officers, 11 European Non-commissioned Officers, 123 Natives, In addition to these numbers, there were 164 conductors and drivers.

Increase –

From 99th Regiment, Mounted Infantry – 4 Non-commissioned Officers and Men.

Total.

Mounted Infantry – 4 Non-commissioned Officers and Men. Her Majesty's Troops – 4 Non-commissioned Officers and Men.

Decrease – Deceased.

Naval Brigade – 1 Officer, 4 Non-commissioned Officers and Men. The Buffs – 2 Officers, 7 Non-commissioned Officers and Men. 99th Regiment – 1 Officer, 8 Non-commissioned Officers and Men. Mounted Infantry, 1 Non-commissioned Officer. Army Hospital Corps – 1 Non-commissioned Officer. Her Majesty's Troops – 4 Officers, 21 Non-commissioned Officers and Men.

Total.

Naval Brigade – 1 Officer, 4 Non-commissioned Officers and Men. The Buffs – 2 Officers, 7 Non-commissioned Officers and Men. 99th Regiment – 1 Officer, 8 Non-commissioned Officers and Men. Mounted Infantry – 1 Non-commissioned Officer. Army Hospital Corps – 1 Non-commissioned Officer. Her Majesty's Troops – 4 Officers, 21 Non-commissioned Officers and Men.

To Mounted Infantry.

99th Regiment – 4 Non-commissioned Officers and Men.

Total.

Staff – 4 Officers, 3 Non-commissioned Officers and Men. Naval Brigade – 8 Officers, 158 Non-commissioned Officers and Men. 11 / 7 Royal Artillery – 1 Officer, 25 Non-commissioned Officers and Men. No. 2 Company Royal Engineers – 4 Officers, 92 Non-commissioned Officers and Men. The Buffs – 19 Officers, 590 Non-commissioned Officers and Men. 99th Regiment – 11 Officers, 368 Non-commissioned Officers and Men, Mounted Infantry – 1 Officer, 22 Non-commissioned Officers and Men. Commissariat Department – 1 Officer, 3 Non-commissioned Officers and Men. Transport Department – 3 Officers, 6 Non-commissioned Officers and Men. Army Hospital Corps – 5 Officers, 15 Non-commissioned Officers and Men. Mounted Volunteers – 11 Non-commissioned Officers and Men. Native Pioneers – 4 Officers, 98 Non-commissioned Officers and Men. Native Contingent – 3 Officers, 11 Non-commissioned Officers and Men, 25 Natives. Her Majesty's Troops – 57 Officers, 1,282 Non-Commissioned Officers and Men. Colonial Troops – 11 Non-commissioned Officers and Men. Native Service – 7 European Officers, 11 European Non-commissioned Officers, 123 Natives.

C.K. PEARSON, Colonel,
Commanding No. 1 Column.

No. 1 Column.
State of the Column at Ekowe on 3rd April, 1879.

Effective.

Staff – 4 Officers, 2 Non-commissioned Officers and Men. Naval Brigade – 6 Officers, 142 Non-commissioned Officers and Men. Royal Artillery – 1 Officer, 23 Non-commissioned Officers and Men. Royal Engineers – 2 Officers, 77 Non-commissioned Officers and Men. The Buffs – 16 Officers, 543 Non-commissioned Officers and Men. 99th Regiment – 7 Officers, 316 Non-commissioned Officers and Men. Mounted Infantry – 1 Officer, 21 Non-commissioned Officers and Men. Commissariat Department – 3 Non-commissioned Officers and Men. Transport Department – 3 Officers, 6 Non-Commissioned Officers and Men. Army Hospital Corps – 5 Officers, 13 Non-commissioned Officers and Men. Volunteer Mounted Rifles – 6 Non-commissioned Officers and Men. Native Pioneers – 4 European Officers, 96 Natives. Native Contingent – 2 European Officers, 8 European Non-commissioned Officers, 25 Natives. Her Majesty's Troops – 45 Officers, 1,156 Non-commissioned Officers and Men. Colonial Troops and Native Levies – 20 Europeans, 121 Natives.

Sick in Hospital and Quarters.

Naval Brigade – 1 Officer, 5 Non-commissioned Officers and Men. Royal Engineers – 2 Officers, 3 Non-commissioned Officers and Men. The Buffs – 1 Officer, 17 Non-commissioned Officers and Men. 99th Regiment – 3 Officers, 10 Non-commissioned Officers and Men. Mounted Infantry – 3 Non-commissioned Officers and Men. Commissariat Department – 1 Officer. Army Hospital Corps – 1 Non-commissioned Officer. Volunteer Mounted Rifles – 5 Non-commissioned Officers and Men. Her Majesty's Troops – 8 Officers, 29 Non-commissioned Officers and Men. Colonial Troops and Native Levies – 5 Europeans.

Attending Hospital.

Staff – 1 Non-commissioned Officer. Naval Brigade – 6 Non-commissioned Officers and Men. Royal Artillery – 2 Non-commissioned Officers and Men. Royal Engineers – 12 Non-commissioned Officers and Men. The Buffs – 23 Non-commissioned Officers and Men. 99th Regiment – 30 Non-commissioned Officers and Men. Mounted Infanty – 1 Non-commissioned Officer. Native Contingent – 1 European Officer, 3 European Non-commissioned Officers. Her Majesty's Troops – 75 Non-commissioned Officers and Men. Colonial Troops and Native Levies – 4 Europeans.

Total.

Staff – 4 Officers, 3 Non-commissioned Officers and Men. Naval Brigade – 7 Officers, 153 Non-commissioned Officers and Men. Royal Artillery – 1 Officer, 25 Non-commissioned Officers and Men. Royal Engineers – 4 Officers, 92 Non-commissioned Officers and Men. The Buffs – 17 Officers, 583 Non-commissioned Officers and Men. 99th Regiment – 10 Officers, 356 Non-commissioned Officers and Men. Mounted Infantry – 1 Officer, 25 Non-commissioned Officers and Men. Commissariat Department – 1 Officer, 3 Non-commissioned Officers and Men. Transport Department – 3 Officers, 6 Non-commissioned Officers and Men. Army Hospital Corps – 5 Officers, 14 Non-commissioned Officers and Men. Volunteer Mounted Rifles – 11 Non-commissioned Officers and Men. Native Pioneers – 4 European Officers, 96 Natives. Native Contingent – 3 European Officers, 11 European Non-commissioned Officers, 25 Natives. Her Majesty's Troops – 53 Officers, 1,260 Non-commissioned Officers and Men. Colonial Troops and Native Levies – 29 Europeans, 121 Natives. In garrison at Ekowe.

Increase.

From 99th Regiment – Mounted Infantry – 4 Non-commissioned Officers and Men. Her Majesty's Troops – 4 Non-commissioned Officers and Men.

Total Increase.

Mounted Infantry – 4 Non-commissioned Officers and Men. Her Majesty's Troops – 4 Non-commissioned Officers and Men.

Decrease – Deceased.

Naval Brigade – 1 Officer, 4 Non-commissioned Officers and Men. The Buffs – 2 Officers, 7 Non-commissioned Officers and Men. 99th Regiment – 1 Officer, 8 Non-commissioned Officers and Men. Mounted Infantry – 1 Non-commissioned Officer. Army Hospital Corps – 1 Non-commissioned Officer. Her Majesty's Troops – 4 Officers, 21 Non-commissioned Officers and Men.

To Mounted Infantry.

99th Regiment – 4 Non-commissioned Officers and Men. Her Majesty's Troops – 4 Non-commissioned Officers and Men.

Total Decrease.

Naval Brigade – 1 Officer, 4 Non-commissioned Officers and Men. The Buffs – 2 Officers, 7 Non-commissioned Officers and Men. 99th Regiment – 1 Officer, 12 Non-commissioned Officers and Men. Mounted Infantry

– 1 Non-commissioned Officer. Army Hospital Corps – 1 Non-commissioned Officer. Her Majesty's Troops – 4 Officers, 25 Non-commissioned Officers and Men.

Strength on 27th January, 1879.

Staff – 4 Officers, 3 Non-commissioned Officers and Men. Naval Brigade – 8 Officers, 157 Non-commissioned Officers and Men. Royal Artillery – 1 Officer, 25 Non-commissioned Officers and Men. Royal Engineers – 4 Officers, 92 Non-commissioned Officers and Men. The Buffs – 19 Officers, 590 Non-commissioned Officers and Men. 99th Regiment – 11 Officers, 368 Non-commissioned Officers and Men. Mounted Infantry – 1 Officer, 22 Non-commissioned Officers and Men. Commissariat Department – 1 Officer, 3 Non-commissioned Officers and Men. Transport Department – 3 Officers, 6 Non-commissioned Officers and Men. Army Hospital Corps – 5 Officers, 15 Non-commissioned Officers and Men. Volunteer Mounted Rifles – 11 Non-commissioned Officers and Men. Native Pioneers – 4 European Officers, 96 Natives. Native Contingent – 3 European Officers, 11 European Non-commissioned Officers, 25 Natives. Her Majesty's Troops – 57 Officers, 1,281 Non-commissioned Officers and Men. Colonial Troops and Native Levies – 29 Europeans, 121 Natives.

C.K. PEARSON, Colonel,
Commanding No. 1 Column.

No. 1 Column.
Nominal Roll of Deaths at Ekowe up to the 3rd April, 1879.

The Buffs – Captain H.J.M. Williams, 12th March; Lieutenant G.R.J. Evelyn, 30th March.

99th Regiment – Lieutenant Davidson, 27th March.

Naval Brigade – Midshipman Coker, 16th March; Artificer J. Moore, 11th February; Seaman J. Radford, 7th March; Private Royal Marines W. Stagg, 17th March.

The Buffs – Private A. Kingston, 1st February; Private W. McLeod, 13th February; Private E. Oakley, 15th February; Lance-Corporal T. Taylor, 21st February; Drummer A. Mortimer, 6th March; Private J. Slack, 9th March; Private A. Tarrant, 27th March.

99th Regiment – Private W. Knee, 21st February, drowned; Private J. Shields, 21st February; Private J. Paul, 4th March; Private J. Tubb, 16th March; Private T. Venn, 17th March; Private W. Kent, 17th March, killed by Zulus when on vedette duty; Private C. Coombs, 21st March; Private W. Roden, 26th March; Private Lewis, 29th March.

Army Hospital Corps – Private W. Barker, 8th March.

Naval Brigade – Seaman A. Smith, 2nd April.

C.K. PEARSON, Colonel,
Commanding No. 1 Column.

CHELMSFORD'S DESPATCHES PUBLISHED ON 21 AUGUST 1879

War Office, 20th August, 1879.

Despatches, of which the following are copies, have been received by the Secretary of State from Lieutenant-General Lord Chelmsford, K.C.B.:-

Head Quarters Camp,
Entonjaneni, Zululand,
6th July, 1879.

SIR,

My last despatch, dated June 28th, will have placed you in full possession of the situation on that date of that portion of Her Majesty's forces under my immediate and personal command, and of our relations with Ketchwayo.

These forces were about to leave this place for the Valley of Umvelosi, with ten days' provisions and about 200 wagons, the remainder of the stores, together with all the tents and wagons, &c., &c.*, being left behind in an entrenched position here. I was at that time aware that a very considerable force was collected on the left bank of the river, and I reported that until I received from Ketchwayo compliance with the demands I had already communicated to you, I should continue my advance to Ulundi.

The advance was commenced on the 30th June, and the camps of the flying column and 2nd Division were formed that day at a distance of nine or ten miles from the Umvelosi River.

Two messengers from Ketchwayo were seen by me about mid-day. I have the honour of enclosing a copy of the message (marked A) sent to him, which, at their request, was reduced to writing; likewise a copy of the written communication (marked A a) received by me through Mr. Fiju, the white man with the Zulu chief. The messengers brought with them the sword of the late Imperial Prince Louis Napoleon, which, for safe custody, was sent back to the fort here. The messengers were desired to take charge of the cattle which had been sent in to me at Entonjaneni, as I wanted to return them now I was advancing; but they refused to take them, on the plea of the delay it would cause in their return to the King.

On the following day (1st July) our advance was continued over a difficult country, where the wagon track passed through bush of cactus and mimosa trees. After considerable labour on the part of the troops in clearing the road and levelling the drifts, the column reached the vicinity of the River Umvelosi about 1 P.M. The enemy's picquets fell back on our approach, and no opposition took place this day to our taking up our positions on the right bank; at one time, indeed, large bodies of Zulus were seen to move from Ulundi to certain positions in our front, which made me anxious to get our camps formed as speedily as possible. By dusk our position was perfectly defensible, and our cattle and horses had been watered at the river.

On the ensuing day (2nd July) the camp of the 2nd Division closed up to that of the column under Brigadier-General Wood, and our entrenched camp, with a small stone fort, was formed on a plan that would enable a small garrison to defend it, leaving the remainder of the force free to operate unencumbered by any wagons, in such manner as might be deemed desirable.

The Zulu force did not show itself this day; no messengers arrived from the King. A large herd of white cattle was observed being driven from the King's kraal towards us but was driven back again shortly afterwards.

As no message had been received from Ketchwayo, the following morning (3rd July), and as considerable annoyance was offered to our watering parties by Zulus firing on them, I arranged for a reconnaissance to be made by Lieutenant-Colonel Buller, C.B., with his mounted men, as soon as the time allowed for meeting my demands had expired. The cattle sent in by Ketchwayo on 29th June, were driven across the river to him during the morning.

Lieutenant-Colonel Buller crossed the river by the lower drift to the right of our camp, and was soon in possession of the high ground on our front and the Undabakaombie Kraal. The object of Lieutenant-Colonel Buller's reconnaisance was to advance towards Ulundi, and report on the road and whether there was a good position where our force could make its stand if attacked.

I was also anxious, if possible, to cause the enemy to show his force, its points of gathering, and plan of attack.

Lieutenant-Colonel Buller completely succeeded in the duty entrusted him. Having collected his mounted men near Undabakaombie from the thorny country near the river, he advanced rapidly towards Ulundi, passing Nondwengo on his right. He had reached the vicinity of the stream Untukuwini, about three-quarters of a mile from Ulundi, when he was met by a heavy fire from a considerable body of the enemy lying concealed in the long grass around the stream. Wheeling about, he retired to the high ground near Nondwengo, where he commenced to retire by alternate portions of his force in a deliberate manner. The Zulus were checked; but in the meantime large bodies of the enemy were to be seen advancing from every direction; and I was enabled with my own eyes to gain the information I wished for as to the manner of advance and points from which it would be made in the event of our force advancing to Ulundi. Though the Zulus advanced rapidly, and endeavoured to get round his flank, Lieutenant-Colonel Buller was able to retire his force across the river with but a few casualties. He informed me of a position which, on the following day, my force occupied, and which subsequent events showed was admirably adapted for the purpose I had in view.

I consider that this officer deserves very great credit for the manner in which he conducted this duty.

That night the Zulus were moving about in large bodies, as testified by the sound of their war songs, but they in no manner interfered with us.

At 4 A.M., the 4th July, the troops were silently roused, the bugles, however, sounding the reveillée at the usual hour – 5.15 A.M.

I left the camp, with all the wagons, oxen, &c., garrisoned by the 1st Battalion 24th Regiment and casualties. Colonel Bellairs, C.B., D.A.G., at my special request, remained in command of them. (Vide Enclosure G).

At 6.45 A.M., the force, as per return enclosed (marked B), crossed the river. Lieutenant-Colonel Buller's mounted men, going by the lower ford, seized the high ground on our front without opposition.

Passing over a mile of very bushy ground, the force marching in a hollow square, ammunition and entrenching tool carts, &c., in the centre, the guns moving also in the square in such positions as to enable them to come into action on each face with delay, reached the high ground between the kraals Undabakaombie and Nondwengo at 7.30 A.M. The mounted men were now out, covering our front and flanks, while the 17th Lancers covered the rear.

By this time our advance from camp was evidently observed, and dark clusters of men could be seen in the morning light on the hill tops on our left and left front. To our right, where the largest number of the enemy were believed to be, we could see but little, as the mist from the river and the smoke of their camp fires, hung heavily over the bush below.

Leaving Undabakaombie to our left (this kraal was burnt by our rear guard), I advanced to the position referred to by Lieutenant-Colonel Buller; this was about 700 yards beyond Nondwengo, and about the same distance from the stream that crossed the road half way to Ulundi; this was high ground uncommanded from any point and with but little cover, beyond long grass, near it.

At this point I wheeled the square half right, so as to occupy the most favourable part of the ground.

The portions of the Zulu army on our left and left front were now formed in good order and steadily advancing to the attack; masses also appeared from the Thorn country on our right and passed round to Nondwengo and to our rear, thus completing the circle round us.

The battle commenced about 8.45 A.M. by our mounted men on the right and left becoming engaged. Slowly retiring until the enemy came within our range, they passed into our square, which now opened fire with artillery and rifles.

Shortly before 9 A.M. the Zulu army attacked us on every side.

The square was formed as shown in enclosure C.

The Nondwengo kraal, a vast assemblage of huts, probably numbering 400 in number, afforded good cover for concealing the movements of a force, which appears to have been the Ulundi, Ngobamakosi, Uve, and Umbakauli Regiments. No order was to be seen in their movements, which was caused (so state prisoners) by these regiments having been taken by surprise by an early and silent advance. Hurrying up from their bivouacs they had no time to form up separately, but, in a cloud advanced to the attack beyond the cover of the kraal; the fire by which they were met however from our right face proved too heavy, and the bulk of these regiments, failing to advance, rapidly passed to their left and joined the Umcityu Regiment, which was pressing up to the attack in a determined manner. As the ground here fell suddenly, and cover was afforded them in this advance, men were killed within 30 yards of the companies of the 21st Regiment forming the rear face at this point.

The fire of the enemy from a few minutes to nine to 9.20 was very heavy, and many casualties, I regret to say, occurred, but when it is remembered that within our comparatively small square, all the cavalry, mounted men, natives, hospital attendants, &c., were packed, it is a matter of congratulation that they were not heavier.

The fire from the artillery and infantry was so effective that, within half an hour, signs of hesitation were perceivable in the movements of the enemy. I then directed Colonel Drury-Lowe to take out the 17th Lancers. Passing out by the rear face, he led his regiment towards the Nondwengo kraal, dispersing and killing those who had not time to reach the shelter of the kraal or the bush below, then wheeling to the right charged through the Zulus who, in full flight, were endeavouring to reach the lower slopes of the mountains beyond.

Numbers of the enemy in this direction, who had not taken part in the actual attack, were now firing, and, momentarily strengthened by those flying, were enabled to pour in a considerable fire on the advancing Lancers below them. Our cavalry did not halt, however, until the whole of the lower ground was swept, and some 150 of the enemy killed. Many of those they had passed in their speed had collected in a ravine to their rear, these were attacked and destroyed by our mounted natives.

The flight of the Zulu army was now general – the slopes of the hills were, however, beyond the reach of our already fatigued cavalry, and, having no fresh troops to support him, Colonel Drury-Lowe exercised a wise discretion in rallying his men.

Lieutenant-Colonel Buller, meanwhile, had posted the mounted infantry so as to fire into the flank of the retiring enemy, and the remainder of his mounted men, making for the country beyond, killed some 450 in the pursuit. Our 9-pounder guns were shortly afterwards moved from the rear and front faces of the square, and made excellent practice on the enemy retreating over the hills to the east on our left rear, and between Ulundi and the River Umvelosi.

As soon as our wounded had been attended to, and were fit to be moved, the force advanced to the banks of the stream near Ulundi, while the mounted men and cavalry swept the country beyond.

Ulundi was fired at 11.40 A.M., and the kraals of Qikazi and Umpambongwena shortly afterwards.

At 2 P.M. the force commenced to return to its camp on the right bank of the Umvelosi, which it reached about 3.30 P.M. by sunset. Every military kraal undestroyed up to this time in the valley of the Umvelosi was in flames. Not a sign of the vast army that had attacked us in the morning was to be seen in any direction.

By the statements of the prisoners attached (marked D), it would appear that nearly the whole available Zulu army was under Ketchwayo's command this day. By Mr. Fiju's statement, it would appear he considered it to be 20,000, by others it is put down at 25,000, or even more, and was larger than that assembled at Kambula; it must have been formed on a circumference of some 10 miles, vide map attached (marked E).

It appears that Ketchwayo himself arranged the disposition of the forces, and that they considered they would have no difficulty in defeating British troops if they advanced in the open, away from their wagons.

I feel I have a right in saying that the results of the battle of Ulundi, gained by the steadiness of the infantry, the good practice of the artillery, and the dash of the cavalry and mounted troops will be sufficient to dispel this idea from the minds of the Zulu nation, and of every other tribe in South Africa for ever.

It is difficult to compute accurately the loss of the Zulus on this occasion, as the extent of ground over which the attack was made, and the pursuit carried on, was so great, but judging by the reports of those engaged it cannot be placed at a less number than 1,500 killed.

The loss of the Zulus killed in action since the commencement of hostilities in January, have been placed at not less than 10,000 men, and I am inclined to believe this estimate is not too great. I regret to state that in addition to the casualties (vide Enclosure I) in killed and wounded, the Honourable

W. Drummond (in charge of my Intelligence Department) is reported missing; it appears he was last seen riding alone near Ulundi, at a time when a considerable number of Zulus were still hovering about.

On the 3rd July Major Upcher, commanding the forts here, reported that Lieutenant Scott-Douglas, of the 2nd Battalion 21st Regiment, in charge of the signalling stations, had not returned here. I enclose a copy of his report (marked F).

I fear it must be considered certain that Mr. Drummond, Lieutenant Scott-Douglas, and the Corporal 17th Lancers, have fallen into the hands of the enemy.

I hope to enclose the name of the Corporal before the post closes (vide Enclosure H). In order that my account of the battle of Ulundi may reach you with as little delay as possible, I have taken upon myself to disregard the instructions I have received, and am sending this despatch direct, furnishing a copy to Sir Garnet Wolseley, who is with General Crealock's Division. I trust that this action will meet with your approval. I avail myself of this opportunity to bring to your notice the names of the following officers who have specially assisted me during the recent operations in Zululand:-

Major-General E. Newdigate, C.B.
Brigadier-General E. Wood, V.C., C.B.
Colonel Drury-Lowe, 17th Lancers.
Lieutenant-Colonel Redvers Buller, C.B., 60th Rifles.
Lieutenant-Colonel Crealock, 95th Regiment, Military Secretary.
Captain W.C. Molyneux, 22nd Regiment, Senior A.D.C.
Captain E. Buller, Rifle Brigade, Commandant at Headquarters.
Lieutenant A. Milne, R.N., A.D.C.
Dr. Scott, Medical Officer in charge at Headquarters.
Colonel Bellairs, C.B., D.A.G.
Major Grenfell, 60th Rifles, D.A.A.G.
Lieutenant-Colonel East, D.Q.M.G.
Lieutenant-Colonel Harrison, R.E., A.Q.M.G.
Deputy Commissary-General Morris.

I have requested Major-General Newdigate and Brigadier-General Wood to furnish me with the names of any officers whom they themselves are anxious to bring to my notice, but it is probable that this list will not be in time to accompany my Despatch.

I feel bound to express my obligations to my Interpreter, Mr. H.W. Longeast, who has, since my first taking the field last January, always been at my side, and who, by his intimate knowledge of the Zulu character and of their country, has proved of the greatest value to me, and during the late operations afforded great assistance as a guide to the leading column.

* 6000 Oxen, 800 Mules, 400 Wagons.

I have, &c.,
CHELMSFORD, L.G.

A.

Message from Lord Chelmsford to Ketchwayo.

30th June, 1879.

Lord Chelmsford sends the following to Ketchwayo:-

1. If the Induna 'Mundula' brings with him (1,000) one thousand rifles taken at Sandhlwana, I will not insist on 1,000 men coming to lay them down if the Zulus are afraid to come. He must bring the two cannon and the remainder of the cattle; I will then be willing to negociate.

2. As he has caused me to advance by the great delay he has made, I must now go as far as the Umvelosi River to enable my men to drink. I will consent, pending negociations, to halt on the further (Ulundi) bank of the river, and will not burn any kraals until the 3rd July, provided no opposition is made to my advance to the position on the Umvelosi, by which day, the 3rd July, by noon, the conditions must be complied with.

3. If my force is fired upon, I shall consider negociations are at an end, and to avoid any chance of this, it is best that 'Mundula' should come to my camp to-morrow at daybreak or tonight, and that the Zulu troops should withdraw from the river and its neighbourhood to Ulundi.

4. I cannot stop the General with the Coast army until all conditions are complied with; when they are so, I will send, as speedily as possible, a message to him.

A A.

Message from Zulu King to Lord Chelmsford, General.

30th June, 1879.

The King called me this morning to write this letter to your Worship General Lord Chelmsford:-

He brings with bearers a dezen as has belonged to the Prince of England (so they say, I do not know, of course), to-morrow morning the two

7-pounder guns and a lot of oxen will leave to-morrow morning to bring at your worship's feet.

For Cetywayo,
C. VIGU, Trader.

SIR,
P.S. – If the English army is in want for the country, please do me a favour to call for me by bearer, that I might get out of the country, I went in to the country to buy cattle for blankets.

And be,
Your obedient servant,
C.V.

P.S. – My really believing is, that the King wants to fight, but the princes or his brothers they want peace, also the people wants to fight.
   The bearers are Umvousie Englishmen.

The following note was written in pencil on the envelope:-

P.S. – Be strong, if the King send in his army, they are about 20,000.

In haste,
Your obedient servant.
C.V.

B.
2nd Division.

Return of Troops proceeding to the Front. Umvolusi River, 4th July, 1879.

Head Quarter Staff – 6 officers, 37 non-commissioned officers and men, 12 horses. 5th Brigade Royal Artillery – 3 officers, 55 non-commissioned officers and men, 26 horses, 1 camp follower, 2 guns. 6th Brigade Royal Artillery – 6 officers, 137 non-commissioned officers and men, 106 horses, 2 camp followers, 4 guns. Staff, Royal Artillery – 3 officers, 6 non-commissioned officers and men, 8 horses. 17th Lancers – 21 officers, 239 non-commissioned officers and men, 285 horses. Dragoon Guards – 2 officers, 24 non-commissioned officers and men, 26 horses. Shepstone's Basutos – 10 officers, 108 natives, 124 horses. Bettington's Horse – 1 officer, 12 non-commissioned officers and men, 14 horses. 2nd Battalion Natal Native Contingent – 19 officers, 385 natives, 25 horses. 2nd Battalion 21st Foot – 10 officers, 200 non-commissioned officers and men, 6 horses, 1 camp follower. 58th Foot – 19 officers, 407 non-commissioned officers and men, 8 horses. 94th Foot – 21 officers, 600 non-commissioned officers and men, 10 horses. Staff Infantry Brigade – 3 officers, 11 non-commissioned officers and men. Army Medical Department – 8 officers, 18 non-commissioned officers and men, 47 natives, 9 horses. Transport Department – 6 non-commissioned officers and men, 35 camp followers.

Total – 132 officers, 1,752 non-commissioned officers and men, 540 natives, 659 horses, 39 camp followers, 6 guns.

Flying Column.

Royal Artillery – 7 officers, 89 non-commissioned officers and men, 79 horses, 1 camp follower, 4 guns, 2 Gatlings. Royal Engineers – 5 officers, 62 non-commissioned officers and men, 11 horses. 1st Battalion 13th Foot – 24 officers, 587 non-commissioned officers and men, 9 horses, 1 camp follower. 80th Foot – 11 officers, 357 non-commissioned officers and men, 3 horses, 20 camp followers. 90th Foot – 22 officers, 688 non-commissioned officers and men, 5 horses, 42 camp followers. Army Hospital Corps – 6 officers, 3 non-commissioned officers and men, 2 horses, 44 camp followers. Army Service Corps – 1 officer, 1 non-commissioned officer, 3 horses. Mounted Infantry – 4 officers, 64 non-commissioned officers and men, 76 horses. Frontier Light Horse – 10 officers, 96 non-commissioned officers and men, 121 horses. Transvaal Rangers – 5 officers, 62 non-commissioned officers and men, 72 horses. Baker's Horse – 6 officers, 86 non-commissioned officers and men, 100 horses. Natal Native Horse – 3 officers, 89 natives, 92 horses. Natal Native Pioneers – 4 officers, 46 natives, 4 horses. – Wood's Irregulars – 6 officers, 330 natives, 26 horses. Natal Light Horse – 3 officers, 54 non-commissioned officers and men, 61 horses. Head Quarters – 5 officers, 10 non-commissioned officers and men, 21 horses.

Total – 122 officers, 2,159 non-commissioned officers and men, 465 natives, 685 horses, 108 camp followers, 4 guns.

Grand total – 254 officers, 3,911 non-commissioned officers and men, 1,005 natives, 1,344 horses, 147 camp followers, 10 guns, 2 Gatlings.

W. BELLAIRS,
Deputy Adjutant-General.

D.

Statement of Undungungunga, son of Umgenene, a prisoner taken at the Battle of Ulundi, on the 4th July, 1879.

The Regiments engaged were:- Undi, Ndhlondhlo (combined), Udhloko, Umxapo, Nodwengu, Umbonambi, Nokenke, Umcityu, Ngobamakosi, and Ingulute (one company Udukuza), these formed the attacking force.

The Undabakaombi Regiment was with the King at Umlambongwenga. They were his body guard.

The king saw the battle from the kraal.

The king said he wanted to make peace, and three days ago he sent 140 of his white cattle as a peace offering to the great chief leading the white army.

These cattle were turned back at the White Umveloosi River at Nodwengu, by the Ukandampemvu Regiment. This regiment refused to let them pass, and said they 'would not have peace,' they 'preferred to fight,' and they turned the cattle back.

The king was then at Ulundi.

Some of these cattle were killed the day before yesterday by the king's orders for the army to eat.

The principal leaders of the army were Tyingwayo, Muyamane, Dabulamanzi, and Mundula (Headman of Nodwengu).

Sirayo and his son, Mehkla Kazulu, were also present.

We had no idea the white force was so strong in numbers till we saw it in the open. We were completely beaten off by the artillery and bullets.

The Zulu army was larger to-day than it was at Kambula, far larger. I was at the Kambula battle. All the army was present to-day. We had not much heart in the fight when we saw how strong the white army was, and we were startled by the number of horsemen.

We were afraid to attack you in the thorns as we knew you would laager the wagons.

We were afraid to cross the river yesterday after the mounted men because of the laager.

We were all, by order, at Umlambongwenga kraal the day before yesterday when the king addressed us.

He said, as the Ukandampemvu Regiment would not let the cattle go in as a peace offering, and wished to fight, and as the white army was not at his home we could fight, that we were to fight the army in the open, to attack it between Nodwengu and Ulundi kraal, where we did fight. The king also told us when we pursued you not to cross the river for fear of the guns that would be left in the laager.

The king himself personally placed the different regiments and gave us our orders.

We were watching and expecting that the army would leave the laager and march for the king's kraal. We saw the force when it started to cross the river, and surrounded it as we had been ordered to do.

Yesterday we all thought we should have an easy victory if you came into the open.

The two cannons taken at Isandhlwana were at Nodwengu and are now at the king's other kraal in the thorns. No one knows how to use them.

The white man who writes the king's letters is a trader. He came trading in the beginning of the year. The king kept him and he is always watched. His property is not touched. He is a lame man.

A white man was taken at the Ulobane and taken to the king who sent him back, and ordered him to be let go near Kambula.

The army is now thoroughly beaten, and as we were beaten in the open, it will not reassemble or fight again.

No force is watching the lower column (Crealock's) and no force has been sent there.

How could there be when all the army was here to-day?

We mustered here by the king's orders at the beginning of this moon (about ten days ago). We had not been called out before.

I have never heard that Dabulamanzi wanted peace or wanted to go over to the white people.

THEOS. SHEPSTONE, Jun., Captain,
Natal Carabineers.

F.

Entonjaneni, 3rd July, 1879.
Assistant-Adjutant-General, 2nd Division.

I regret to state that Lieutenant Douglas, 1st Battalion 21st Regiment, has not returned to this station.

It appears that on the 1st July, the day being cloudy, Lieutenant Douglas left his escort of ten mounted men, Baker's Horse, and the signalling party, and rode in to Fort Evelyn, to try and forward a message to Fort Marshall, which he was unable to transmit by heliograph, taking with him only one corporal of the 17th Lancers.

There is evidence to prove that he, with the corporal, was at Fort Evelyn on the 1st, but had left before night.

The signalling party, on returning here on the evening of the 1st, reported that Lieutenant Douglas had ridden in to Fort Evelyn, and I expected that he would have rejoined the signalling party on the next day.

Hearing that he had not done so, I reported to you, and sent out a party of natives in the direction of Fort Evelyn, but without any success.

To-day I sent out all available Basutos along the Fort Evelyn-road, and to the left of the road to Ramagwasa. They report seeing about (500) five hundred Kafirs near the mission station, and interchanged shots at long range.

A wagon conductor, who arrived this evening from Fort Evelyn, states that he saw Lieutenant Douglas and the corporal, 17th, leave that place on the afternoon of 1st instant in the direction of Fort Marshall.

The signalling party has an escort of twelve mounted men detailed daily; but the day in question, owing to the very bad state of the horses here, only ten horses were sent. [End of Extract.]

> R. UPCHER, Brevet-Major,
> 1st Battalion 24th Regiment, Commanding,
> Entonjaneni.

Extract from Memorandum by Captain Churchill, 58th Regiment, Commanding at Fort Evelyn. To the Deputy Quartermaster-General.

5th July, 1879.

No news of Scott-Douglas, who started from here on the 1st, at 3 P.M. back to his signalling party. A mist came on about 5 P.M. I sent out a party to search for him and the corporal of the Lancers, but in vain. They were out two nights.

> M. CHURCHILL.

G.

2nd Division.

Troops, &c., remaining in Lagaar.

Umvolosi, 4th July, 1879.

Head-quarters Staff – 6 non-commissioned officers and men, 6 camp followers. Royal Artillery – 10 non-commissioned officers and men, 4 horses, 25 camp followers. 17th Lancers – 6 non-commissioned officers and men, 8 horses, 2 camp followers. Shepstone's Basutos – 2 natives. Bettington's Horse – 1 non-commissioned officer, 1 horse. 2nd Battalion Natal Native Contingent – 6 non-commissioned officers and men, 91 natives, 4 horses. 2/21 Foot – 3 non-commissioned officers and men, 11 camp followers. 1/24 Foot – 23 officers, 410 non-commissioned officers and men, 8 horses, 3 camp followers. 58th Foot – 4 non-commissioned officers and men, 22 camp-followers. 94th Foot – 21 non-commissioned officers and men, 23 camp followers. Army Medical Department – 2 officers, 7 non-commissioned officers and men, 3 horses, 18 camp followers. Deputy Commissary-General

– 9 officers, 15 non-commissioned officers and men, 13 horses, 4 camp followers. Staff Infantry Brigade – 6 non-commissioned officers and men, 2 horses, 2 camp followers.

Total – 34 officers, 495 non-commissioned officers and men, 93 natives, 43 horses, 116 camp followers.

Flying Column.

Royal Artillery – 10 non-commissioned officers and men, 1 horse, 1 Gatling. Royal Engineers – 3 officers, 72 non-commissioned officers and men, 6 horses. 1/13 Foot – 18 non-commissioned officers and men, 7 horses. 80th Foot – 12 non-commissioned officers and men, 6 horses. 90th Foot – 22 non-commissioned officers and men, 15 horses. Army Hospital Corps – 2 officers, 6 non-commissioned officers and men, 3 horses, 19 camp followers. Army Service Corps – 1 officer, 6 non-commissioned officers and men. Mounted Infantry – 8 non-commissioned officers and men, 6 horses. Frontier Light Horse – 8 non-commissioned officers and men, 18 horses. Natal Light Horse – 17 non-commissioned officers and men, 14 horses. Transvaal Rangers – 1 officer, 11 non-commissioned officers and men, 12 horses. Baker's Horse – 2 officers, 16 non-commissioned officers and men, 18 horses. Natal Native Pioneers – 1 officer, 40 natives, 1 horse. Wood's Irregulars – 1 officer, 60 natives, 2 horses. Transport Department – 4 officers, 13 non-commissioned and men, 14 horses. Total – 15 officers, 219 non-commissioned officers and men, 110 natives, 141 horses, 19 camp followers, 1 Gatling.

Grand total – 49 officers, 714 non-commissioned officers and men, 203 natives, 184 horses, 135 camp followers.

W. BELLAIBS,
Deputy Adjutant-General.

H.
17th Lancers.

Casualty Return.

21st Foot – Lieutenant Scott-Douglas, missing from Fort Evelyn.
17th Lancers – Corporal Cotter, missing from Fort Evelyn.

J. GRENFELL, Major,
Deputy Assistant Adjutant-General.

Intonyaneni Camp, 6th July, 1879.

I.

Flying Column.

Return of Officers, Non-Commissioned Officers and Men killed in Action, 4th July, 1879.

11th Brigade 7th Battery Royal Artillery.
1697 Corporal C. Carter.

1st Battalion 13th Foot.
2037 Bugler J. Burns.
 173 Private W. Bradley.

80th Regiment.
1892 J. Floyd.
Natal Native Horse – Trooper Jonas.

Return of Wounded in Action at Ulundi, Zululand, on the 4th July, 1879.

Brigadier-General Wood's Flying Column.
1st Battalion 13th Foot.
Lieutenant G.A. Pardoe, dangerously.

10th Battery 7th Brigade Royal Artillery.
1782 Gunner T. Morton, dangerously.
2548 Gunner W. Moorhead, severely.

Royal Engineers.
9471 Sergeant R. Wood, severely.

1st Battalion 13th Foot.
1467 Private J. Davis, dangerously.
1934 Private J. Bourne, severely.
 402 Private H. Owens, severely.
1811 Private W. Sheppard, dangerously.
1798 Private C. Johnson, severely.
  27 Private W. Hart, severely.
2042 Private T. Stokes, slightly.
 290 Private .T. Swain, severely.
1769 Bugler M. Cockling, dangerously.

80th Foot.

249 Sergeant T. O'Neil, severely.
669 Private P. Tulley, dangerously.
636 Private A. Beecroft, severely.
1213 Private W. Lunt, dangerously.
1616 Private M. Duffy, severely.

90th Foot.

1127 Private J. Flood, severely.

Baker's Horse.

82 Trooper P. Legge, severely.

Wood's Irregulars.

Captain S.S. Horber, severely.
Lieutenant J. Cowdell, severely.

Mounted Basutos.

Trooper Salem, severely.
Trooper Leardo, dangerously.

C.T.D. CUFFE, Surgeon-Major.

2nd Division.

Return of Officers, Non-Commissioned Officers, and Men killed in the Engagement before Ulundi, 4th July, 1879.

17th Lancers – Captain Wyatt-Edgell.
17th Lancers – Farrier-Sergeant Taylor.
58th Foot – Corporal Tomkinson.
94th Foot – Private Coates.
94th Foot – Kent.
Shepstone Horse – Trooper Lisoma.

2nd Division.

Return of Wounded and Missing in the Battle of Ulundi 4th July, 1879.

Staff.

Lieutenant A.D.C. Milne, slightly.
Lieutenant and Captain the Honourable S. Cotton, slightly.
Lieutenant Phipps A. Barry, severely.
Lieutenant Liebemwood, severely.

17th Lancers.

Colonel Drury-Lowe, slightly.
Lieutenant James, slightly.
Lieutenant Jenkins, dangerously.
Private Jones, dangerously.
Private Waite, dangerously.
Private Keegan, slightly.
Private Wright, slightly.

Royal Artillery.

Driver Brennan, severely.

2nd Battalion 21st Foot.

S.F. Major Winslow, severely.
Private Calder, dangerously.
Private Dowble, dangerously.
Private Brown, severely.
Private Fidler, severely.
Private Davinning, severely.
Private Bevan, dangerously.
Private Hennessey, slightly.
Private King, slightly.
Private Smith, slightly.
Private McKae, slightly.

1st Battalion 24th Foot.

Private Aly, slightly.

58th Foot.

Major Bond, severely.
Colour-Sergeant Piper, severely.
Colour-Sergeant Wallingford, severely.

58th Foot.

Private Leverett, dangerously.
Drummer Stewart, dangerously.
Private Tosh, dangerously.
Private Howe, dangerously.
Private Smith, dangerously.
Private Garrotly, dangerously.
Private Lacey, severely.
Private Donolly, slightly.

94th Foot.

Lieutenant Brooke, slightly.
Sergeant Popple, severely.
Sergeant Hunt, dangerously.
Private Murtha, dangerously.
Private Godden, slightly.
Private Penfold, dangerously.
Private Campbell, dangerously.
Private Cotterill, dangerously.
Private Boyles, slightly.
Lance-Corporal Grimes, slightly.
Private Mulholland, severely.
Sergeant McNally, dangerously.
Private Croxford, dangerously.

2nd Natal Native Contingent.

Lieutenant Sukin, slightly.
Lieutenant Moncrief, slightly.
Private Pender, slightly.
Private Mori, severely.
Private Hea, severely.
Private Tulman, dangerously.

Shepstone's Native Horse.

Private Umzaaza, dangerously.

Hospital Bearers.

Private Umbiquito, severely.

Shepstone's Native Horse.

Two Privates not named, slightly.

Nominal Return of Wounded in Action at White Umvolosi, Zululand, on the 3rd July, 1879.

Frontier Light Horse – Private J. Tracey, slightly.
Natal Light Horse – Private A. Kantz, dangerously.
Transvaal Rangers – Private E. Meyles, dangerously.

C.T.D. CUFFE,
Surgeon-Major S.M.O., Flying Column.

From Lieutenant-General Lord Chelmsford, K.C.B., to the Right Honourable the Secretary of State for War.

Head Quarter Camp, Entonjaneni,
Zululand, 7th July, 1879.

SIR,

I have the honour to forward, in continuation of my Despatch of yesterday's date, the accompanying reports and enclosures from Major-General Newdigate, commanding 2nd Division, and Brigadier-General Evelyn Wood, V.C., C.B., bringing to notice the names of those serving under their immediate command whose services they consider deserving of recognition.

These reports not being before me when I wrote my Despatch, I contented myself with mentioning the names of those officers whose good services had come under my personal observation, in order that it might not be considered I was unmindful of the assistance they had rendered.

I now submit with confidence these additional lists, and trust that you will see fit to submit to Her Majesty the names of the officers therein mentioned, in view to their being granted such honours and rewards as may be considered commensurate with the good services performed by them.

I cannot refrain from again bringing to your special notice the names of Brigadier-General Evelyn Wood, V.C., C.B., and Lieutenant-Colonel Redvers Buller, C.B., 60th Rifles, whose services during the advance towards Ulundi from the advanced base, and during the recent successful operations near Ulundi, have been invaluable. Brigadier-General Wood, although suffering at times severely in bodily health, has never spared himself, but has laboured incessantly night and day to overcome the innumerable difficulties which have had to be encountered during our advance through a country possessing no roads.

I can but endorse all that Brigadier-General Wood has said regarding the services of Lieutenant-Colonel Redvers Buller, but I would wish to add my conviction that the victory of Ulundi would not have been gained so easily had not he, by his gallant reconnaisance the day before, discovered the excellent position on which the battle was fought.

In conclusion, I would bring to your notice the excellent service which the several Colonial mounted corps have rendered during the recent operations. The Basutos, either as scouts or as fighting men, have proved themselves invaluable. No column operating in Zululand can be considered complete without them.

I have, &c.,
CHELMSFORD, Lieutenant-General.

Camp Entonjaneni, Zululand,
6th July, 1879.

SIR,

I have the honour to report that in accordance with orders the division under my command* moved from Birmack on the right bank of the Umvolosi River towards Ulundi, at day break on the 4th instant, immediately after the flying column. It formed the rear half of a hollow square, of which Brigadier General Wood's column formed the front half. Artillery, ammunition, and tool carts, hospital stretchers, and led horses moved inside the square.

The men carried two days' provisions, and 70 rounds of ammunition per man, 30 rounds were carried in the mule carts, and a reserve of 12 boxes was carried in ox carts. Entrenching tools were also carried.

The remainder of our stores and provisions were left in the laager which was strongly entrenched and protected on the west side by a stone fort. It was of vital importance to our force that the post should be held. We were aware of the presence of large bodies of Zulus, not only in front in the large military kraals, but also in the thorn country to our right rear and on our left. For this important duty I detailed the 1st Battalion 24th Regiment. I enclose a satisfactory report from Major Dunbar, commanding the regiment, who was ordered to hold the post to the last extremity, by which it will be seen that the men were only too anxious to be attacked, an event which those well acquainted with Zulu warfare, led me to believe was as certain to take place as that we should be attacked on the march. Had this taken place, the men would have had an opportunity of avenging the Isandhlwana disaster.

During the advance of force our rear and flanks were covered by the 17th Lancers and Shepstone's Basutos.

The Umvolosi River, and a sprint about a quarter of a mile further on, were crossed without opposition, and open undulating country reaching as far as Ulundi was gained. The hollow square was, therefore, able to advance, in readiness at any moment to halt and show front in every direction to resist an attack. Guns were placed in the angles and in the centre of each face of the square. Reports from Colonel Lowe made us aware that the enemy was coming rapidly on in great numbers in rear and in both flanks. Large numbers of Zulus could be seen coming quickly towards us from the surrounding hills and the Nodwengo Kraal. As they approached the cavalry were brought inside the hollow square. The Basutos, however, were loth to give up the fight in which they were engaged, and were not inside the square as quickly as I wished, this prevented my opening fire with the infantry.

As soon as the enemy had been repulsed by fire from the square, the cavalry were sent out in pursuit. I cannot speak too highly of the conduct of the 17th Lancers on this and all occasions when they have been engaged; this, however, was the first opportunity they have had of a pursuit, and their lances proved to be a very efficient arm. The Zulus lie down when pursued, and by this means frequently escaped swordsmen. Colonel Lowe's conduct on this day was in every way deserving of high commendation. He was wounded whilst waiting in the hollow square, but this did not prevent his leading the cavalry when the moment came for the pursuit. He has given me the greatest assistance ever since he has been with my division, and is a very valuable officer. All the officers behaved gallantly, but I would also bring to notice the dashing manner in which Major Boulderson led his squadron against the enemy. Captain Shepstone's Basutos and Captain Bettington's troop of Natal Horse behaved well. The Basutos are good fighting men, and are excellent scouts. Both of the above-named officers are deserving of notice. I enclose Colonel Lowe's report upon the action. Lieutenant-Colonel Harness, R.A., was in command of the artillery of the division during the day. On the right rear angle of the square two 9-pounder guns were in action, at first on a slight rise of ground outside the square; as the enemy advanced, they were drawn back into the line of infantry, and were served with great effect during the action, under the direction of Lieutenant French, R.A., whose conduct on the occasion was especially deserving of commendation. All the officers and men of the artillery were particularly steady under fire. I enclose a report upon this arm from Colonel Browne.

With regard to the infantry, I am able to make a most satisfactory report. The fact that the average number of rounds fired by men actually in the ranks was only 6.4 rounds per man, and that, with this small number, the determined attack of the Zulu army was repulsed, speaks for itself. The men were very steady and the firing was well controlled. Volley firing by sections was generally practised, and although for a short time, this degenerated into rapid independent firing, it was soon restrained, and volleys were resumed, which is highly creditable both to officers and men.

The effect of the volleys was most satisfactory on the left of the 2nd Battalion 21st Royal Scots Fusiliers. The enemy were coming up in great numbers. The ground enabled them to creep up to within about 80 yards without being under fire. The long grass there nearly concealed them, a steady volley from the left of the 2nd Battalion 21st at a critical moment (for it was necessary to wait until the smoke had sufficiently cleared away) completely repulsed the attack. At this point Major Hazlerigg, who was in command of the 2nd Battalion 21st, was most active and zealous in attending to the steadiness of his men during the action.

The 58th Regiment occupied the rear half of the right face of the square. Lieutenant-Colonel Whitehead commanded his battalion well. The right of his regiment especially was under a very heavy fire, and the conduct of the men and officers was all that could be desired. The firing was very good. The 94th Regiment occupied the rear face with its left adjoining the right of the 2nd Battalion 21st, and also the left face of the square. Colonel Malthus commanded his battalion most efficiently. The companies in the rear face were under the command of Major Anstruther, whose conduct during the whole day is deserving of high commendation. The Adjutant of this regiment, Lieutenant Brooke, and also the Adjutants of the 2nd Battalion 21st and 58th, Lieutenants Lambert and Lovegrove, rendered great assistance.

The Infantry Brigade was commanded by Colonel Glyn, C.B. I received every assistance from him during the action, and enclose his report. The officers on the staff of my division have given me great satisfaction on this occasion, and, indeed, ever since the formation of the division, although warfare in South Africa was new to most of them, they have diligently endeavoured to carry out their duties. I would especially mention Captain Lane, Rifle Brigade, my Aide-de-Camp, who is a most useful staff officer under fire. He is cool and courageous, and on the march he is always first to give a helping hand wherever he can make himself useful. Major Robinson, Rifle Brigade, Assistant Adjutant-General, Major Gosset, 54th Regiment, Assistant Quartermaster-General, Lieutenant-Colonel Montgomery, Scots Guards, Deputy-Assistant Quartermaster-General, and Captain Sir W. Gordon Cumming, my Extra Aide-de-Camp, all worked hard, and were present during the action. Captain the Honourable S. Cotton, Scots Guards, not being required for transport duties, acted as my orderly officer during the engagement.

The duties of the Commissariat Department have been most ably and satisfactorily performed by Deputy Commissary-General Morris.

The medical officers performed their duties well in the field. I enclose a report from the principal medical officer. I regret to say that there is a long list of wounded officers and men: 57 in all, the greatest proportion of which are dangerous and severe. I also lament the death of Captain Wyatt-Edgell, 17th Lancers, who was shot through the head whilst leading his troop. Five men were also killed. The nominal list of killed and wounded has already been forwarded to you. The number of horses killed was 18, and wounded 29.

* Europeans. – Officers 100; non-commissioned officers and men 1,712; horses 316; guns 8. Natives – Officers 29; non-commissioned officers and men 545; horses 149.

I have, &c.,
EDWARD NEWDIGATE, Major-General,
Commanding 2nd Division, South African Army.

P.S. – The 2nd Battalion of Natal Native Contingent acted in reserve during the action. This battalion has been well commanded by Major Bengough, who is a very good and active officer. His battalion has done very good service in outpost and scouting duties during the whole time they have been in the field. E.N.

7th July, 1879.

P.S. – I omitted in my report furnished yesterday to bring as prominently forward as I had intended the name of Captain Shepstone, commanding the Basutos. This officer, at great personal sacrifice, raised a regiment of Basutos, who, under his able leadership, have on every occasion rendered me very valuable assistance; they are brave soldiers and excellent scouts. He is deserving of the highest commendation.

EDW. NEWDIGATE,
Major-General.

2nd Division.

Return of Horses Killed and Wounded in the Battle of Ulundi on 4th July, 1879.

Staff, 2nd Division: – 2 wounded. Army Medical Department: – 1 killed, 1 wounded.

Cavalry, 17th Lancers: – 8 killed, 2 of these are missing, 19 wounded. King's Dragoon Guards – 1 killed. Shepstone's Horse: – 5 killed, 5 wounded. Royal Artillery, N 5 Battery: – 1 killed. N 6 Battery: – 2 killed, 2 wounded. 2nd Battalion Natal Native Contingent: – 2 wounded.

Total – 18 killed; 31 wounded and missing.

EDWD. NEWDIGATE,
Major-General, Commanding 2nd Division.

From Colonel Glyn, C.B., Commanding Infantry Brigade, to Assistant Adjutant-General, 2nd Division.

Camp, Entonjaneni, 5th July, 1879.

SIR,

I have the honour to submit the following report of the action near Ulundi on the 4th instant, in which my brigade was engaged.

The Infantry Brigade, consisting of two companies and head-quarters 2nd Battalion 21st Regiment, under command of Major Hazlerigg, the 58th Regiment under Colonel Whitehead, and the 94th under Lieutenant-Colonel Malthus – strength as per margin,* paraded before daylight and moved off in double column of fours, with regimental ammunition, carts, and entrenching tools, crossing the Umvelosi River about 7 A.M. immediately in rear of the Flying Column.

The broken ground in the valley on the other side was traversed in this formation until the plain was reached, about a mile and a half distant from the drift, when the hollow square commenced by the Flying Column was completed by the Infantry Brigade, the 58th Regiment finishing the right face, the 94th Regiment the left and half of the rear face, and the 2nd Battalion 21st Regiment the right half of the rear face. In this formation the column moved on until about 600 yards clear of Nodwengo's kraal, where the square wheeled to the right front face turned towards Ulundi. The column was then halted, the faces formed fours outwards, the men in the fourth ranks filling the intervals between the men of the third ranks, first and second ranks kneeling, remainder standing, and all with fixed bayonets. About this time I observed a large force of the enemy advancing in columns of companies, with skirmishers in front, from a hill to our left rear. The action, so far as my brigade was concerned, commenced on the right, the enemy's first attack being directed from the neighbourhood of Nodwengo. The fire on the enemy at a range of 400 to 500 yards was so severe as to check them and divert the attack up a valley which ran along our rear and afforded them complete shelter to a point within 150 yards of our right rear corner. Here the enemy collected rapidly and made a dash at the 9-pounder guns situated between the right of the 58th and left of 21st, many casualties occurring to the brigade and others.

The Zulus got within 30 yards of our line at this point, when their advance was checked by a most galling and destructive fire which caused them to retreat.

In the meantime the columns of the enemy which I had noticed at first had moved round to the back of a ridge about 300 yards from our left rear and opened a brisk fire on the 94th Regiment, from which they suffered some loss. The enemy were, however, dislodged from there by steady volleys fired by sections of this regiment. All the brigade behaved well and with great steadiness, and I specially bring under your notice the conduct of the companies 2nd Battalion 21st and 58th Regiments posted near the guns at the corner. I attribute the steadiness of the regiments of my brigade in a great measure to the influence and example of their respective commanding officers. From my staff I have received every assistance, and especially from my Brigade-Major, Major Dalrymple, 88th Regiment, who has worked hard and well since he held that office. I regret to add that my two Orderly Officers, Lieutenant Liebenrood, 58th Regiment and Lieutenant Phipps, 1st Battation 24th Regiment, were both wounded during the attack on the guns. The former, although wounded in the ankle, remained with me until he was wounded a second time in the right arm.

I beg to bring all these officers to your favourable notice.

I have, &c.,
R.T. GLYN, Colonel, 1st Battalion 24th Regiment,
Commanding Infantry Brigade.

* 2nd Battalion 21st Regiment, 11 officers and 205 non-commissioned officers and men; 58th Regiment, 19 officers and 407 non-commissioned officers and men; 94th Regiment, 21 officers and 616 non-commissioned officers and men.

P.S. – I append two reports from officers commanding 2nd Battalion 21st and 58th Regiments.

Camp, 6th July, 1879.

SIR,

I have the honour to report that the cavalry under my command formed the rear guard of the force which left Camp, Umvelosi River, on the morning of the 4th instant in the direction of Ulundi, with orders to take advantage of any opportunity to harass the enemy during the advance, and if hard pressed and unable to break through the enemy's line in a good open country, to bring the cavalry inside the infantry square. No such opportunity offered itself, and the cavalry closed in on the rear of the force very rapidly, advancing under cover of two large kraals; I therefore entered the square of infantry and guns under a sharp fire from the Nodwengo kraal The enemy's attack on the square having developed itself in a most determined manner from all four sides and being eventually repulsed, I received the order to pursue and sweep the ground of the retiring Zulus, who were making for the hills to the rear face of the square.

This pursuit was carried out in a most determined manner by five troops of the 17th Lancers and 24 men King's Dragoon Guards (one troop remained inside the square unknown to me). The Zulus fled in every direction, and were pursued for a distance of some three miles across the slope of the hills before mentioned, very many being killed with the lances, which proved their decided superiority to the sword in a pursuit. It would, I think, be invidious to point out any particular officer or man when all, I think, showed the same eagerness to reach the enemy and rode with the greatest determination into the scattered Zulus, for the most time under a galling fire from the hills, where the enemy formed themselves into groups and kept up an incessant fire. I may, however, mention that Major Boulderson, who at first had charge of a supporting squadron, which gradually merged into the general line, led the squadron most gallantly.

I was subsequently joined by Captain Bettington and his men, who did considerable execution amongst Zulus who had hidden in the long grass after being cut off by the advance of the Lancers.

Captain Shepstone, with his Basutos, performed excellent service in another direction, but were not under my immediate notice.

Captain Shepstone's own report is herewith forwarded.

I have &c.,
DRURY LOWE, Colonel,
Commanding Cavalry 2nd Division.

To the Assistant Adjutant-General 2nd Division.

Camp, 2nd Division, Entonjaneni,
5th July, 1879.

SIR,

Referring to your memorandum of this day's date, I have the honour to report, for the information of the Major-General Commanding, as to the part taken by the officers and men under my command in the action of yesterday. I am happy to state that nothing could exceed the zeal with which the wounded were attended by Surgeon-Major Stafford and Surgeon Brown, also by Surgeon-Major Hunt, who voluntarily attended to that duty. Surgeon-Major Townsend assisted also at the dressing station in addition to the 2nd Battalion 21st Regiment.

The men of the Army Hospital Corps, 12 in all, behaved exceedingly well on this occasion. I regret I cannot speak equally well of the half Bearer (Native) Company, who showed great reluctance in carrying the wounded to the dressing station, and could hardly be got hold of to carry away the wounded when required from the field of action. Hospital Dresser Mr. Schultz rendered great assistance in bringing the native bearers to the performance of their duties.

I have also to state that Lieutenant of Orderlies Pike materially assisted at the dressing station, where everything was obtainable as regards medicines, medical comforts, and surgical materials conducive to the welfare of the wounded in action of the 2nd Division and Flying Column.

I have, &c.

AND. SEMPLE, M.D.,

Surgeon-Major,

Staff Medical Officer 2nd Division.

From Officer Commanding Royal Artillery 2nd Division to Assistant Adjutant-General 2nd Division.

Camp, 2nd Division,

5th July, 1879.

SIR,

I have the Honour to report that the Artillery of the 2nd Division under my command who took part in the action of yesterday were posted as follows*:-

Lieutenant-Colonel Harness took command of the whole of these guns, as I had general command of the artillery in action.

The whole of the officers and men were very steady under fire, losing no opportunity, and at the same time not firing at random.

The total expenditure of ammunition was 90 rounds and 3 rockets, these latter were fired at Nodwengo kraal.

The casualties were N-5 1 horse killed, N-6 1 driver wounded, 2 horses killed, and 2 wounded.

Total, 1 driver wounded (severe gunshot wound in arm), 3 horses killed, 2 wounded.

The fuzes and ammunition were good, and from officers who crossed the field in pursuit, I heard that the effects of our fire were marked. Lieutenant-Colonel Harness, who had had experience in South African wars, gave me every assistance, and I was much pleased with the steady and, accurate fire of Major Le Grice's 9-pounder. Captain Alleyne, my Adjutant, was, as he has been through the campaign, of great use to me, and so was Captain Alexander, who acted as Orderly Officer.

I have, &c.

TATTON BROWNE,

Lieutenant-Colonel, R.A.

* N-5, Major Le Grice's 9-pounder battery. 2 guns under Lieutenant Eliot on left front angle of the square. 2 guns under Captain Crookenden and Lieutenant Woodehouse, about two-thirds right face. 2 guns under Lieutenant French at rear end of right face. N-6, Lieutenant-Colonel Harness' 7-pounder

battery. 2 guns under Lieutenant Parsons on the rear of the left face. N-5, 2 guns fired 22 rounds, N-6, 6 guns fired 68 rounds and 3 rockets.

From Brigadier-General Evelyn Wood, Commanding Flying Column, to the Deputy Adjutant-General.

Camp, Umvolosi Valley, near Ulundi,
5th July, 1879.

SIR,

His Excellency the Lieutenant-General Commanding having planned the operations of yesterday, and personally commanded the troops throughout the action, I do not presume to offer any remarks on such points, as I feel sure his Excellency must have observed, but I desire to bring to notice one or two facts which affect those under my command.

2. In obedience to his Excellency's instructions, and acting in my capacity as Political Agent, I had the cattle sent in by Cetewayo, on the 27th June, driven back across the Umvolosi River, above the wagon drift, punctually at noon, on the 3rd instant.

These cattle were, it will be remembered, accepted only on the condition that Cetewayo complied with certain demands made on him.

3. About the same time Colonel Buller crossed the river lower down, with the mounted men of this column, and advanced very rapidly towards Ulundi to reconnoitre the ground in that direction.

Moving out parties to cover his flanks, he pushed forward in a very dashing manner to within two hundred yards of the Ulundi River. Here he came on about five thousand Zulus lying concealed in the valley. The latter opened fire on the advancing horsemen, while bodies of from three thousand to four thousand of the enemy, moving down on each flank, tried to cut off his retreat.

At the Ulundi River the long grass had been carefully plaited near the banks to impede or trip up the horses while the enemy lay concealed in the river bed.

4. Colonel Buller, having effected the purpose for which he had gone forward, now withdrew his men. He suffered a loss, however, of three men killed, notwithstanding the gallant exertions of his officers to save them. Commandant D'Arcy took up behind him on his own horse Trooper Raubenheim, Frontier Light Horse, but the horse fell, and Commandant D'Arcy was much injured thereby. The trooper was so shaken that he was unable to mount again.

In a similar manner Trooper Peacock, Natal Light Horse, was put up by Lieutenant-Colonel Buller and Captain Prior, behind Sergeant Kerr,

Natal Light Horse. Sergeant Kerr behaved exceedingly well, but was eventually pulled off by Trooper Peacock, who was either killed or so stunned that he was unable to rise again. Lord William Beresford and Lieutenant Hayward also brought dismounted men out of action. Considering that in each of these cases crowds of Zulus were rushing on these courageous men and were only about 150 yards off, their noble conduct will doubtless be noticed by his Excellency the Lieutenant-General Commanding.

The entire number of casualties were three killed and four wounded.

Much, though the loss of these brave men is to be regretted, the information about the enemy and the nature of the ground beyond the Umvolosi River proved of the greatest advantage in the operations of yesterday.

5. In compliance with orders the column under my command moved across the Umvolosi River at at 6.45 A.M. yesterday, strength about 2,000 white men and 400 natives.

Here, again, Colonel Buller gave us such aid as has seldom been afforded by light cavalry to a main body of troops. Crossing the river in advance of our infantry, he pushed on and selected the position his Excellency the Lieutenant-General Commanding eventually occupied, a choice which materially aided us in obtaining so cheaply bought a victory.

6. During the action of yesterday, the men were as steady as walls and as much under the control of their officers as at a drill in England.

7. The Gatling guns under Major Owen, Royal Artillery, and Lieutenant Rundle, Royal Artillery, came into action a little in advance of the front face of the square. Combined with the fire of the infantry they effectually checked the daring attempt of the enemy to come to close quarters.

8. I received during the action every support from the officers of the staff and corps of the column.

9. The wounded were carefully treated under a very hot fire by Surgeon Anderson and Surgeon A. Lennox Brown, and on their being brought into camp by Surgeon-Major Cuffe and Civil-Surgeon Glanville. Surgeon-Major Cuffe speaks in the highest terms of the skill and attention of this gentleman. Surgeon Anderson particularly mentions the assistance he received from Private Lanning, Army Hospital Corps, during the engagement.

10. His Excellency has frequently been good enough to speak with approbation of the order, regularity, and celerity of the movements of this column. I feel that eighteen months of incessant work in the field, which has not been without anxiety, more or less constant, makes it advisable, both in the interest of the service, and for the sake of my own health and efficiency, that I should

have a relaxation of work, if only for a short time. I desire, therefore, to place on record that the good service done by this column is due to the cheerful, untiring obedience of soldiers of all ranks which has rendered my executive duties a source of continued pleasure, and to the efforts of the under-mentioned staff, regimental, and departmental officers, many of whom have worked day and night to carry out my wishes:-

Major Clery, half-pay 32nd Light Infantry, was, to my great regret, removed to No. 3 Column in December, but his Excellency allowed him, at my special request, to rejoin me as my Senior Staff Officer on 1st May.

Energetic and untiring, well versed in the theory of his profession, and from his services as Adjutant of his Regiment, thoroughly acquainted with regimental duties, he has rendered me great assistance. Since he rejoined me I have practically left in his hands all the routine of the column duties.

I have frequently had the pleasure of bringing to notice the good service done by Captain E.K.P. Woodgate, 4th King's Own Regiment.

Singularly calm and collected under fire, he has a quick eye for ground, and I have seldom or never desired to change the choice he has made for our positions. He has done all the work of the Quartermaster-General's Department, and has yet found time to execute a survey of a tract of country of about fifty miles square, which is the only one I have seen with any pretence to accuracy.

Lieutenant Lysons, A.D.C., 90th Light Infantry, has done good service.

His Excellency the Lieutenant-General Commanding has observed with approbation the prompt and soldier-like way in which he took forward my personal escort under fire on the 2nd instant, to recover some cattle which had strayed across the river.

Colonel the Honourable R. Needham, late Grenadier Guards, and Captain Thornbury Cropper, West Kent Militia, Orderly Officers, have worked continuously in assisting to get the column transport forward on the line of march. Indeed I had employed Lieutenant Lysons and them daily as staff officers.

To the several commanding officers of corps my best thanks are due. Their example has been well followed by the troops they ably command.

Major E.J.T. Tremlett, Commanding Royal Artillery.
Major J.F.O. Owen, R.A., Commanding Gatling Battery.
Captain H.R.G. Browne, Commanding 7-pounder Battery.
Captain J. Jones, Commanding 5th Company Royal Engineers.
Major E.L. England, Commanding 1st Battalion 13th Light Infantry.
Major C. Tucker, Commanding 80th Regiment.
Major R.M. Rogers, V.C., Commanding 90th Light Infantry.

Commandant L. White (Wood's Irregulars).

Captain J. Nolan, Commanding Natal Pioneers.

Major C.J. Moysey, Commanding Royal Engineers, has served with me since December.

Not content to render me all the assistance derivable from the technical knowledge of his branch of the service, he has done every kind of staff work for me in turn, and has assisted me materially.

Commissary E. Hughes joined me in December. I was then in difficulties as regards our commissariat arrangements. Since Mr. Hughes's arrival I have had no trouble. Far seeing and painstaking, he unites in his character the unusual faculty of pleasing commanding officers and their men, while watching closely the interests of the public. I am very anxious his services should be rewarded. Deputy Commissary Coates has been acting as Director of Transports under Commissary Hughes, and has done his work remarkably well, as, indeed, he did in 1873, in the Ashantee expedition. Commissary of Ordnance C. Campbell has rendered me all the assistance in his power. His departmental duties were greatly increased by the want of ordnance stores at his command, which obliged me to direct him to purchase largely in the district. Commissary of Ordnance Campbell has also given great assistance daily on the line of march in transport work. In recognition of the hard work he and Commissary Hughes have done I took them into action yesterday as Orderly Officers.

Captain Vaughan, R.A., with local rank of Major, was in charge of our line of communications and Director of Transport, from January to April. During this period, the transport arrangements received the approval of his Excellency. Captain Bradshaw, 13th Light Infantry, has been employed as Assistant Director of Transport for seven months. He possesses sound judgment and great energy, and has done excellent service.

The movements of this column have been so constant, that the Reverend Coar and the Reverend Bandry, have had very little opportunity of exercising their sacred functions. Both these gentlemen, at their special request, however, accompanied the troops in action yesterday, to render the last rites of the Church to those requiring them.

Surgeon-Major Cuffe has been indefatigable in endeavouring to perfect the medical arrangements of this column. I consider he has made the utmost of the means at his disposal, and he possesses that great quality in an Army Medical Officer, of making the best of every available resource. He has worked incessantly.

In transmitting the accompanying report from Colonel Buller, I wish to record here again how much I owe to this officer. He has never failed to cover the column with his mounted men, for from ten to twelve miles in front, and on the flanks. Constitutionally fearless, he is prudent in counsel, and though resolute, is very careful of the lives of his troops in action. He possesses, in my opinion, all the attributes of a perfect leader of Light Cavalry.

I have &c.,
EVELYN WOOD,
Brigadier-General.

Camp, Umfelosi River, Zululand,
5th July, 1879.

SIR,

In compliance with instructions, I have the honor to report that I marched from bivouac at 5.45 A.M., on the 4th July, with the Mounted Corps under my command and occupied positions covering the advance of the column to the ground I had selected the day before.

As soon as the troops had formed up we advanced towards the points where the Zulus were bivouacing.

We were soon heavily engaged on three sides, and the different corps retired independently upon the infantry square, with regularity and steadiness, and it was due to the personal exertions of the several commanding officers that this difficult movement was executed without the slightest confusion.

As soon as the Zulu attack wavered, Captain Brown and the mounted infantry moved out in support of the 17th Lancers, and the rest of the mounted corps went out in other directions.

The enemy were pursued with spirit; the Natal Native Horse, under Captain Cochrane, 32nd Light Infantry, specially distinguishing themselves, as, getting off with a flying start, they reached the Zulu reserve beyond Ulundi, inflicting great loss upon them with comparative impunity.

Having pushed the pursuit to the slopes of the hills forming the amphitheatre we were engaged in, we returned to the infantry, and then, by the direction of the Lieutenant-General Commanding, we burnt Ulundi and the military kraals near.

In this we met with no resistance. I estimate that during the day we inflicted a loss of at least 450 men upon the enemy. Our casualties were, I am thankful to say, very small.

Both the Lieutenant-General Commanding and yourself have from time to time been pleased to express approval of the operations of the corps under my command, and I take this opportunity to bring to your notice the fact that these operations would have been impossible but for the manner in which my efforts to secure the repose and safety of the flying column and to carry out your orders have been seconded by the officers and men serving under me.

Very few of these gentlemen have had the advantage of military training, but, as regards their executive duties, no ill effects have resulted from this want.

In the peculiar warfare in which I have been generally engaged the rough practical knowledge of the Colonist has proved more valuable than the trained service of military troops, while their cheerful self-imposed obedience has fully compensated for the absence of discipline.

In carrying out your wishes my task has been materially lightened by the efforts of the under-mentioned officers, Captain Lord William Beresford, 9th Lancers, my Staff Officer, who came from India for the Zulu war, has been of immense assistance to me. Energetic and untiring, he is always at hand when wanted, while his marked gallantry in the field and his pleasant address, secured the respect and ready obedience of the men.

Captain E. Prior, 80th Regiment, served for some time in the Frontier Light Horse until you were obliged to send him back to his regiment, then greatly in want of officers. I gladly availed myself of the first opportunity I had of regaining his services. He has been my orderly officer since the end of May.

Sir T. Hesketh, Bart., who is visiting Natal, volunteered his services to me as galloper, and has always been willing and anxious to do his best.

Captain Brown, 1st Battalion 24th Regiment, commanding 1st Squadron Mounted Infantry, is an officer who can be thoroughly depended on, while his coolness and personal courage under fire render him an excellent troop leader.

Commandant Raaff, Transvaal Rangers, is a perfect type of a border soldier, brave, indefatigable, and deeply versed in African warfare. I have profited equally by his assistance and by his advice.

Commandant D'Arcy, Frontier Light Horse reckons neither personal inconvenience nor danger in the execution of any order, determined and bold; he has frequently shown great personal gallantry, and has always given a fine example to his men.

Commandant Baker, Baker's Horse, though not strong in health, is singularly happy in his power of leading men in action and of controlling them in camp.

Commandant Whalley, Natal Light Horse, is a brave, straight-forward gentleman, whom I have known for the last fifteen months, and who has always done well.

Captain Cochrane, 32nd Light Infantry, has commanded the Natal Native Horse throughout the operations; the corps has been most efficient, and this I attribute in a great measure to the tact and good management of Captain Cochrane.

In the above-mentioned corps are many excellent officers, whose names I hope hereafter to bring to the notice of the Lieutenant-General Commanding;

but Captain Alfred Blaine, Frontier Light Horse, deserves special mention. He has served under me for fifteen months, and has never failed in any duty. I had occasion to bring his name forward for gallantry during the Kaffir War, and again in the operations against Sekukuni, and he merits similar mention now.

Throughout the operations the sick and wounded of the mounted corps have had the advantage of the services of Civil Surgeons Connolly and Jolly. These two gentlemen have been alike remarkable for the readiness with which they have treated wounded men under fire, and for the kindness and attention they have paid to them in camp. During the retreat from Hlobana Mountain, on the 28th March, these two gentlemen not only remained with the rear guard to treat wounded, but, when not so employed, greatly assisted the rear guard, using the rifles of the wounded.

Veterinary-Surgeon Duck, R.A,, has been attached to the Frontier Light Horse for twelve months, and has had charge of the horses of all mounted corps. We have to thank his skill and unremitting attention for their efficiency. Mr. Duck has also accompanied the troops on all large patrols, and has frequently rendered me great assistance in action.

I have, &c.,
REDVERS BULLER, Lieutenant-Colonel,
Commanding Mounted Corps Flying Column.

The Brigadier-General
Commanding Flying Column.

Return of Casualties on 3rd July, 1879, at Umvolozi River.

Mounted Force.

Frontier Light Horse – Trooper G. Pearce, killed.
Frontier Light Horse – Trooper Rauhenheim.
Natal Light Horse – Trooper Gr. Peacock.

REDVERS BULLER, Lieutenant-Colonel,
Commanding Mounted Corps.

From Lieutenant-General Lord Chelmsford, K.C.B.,
to the Secretary of State for War.

Forwarded in continuation of my despatch of yesterday's date.

CHELMSFORD, Lieutenant-General.
Entonjaneni, 8th July, 1879.

Camp, 8th July, 1879.

SIR,

I should deem it a favour if you will kindly submit to the Major-General Commanding the following remarks on the action of the cavalry under my command at the Battle of Ulundi. My previous report was written whilst in considerable pain on my bed. The detachment of 24 rank and file of King's Dragoon Guards was under command of Lieutenant Brewster, who ably led his men in the charge and pursuit of the Zulus. At the moment of leaving the square, Captain Brownloe, King's Dragoon Guards, volunteered, with the sanction of the Major-General, to act as my orderly officer. This officer, as also my own orderly officer, Lieutenant Neild, were most useful in carrying orders throughout the day, and were constantly exposed to the fire of the enemy in so doing. I have still no wish to particularize any individual officer where all behaved with equal gallantry and prompt attention to orders. I am, however, much indebted to my second in command, Major Boulderson, for the coolness and judgment displayed throughout the day, no less than for the gallantry displayed in leading his particular command (the support), which by the nature of the pursuit, became merged in the first line.

The admirable manner in which the troops, after a rapid pursuit of some three miles, reformed when a change of direction was required to continue the pursuit, after crossing a rather deep donga, is worthy of record, being as quietly and rapidly effected as if on parade, although actually under fire.

The interpreter to my regiment, Mr. Philip Doyle, accompanied me throughout the pursuit, and used his carbine very effectively.

The casualties, I regret to say, are heavy, but many occurred before leaving the square. I have, however, deeply to deplore the loss of Captain the Honourable Wyatt-Edgell, shot dead whilst leading his squadron in the charge, and a more gallant leader never rode in a charge. A complete return of casualties in men and horses has already been furnished.

I have, &c.,
DRURY LOWE, Colonel,
Commanding 17th Lancers and Cavalry 2nd Division.

To the Assistant Adjutant-General,
2nd Division.

Return of Casualties at Ulundi, Zululand, on 4th July, 1879.

Killed – 2 officers, 13 non-commissioned officers and men, 3 natives. Total, 18.
71 horses killed, wounded, and missing.

Wounded – 19 officers, 59 non-commissioned officers and men, 7 natives. Total, 85.

Grand total – 21 officers, 72 non-commissioned officers and men, 10 natives. Total, 103.

F.W. GRENFELL, Major,
Deputy Assistant-Adjutant-General.

Return of Casualties amongst Officers at Ulundi, Zululand, on 4th July, 1879.

17th Lancers – Captain Wyatt-Edgell, killed.
Interpreter Honourable W. Drummond, missing.
Staff – Lieutenant Milne, R.N., A.D.C., slightly wounded.
Staff – Lieutenant and Captain Honourable R. Cotton, slightly wounded.
Staff – Lieutenant Barry Phipps, severely wounded.
Royal Artillery – Lieutenant Davidson, slightly wounded.
Staff – Lieutenant Liebenrood, severely wounded.
17th Lancers – Lieutenant-Colonel Drury-Lowe, slightly wounded.
17th Lancers – Lieutenant James, slightly wounded.
17th Lancers – Lieutenant Jenkins, dangerously wounded.
21st Foot – Major Winslow, severely wounded.
58th Foot – Major Bond, severely wounded.
94th Foot – Lieutenant Brooks, slightly wounded.
1st Battalion 13th Foot – Lieutenant Pardoe, dangerously wounded.
Natal Native Contingent – Lieutenant Lukin, slightly wounded.
Natal Native Contingent – Lieutenant Moncrief, slightly wounded.
Wood's Irregulars – Commandant White, slightly wounded.
Wood's Irregulars – Captain Horton, severely wounded.
Wood's Irregulars – Lieutenant Cowdell, severely wounded.
Natal Native Pioneers – Lieutenant H. Hickley, slightly wounded.
Natal Native Pioneers – Lieutenant F. Andrews, slightly wounded.
Total – killed 1; wounded 19; missing 1.

F.W. GRENFELL, Major,
Deputy Assistant Adjutant-General.

WOLSELEY'S DESPATCHES PUBLISHED ON 10 OCTOBER 1879

War Office, 10th October, 1879.

A despatch, of which the following is a copy, has been received by the Secretary of State for War from General Sir Garnet Wolseley, G.C.M.G., K.C.B., commanding the Forces in South Africa:-

Army Head Quarters, Camp, Ulundi,
Zululand, 3rd September, 1879.

SIR,

I have the honour to report that after a well sustained pursuit through a most difficult country, extending over sixteen days, Ketchwayo, the ex-King of Zululand, was captured on the 28th ultimo by a patrol under the command of Major Marter, King's Dragoon Guards, to whom every praise is due for the skilful manner in which the capture was effected.

Ketchwayo is now on his way to Cape Town, accompanied by some of his wives and servants. He will be detained as a State prisoner at large in the Cape Colony, under the authority of an Act to be passed for that purpose by the Cape Parliament.

On the 1st instant I held a meeting attended by nearly all the great chiefs of Zululand, most of those who from bodily infirmities, or other sufficient causes were unable to attend, being represented by their principal councillors. I explained to the assembled chiefs how the country is in future to be divided amongst them, and the terms upon which they are to be appointed to rule over their respective territories as independent chiefs. I have addressed a despatch to the Secretary of State for the Colonies giving full details of the arrangements I have made for the future government of the country, through which I have every reason to believe that peace will be permanently secured, and the Zulu military power, which has so long threatened the peace of South Africa, be for ever broken up.

I now feel, therefore, in a position to report that the Zulu War has been satisfactorily concluded. Her Majesty's troops can now return to Natal, where, with the exception of those to be retained for the garrisons of South Africa, they will be encamped at Pinetown to await the arrival of transports to take them to their respective destinations. The 1st Battalion 13th Light Infantry and the 1st Battalion 24th Regiment have already embarked for England.

Lieutenant-Colonel Clarke's Column is now on the march to Natal, viâ St. Paul's and Entumeni. It will cross the Tugela at the Middle Drift. Upon reaching Natal, all the levies and irregular troops belonging to it will be disbanded. Lieutenant-Colonel Baker Russell's Column will be broken up as soon as Oham, Ketchwayo's brother, has been re-established in his own district, and when, with the assistance of Lieutenant-Colonel Honourable G. Villiers, whom I appointed Special Commissioner to Oham's armed forces, Lieutenant-Colonel Russell has obtained the submission of the turbulent and semi-independent tribes inhabiting the north-west corner of Zululand, and the disputed territory there bordering upon the Transvaal. I expect that a show of force in the district will be sufficient to effect this object in a very short time.

I have already had the honour of reporting to you the strength of the garrisons I propose retaining at least for the present in the several provinces of South Africa, and from which detachments will be provided for Mauritius and Saint Helena.

Almost all the hired land transport is now being discharged, and I hope I may soon be in a position largely to reduce the amount of Government transport still retained.

To-morrow I intend marching from this with the Head Quarter Staff and a small personal escort direct to Utrecht, en route for Pretoria, which place I hope to reach about the 1st proximo.

Our patrols have visited the most distant localities of Zululand, testing thereby the completeness of the submission of the chiefs, and the peaceable condition of the country. I have in this way been able to extend our topographical knowlege of Zululand, and by actual survey, as well as by reconnaissances, to lay down on paper with very tolerable accuracy its rivers, mountains, &c.

I believe that at least 5,000 stand of arms have been now collected and destroyed. Those upon whom I rely most for information estimate at about 8,000 the total number of guns in Zululand before the war. Assuming that this somewhat under estimates the number, I think we may calculate that at least one-half of the firearms in the country have been taken or voluntarily surrendered by the chiefs coming in to submit. A considerable amount of gunpowder and ammunition has also been destroyed.

The successful action fought near this spot on the 4th July last, has been the only engagement with the enemy since I assumed command of the troops in South Africa. In that action I took no part, Lieutenant-General Lord Chelmsford having commanded there in person, and made all preliminary arrangements, all the merit of that victory is due to him. The subsequent operations have happily been of a bloodless character, but their successful accomplishment depended upon a nicety of calculation and a precision of arrangement only to be expected from a very able and experienced staff, such as that which I am fortunate enough to have with me, presided over by that ablest of Staff Officers Brigadier-General Sir George Pomeroy Colley.

These operations, immediately leading to the capture of the King have been carried out by the troops of the column under Lieutenant-Colonel Clarke, 57th Regiment, who has performed the duties of his responsible command in the most highly efficient manner. The officers and men under him have worked most cheerfully, though the stimulus to exertion given by the presence of an armed enemy was wanting; indeed the conduct of all the troops in the field, British and Colonial, since I assumed command, has been admirable.

Of those who have toiled unremittingly throughout this war, no one is more deserving of special mention than Major-General the Honourable H.H. Clifford. Since his arrival in South Africa, he has been in charge of the base, and of the lines of communication, a charge which I thought it necessary to extend when I assumed command. On him has devolved the heaviest part of the work connected with the concluding operations and reduction of the force. No one could have worked with more earnest zeal than he has done, not only to keep the troops in the field supplied with everything they required, but to do so without unnecessary or extravagant expenditure of public money. By him great economy was introduced into the administration, and a most salutary check established over the outlay of all public money.

As this Despatch is to announce to Her Majesty's Government the successful termination of the military operations in Zululand, and the peaceable settlement of the country, I venture to send it to you in charge of my Aide-de-Camp, Captain Lord Gifford, V.C., whom I recommend to your favourable consideration. Lord Gifford was actively engaged in pursuit of Ketchwayo from the day when the first patrol was sent out; and, at the time when the capture was made, was watching with a small body of men the kraal into which he had traced the King, with the intention of effecting the capture at night-fall.

I have &c.,
G.J. WOLSELEY, General.
The Right Honourable the
Secretary of State for War,
War Office, London,

War Office, 15th January, 1880

Despatches, of which the following are copies, have been received by the Secretary of State for War from General Sir Garnet Wolseley, commanding the troops in South Africa:-

> Army Head Quarters, Camp,
> Sekukuni's Town, Transvaal,
> South Africa, 1st December, 1879.

SIR,

I have the honour to forward for your information the enclosed report from Lieutenant-Colonel Baker Russell, C.B., 13th Hussars, commanding the Transvaal Field Force, of the action fought here on the 28th ultimo, the successful result of which I communicated to you by telegram on that same evening.

The conduct of the troops, both regulars and volunteers, was everything that could be desired. The steadiness of Her Majesty's young soldiers in action, their fire, discipline, and the dashing manner in which they assaulted the 'Fighting Koppie' showed they were as well capable of sustaining the military reputation of the British army as any men who have ever served in it.

The skill and gallantry with which the Volunteer Corps worked over those scarped and difficult mountains was most conspicuous, and I have great pleasure in bringing especially to your notice the invaluable services performed by Commandant Ferreira, of Ferreira's Horse.

The action began at 4.30 A.M. and lasted until 10 A.M., when the 'Fighting Koppie' was stormed by a general charge of all the corps engaged, the assault being led by Colonel Russell in person.

Of Colonel Russell, who had his horse shot under him, I cannot speak too highly; the force under his command, which may be roughly estimated as consisting of about 2,200 British and about 10,000 Natives, was hastily collected from all sides, and where native levies are concerned, it is no easy matter to plan and carry out an extensive operation extending over some miles of a very difficult mountain country with the skill, accuracy, and success which have characterized Colonel Russell's operations here.

The Chief, Sekukuni, who did not personally take any part in the action, is now in a cave about fifteen miles from this. The cave is closely surrounded by troops, and I hope that want of water will soon compel him and those with him to surrender.

In a few days more I hope to clear out all the robber chiefs living in these Zulu mountains, when the Transvaal Field Force will be broken up.

I believe that the success which has attended this little campaign will confer lasting benefit upon the Transvaal by securing peace to a district where neither life nor property has been safe for many years past.

The destruction of Sekukuni's stronghold and of his power, and the breaking up of the robber clans who looked up to him as their King, cannot fail to have a quieting effect upon the native mind generally in South Africa, and will, I am sure, go far towards settling all native difficulties in the Transvaal.

In the organization and concentration of the forces engaged in these operations, and in all the many complex arrangements required for supplying them with stores, food, &c., &c., during the campaign, I have received the most efficient and able assistance from Lieutenant-Colonel H. Brackenbury, Royal Artillery, who is acting as my chief of the Staff.

Surgeon-Major Jackson, C.B., who is attached to my head quarters did good work during the action in attending to the wounded, many of whom he dressed under fire.

Captain Maurice, Royal Artillery, my Camp Commandant, acted as Staff officer to one of the attacking columns, and did excellent service until he was unfortunately wounded.

My Aides-de-Camp, Major McCalmont, 7th Hussars, and Lieutenant A.G. Creagh, Royal Artillery, both performed their duties to my entire satisfaction.

I have, &c.,
G.J. WOLSELEY, General,
The Right Honourable
the Secretary of State for War,
War Office, London.

NAVAL BRIGADE DESPATCH PUBLISHED ON 7 NOVEMBER 1879

Admiralty 7th November, 1879.
The following Despatches and Communications, relative to the proceedings of the Naval Brigade in Zululand, are published by desire of the Lords Commissioners of the Admiralty:-

H.M.S. 'Active Sierra Leone,
3rd September, 1879.

SIR,
I have the honour to submit, for the information of the Lords Commissioners of the Admiralty, a short account of the proceedings of the naval forces, lately under my command, landed for service in the Zulu war.

2. Enclosure (A.) shows the total of officers and men landed from the fleet, with other particulars.

3. Enclosure (B.) shows the strength of the 'Active's' party landed at Durban in November, 1878. This force at once marched to the Lower Tugela, of which place, and Fort Pearson, it formed the garrison until the concentration of No. 1 column under Colonel Pearson, took place.

This party established the pont, and collected boats preparatory to the passage of the Tugela, which took place on 12th January; the river was, at this time a torrent 270 yards across, rendering the work both difficult and dangerous. More than once the pont upset, drowning William Martin, A.B., of H.M.S. 'Active,' while Lieutenant Craigie and others narrowly escaped.

The entire responsibility of transporting the column, with its immense quantity of stores, &c., fell on the Royal Navy, and was rapidly and successfully performed.

4. On 7th January, 1879, a detachment of of 50 men from H.M.S. 'Tenedos' (C.) joined the Naval Brigade. This party took charge of the pont and general working of the river on 18th January, when the 'Actives' advanced with No. 1 column into Zululand, they (the 'Tenedos') advanced with Lord Chelmsford's army to the relief of Ekowe, and were present at the battle of Gingilhovo; shortly after they re-embarked.

5. On 22nd January the 'Actives' took a distinguished part at the battle of Inyezane, sustaining a loss of seven wounded.

Lord Chelmsford described the part, taken by the Royal Navy 'on this occasion, as one of the finest incidents of the war.'

This party formed part of the garrison of Ekowe from 24th January to 4th April, 1879, sustaining considerable hardships; one officer and four men having died during the siege, while three more died soon afterwards from diseases contracted there.

6. Ekowe was relieved on the 3rd April, and the following day I assumed command of all the naval forces landed, amounting to 858 men. This force was divided between the Lower Tugela and Fort Chelmsford, Commander Brackenbury being in command of the detachment at the latter place.

On the 19th June, the main naval forces, consisting of 545 officers and men of H.M.'s ships 'Active,' 'Boadicea,' and 'Shah,' with three 9-pounder guns, six rockets, and five Gatling guns, were concentrated at Fort Chelmsford, from which they advanced with General Crealock's army to Durnford, employed there disembarking provisions and stores till 21st July, when, after a review by Sir Garnet Wolesley, the detachments of 'Active' and 'Shah' embarked, leaving the detachment of 'Boadicea' to continue the work of landing.

Sir Garnet made a flattering speech after the review, and then handed me a General Order, (Enclosure D).

I also annex extracts from a letter addressed to me by General Crealock, (Enclosure E), who having been relieved from the chief command of 1st Division, could not address the Royal Navy officially.

7. Commanders Brackenbury and Romilly, commanding the two divisions of seamen, as well as Captain Philips commanding the Royal Marines, have most ably seconded me in all respects, and I cannot speak too highly of the zeal and ability displayed by both officers and men acting under any orders. General efficiency was the result, while punishment was almost unknown.

8. Lieutenant Craigie, R.N., first as acting adjutant of 'Actives' detachment, and afterwards as staff officer to the whole brigade, rendered most valuable services throughout; and I most strongly desire to respectfully urge his claims for some mark of their Lordships' approval. Enclosed is a medical report by Fleet Surgeon Norbury, who as P.M.O. to No. 1 column, and then as P.M.O. to the Naval Brigade, has rendered most important services; he has shown marked zeal and ability.

10. It will be observed by reference to Table (A.) and to the medical report, that the detachment of H.M.S. 'Active' was much longer landed, and suffered

far more than those of the other ships; I trust therefore that their Lordships will permit me, before the ship pays off to submit the names of the officers and men who have distinguished themselves while on active service before the enemy.

I have, &c.,
(Signed) H. FLETCHER CAMEBELL,
Captain R.N.,
late commanding Naval Brigade,
Zululand.

The Secretary of the Admiralty.

A.

A Return of the Naval Forces landed for Service in Zulu War.

H.M.S. 'Active'. – Date of landing, 19th November, 1878. Date of embarkation, 21st July, 1879. Time landed, 8 months. Died, 11. Officers, 10; men, 163. Total 173.

H.M.S. 'Tenedos'. – Date of landing, 1st January, 1879. Date of embarkation, 8th May, 1879. Time landed, 4¼ months. Died, 1. Officers, 3; men, 58. Total, 61.

H.M.S 'Shah'. – Date of landing, 7th March, 1879. Date of embarkation, 21st July, 1879. Time landed, 4½ months. Died, 4. Officers, 16; men, 378. Total, 394.

H.M.S. 'Boadicea'. – Date of landing, 18th March, 1879. Date of embarkation, 31st July, 1879. Time landed, 4½ months. Died, 3. Officers, 10; men, 218. Total, 228.

H.M.S. 'Flora'. – Date of landing, 20th April, 1879. Date of embarkation, 31st July 1879. Time landed, 3½ months. Officers 2. Total, 2.

B.

Landing Party of H.M.S. 'Active.'

Commander H.J.F. Campbell, commanded at Lower Tugela, from 24th November, 1878, to 4th January, 1879; Lieut. R.W. Craigie, Lieut. W. des V. Hamilton, Sub.-Lieut T.G. Fraser, Nav. Sub.-Lieut. J.G. Heugh, Boatswain J. Cotter, Midshipman L.C. Coker, Staff Surgeon Norbury, Surgeon Thompson, Lieut. T.W. Dowding, R.M.L.I., total, 10 officers. Seamen, 100; idlers, 5; marines, 42; krooman, 14; hospital, 2 – 163 men; total, 173.

Armament of above: 12-pr. B.L. guns, 2 in number; 22-pr. rockets, 2 in number; Gatling, 1 in number; In addition to the above, two 7-pr. army mountain guns were in charge of and worked by the 'Active's' from December to March.

C.

Landing Party H.M.S. 'Tenedos.'

Lieut. King Scott, commanded at lower Tugela from 18th January to 14th February, 1879, Sub-Lieut. Starting. Staff Surgeon Longfield, 3 officers and seamen and marines 47. Total 50. This force was afterwards increased.

Armament of Above.

9-pr. gun, 1 in number; 7-pr. gun, 1 in number; 24-pr, rocket, 1 in number.

D.

Copy of General Order by Sir G. Wolseley.

Camp, Port Durnford,
21st July, 1879.

As the Naval Brigade is now, about to embark, General Sir G.Wolseley wishes to place on record his very high appreciation of the services it has rendered while acting on shore.

The conduct of the men has been admirable, and their bearing in action every way worthy of the service to which they belong, while they have worked hard and cheerfully on those arduous labours which constitute so important a part of military operations.

In returning to their ships they will have the satisfaction of knowing that all recollections of the Zulu war will ever be associated with the Naval Brigade which has borne so distinguished a part in it.

By order,
(Signed). G. POMEROY COLLEY,
Staff Officer.

E.

General Crealock to Commander Campbell.

. . . I am deprived from publicly thanking the officers and men of the Naval Brigade under your command for the good services they have performed since I assumed command of the 1st Division.

But I cannot part company without writing to thank you, Captains Romilly and Brackenbury, and the rest of the naval officers and men, for your valuable assistance in working this campaign to an end. . . . . Good bye, and good luck to you all wherever you go.

(Signed) H. HOPE CREALOCK,
M. General.

Medical Report on the Naval Brigade, engaged in the Zulu War,
from 19th November, 1878, to 21st July, 1879.

The total force landed in the Zulu war consisted of 41 officers and 817 men, 858 in all. The men of H.M.S. 'Active' were on shore 245 days, those of the 'Tenedos' 129 days, 'Shah' 136 days, and 'Boadicea' 131 days.

The 'Active's' men were incarcerated at Fort Ekowe, they then passed some time at the Lower Tugela to recruit their health, and again advanced along the coast district with General Crealock's division; those of the 'Shah' and 'Boadicea' were, principally quartered at Fort Chelmsford, situated in a malarious neighbourhood with a supply of very impure drinking water, they consequently suffered much from remittent fever and dysentery; while the small contingent of the 'Tenedos' passed nearly all its time at the Lower Tugela, with the exception of some three weeks when it advanced with Lord Chelmsford's column, to relieve Ekowe, and consequently, having but few hardships to endure, suffered little in health.

The principal diseases from which the Naval Brigade suffered were fevers, continued remittent and enteric dysentery, diarrhoea, congestion of the liver and tape worm. From April 30th to June 30th, 123 cases of remittent fever were received at the Naval Field Hospital at the Lower Tugela all from Fort Chelmsford, 85 of them belonged to the 'Shah,' and 38 to the 'Boadicea.' The most sickly men of the Naval Brigade were those of the 'Shah,' this ship having at a period of great emergency landed every available man, and among these there was a large number of time expired, sickly, and other men who had been long serving abroad in gunboats and other vessels, and who were taking passage home; these easily succumbed in a practically tropical climate. The men of the 'Active' at Ekowe suffered a great deal from similar diseases; the fort was situated on an unhealthy site which it was necessary to occupy for military reasons; the weather was often extremely wet, and being surrounded on all sides by high earthworks there was a certain stagnation of air. The cubic space too was limited, affording only 3½ square yards per man; then the reduced scale of diet, which obtained during the entire period, combined with the very hard work to which the men were subjected, told severely on their constitutions. In action with the enemy, the Naval Brigade had one man killed and two officers and 13 men wounded. The man killed and nine of the wounded belonged to H.M.S. 'Active,' three to the 'Boadicea,' two to the 'Shah,' and one to the 'Tenedos.'

Table of Killed and Wounded of Naval Brigade.

Isandlhwana. – W. Aynsley, signalman, 'Active,' killed.

Ulundi. – Lieut. A. Milne, R.A., 'Active,' slightly wounded.

Inyezana. – G. Bearyman, O.S., 'Active,' severely wounded. G. Doran, O.S., 'Active,' dangerously wounded. H. Gosling, A.B., 'Active,' severely wounded. E. White, Capt. Forecastle, slightly wounded. J. Butler, signalman, slightly wounded. J. Ropeyarn, krooman, slightly wounded. J. Lewis, krooman, slightly wounded.

Ginginlhovo. – J. Porteous, Capt. foretop, 'Active,' slightly wounded. F. Parfitt, gunner, R.M.A., 'Boadicea,' dangerously wounded, P. Corday, Captain's Mate, 'Boadicea,' dangerously wounded. W. Hinchley, bugler, 'Boadicea,' dangerously wounded. J. Bird, A.B., 'Shah,' severely wounded. J. Bugler, A.B., 'Shah,' severely wounded. Mr. W. Longfield, staff surgeon, 'Tenedos,' dangerously wounded.

All the above wounded officers and men recovered, most of them sufficiently to return to duty, the remainder to be sent home in a transport ship.

From the effects of disease there were 17 deaths, including one officer, Mr. L. Coker, Midshipman, H.M.S. 'Active,' and one man, also of the 'Active,' was drowned in the Tugela when attending to his duties on board the pont. Of those who died from disease nine belonged to the 'Active,' and five of them occurred during the occupation of Ekowe; three to the 'Boadicea,' four to the 'Shah,' and one to the 'Tenedos.' Two succumbed to pneumonia, six to dysentery, three to enteric fever, three to remittent fever, one to peritonitis, one to continued fever, and one to sunstroke.

(Signed) HENRY F. NORBURY,
Fleet Surgeon,
P.M.O. Naval Brigade.

Report on the Services rendered by the Officers and Men of the Squadron during Zulu War.

No. 158.

'Boadicea' in Simon's Bay,
13th September, 1879.

SIR,

The Zulu King being now a captive in this harbour, and the war having come to an end, I desire to bring generally to the notice of my Lords

Commissioners of the Admiralty the services which have been rendered by the officers and men of the squadron under my command throughout its course.

2. From the despatches of my predecessor, Commodore Sullivan, which I observe have been duly published in the London Gazette, I have seen that he has done full justice to the good services performed by Captain (then Commander) Campbell, and the officers and crew of H.M.S. 'Active,' and of the gallantry displayed by them at the action on the Inyzane on 22nd January, and also to the services of the officers and crew of the 'Tenedos,' from the date of their first landing in Natal, the 'Active' on 19th November 1878, and the 'Tenedos' on the 1st January, 1879, to the 17th March, when he resigned the command of the squadron to me.

3. As their Lordships are aware, the 'Shah' arrived at Natal with reinforcements on the 6th March, and the 'Boadicea' on the 15th, and contingents from these vessels were immediately landed and pushed forward to the Lower Tugela, where they arrived in time to take part in Lord Chelmsford's advance for the successful relief of Ekowe, in which the 'Tenedos' contingent took part also. My despatches of 11th April, Nos. 18 and 19, with enclosures, have acquainted their Lordships with the particulars of that expedition, and of the part taken by the Naval Brigade in the action at Ginginhlovo.

4. Commander Brackenbury, of H.M.S. 'Shah,' commanded the Naval Brigade in that action, and the conduct of the officers and men on the occasion under my own personal observation was everything that could be desired, and fully justified the high encomiums passed upon it by the General Commanding-in-Chief.

5. On the 4th April, at Ekowe, I appointed Acting Captain Campbell, of the 'Active,' to the command of the United Naval Brigade in the field, a force numbering over 800 men; he retained command until re-embarked at Port Durnford on the 22nd July.

6. On the relief of Ekowe, the 'Active's' crew returned to the Tugela to recruit, after their long confinement of ten weeks, and Captain Campbell remained at head-quarters there with General Crealock until the advance of the First Division on 17th June.

7. Between these dates, or covering a period of considerably over two months, Commander Brackenbury remained in command of that part of the Brigade consisting of the contingents from the 'Boadicea,' 'Shah,' and for some time of the 'Tenedos,' which served with the advanced force under Brigadier-General Clarke on the banks of the Inyzane river.

8. This was a period of much trial and hardship for officers and men. When, for sanitary reasons, the position at Ginginhlovo was abandoned, and Fort Chelmsford (in the construction of which the Brigade took an active part) was built, the men were continually employed on convoy duty between that position and Fort Crealock on the banks of the Amatakulu, or on fatigue duty of one kind or another. The weather was very bad, with much heavy rain for a great part of the time, and sickness to a serious extent prevailed, every week bringing its convoys of ambulances full of fever and dysentery cases down to the Tugela. No matter what the weather was, the trenches had to be manned every morning at four o'clock, and kept manned until clear daylight. For the greater part of the time there were no tents; but every duty was performed with a cheerful readiness deserving of all praise.

9. During this period Commander Brackenbury was ably supported by Commander Romilly of the 'Boadicea,' and by Captain Phillips, R.M.L.I., commanding the Marines of the Brigade, and the bright and cheerful manner of these officers could both fail in its effect upon the officers and men under their orders. Brigadier-General Clarke has frequently testified to the great support and assistance he derived from the officers and men of the navy during this trying period.

10. During the occupation of Fort Chelmsford several reconnaisances were made for the examination of the different drifts for the passage of the Emlalazi river, in which Commanders Brackenbury and Romilly, Sub-Lieutenants Startin and Smith-Dorrien, took part. These reconnaisances were made under fire.

11. On the 17th June General Crealock advanced from the Tugela, and crossed the Emlalazi river on the 22nd without opposition.

12. The division encamped on the Emlalazi plain on the coast, at the position known as Port Durnford, and on the arrival the following day of the 'Forester' with the surf boats and store ships for the purpose of opening communication with the shore at that place, the services of the brigade were immediately put in requisition for this operation, and so well was the work done that in three weeks time over 2,000 tons of commissariat and ordnance stores had been landed on the open beach, to the entire relief of the land transport.

13. On the 7th July Sir Garnet Wolseley arrived in camp to assume the chief command of the army, and intelligence having been received of the victory of Lord Chelmsford at Ulundi, the General informed me that the services of the naval forces on shore would no longer be required, and accordingly, on his return to Port Durnford from his meeting with Lord Chelmsford at St. Paul's,

he inspected the brigade on 21st July, and with the exception of the 'Boadicea's' crew, who remained to work the landing, they were embarked the same day for return to their ships, the 'Boadicea's' following on 27th.

14. In my despatch of the 11th April, I mentioned the name of Commander Brackenbury (and enclosed the report of that officer, who commanded at the action of Ginginhlovo) of Lieutenants Carr, Lindsay, and Kingscote, R.N., and of Captain Phillips, who commanded the marines of the brigade, and who was ably seconded by Captain Burrowes, R.M.A., and the other officers of the Royal Marine Regiments.

15. Where all did good service and were animated by an excellent spirit, it is not possible for me to mention every officer individually where so many were engaged, but I enclose for their Lordships' consideration a complete list of all the officers who took part in the operations on shore during the war.

16. A finer and more efficient body of men than were paraded by Captain Fletcher Campbell on the plains of the Emlalazi, for the inspection, of Sir Garnet Wolseley on the completion of their service, could not have been seen.

17. Of the services of Staff (now Fleet) Surgeon Norbury, Staff Surgeons Longfield, Shields, Grant, and the other medical officers of the Brigade, I cannot speak too highly.

18. Lieutenant Commander Smith, Sub-Lieutenants Bourchier-Wrey, Theed, and the officers and crew of the 'Forester,' performed most excellent service on the coast, and by their careful survey contributed mainly to the complete success of the landing operations at Port Durnford, which were effected without accident to any of the vessels employed on this dangerous and imperfectly surveyed coast.

19. The transport arrangements at Durban and Port Durnford have through-out been most ably conducted by Captain Twiss, R.N., principal transport officer, and the officers of his department, Commander Caffin, Lieutenant Gardiner of the 'Shah,' and Mr. Ramsay, paymaster. The operation of disembarking so many thousand men, horses and mules, and thousands of tons of stores, at the exposed anchorage at Durban , where ships are continually rolling to an inordinate degree, and conveying them over the heavy bar, has been conducted with the most complete success, and without a single accident from first to last.

20. I have received the most cordial assistance throughout from Captain Bradshaw of H.M.S. 'Shah,' who has also conducted the duties of senior officer at Durban during my absences at the front.

21. Captain Adeane, of H.M.S. 'Tenedos,' acted as senior officer at Simon's Bay from February until the departure of the 'Tenedos' for England on the 20th June, and has rendered the best service during the great strain thrown upon the resources of the Navy in coaling and forwarding the many transports arriving almost simultaneously, and in expediting the clearing of the colliers.

22. The work done at Simon's Bay dockyard during the long continued strain upon this small establishment has been immense, and the cheerful and continued assiduity shown by Staff Commander Rowe, Mr. White, chief engineer, Mr. Fynmore, storekeeper, and Mr. Gillham, carpenter and superintendent of repairs, commands my highest admiration.

23. During this war it has been necessary for the complete efficiency of the service, that I should keep two offices open, the one at Durban and the other at Simon's Bay. The clerical labour has been very great, and communication and arrangement of details of transport and other services between Durban and the Cape, and with the military authorities, has been incessant. The telegraph was constantly at work; and in this duty the services of Mr. Carlisle, my secretary at Durban, and of Mr. Trew, assistant paymaster at Simon's Bay, have been invaluable, and I have much pleasure in recommending both these officers to the most favourable consideration of their Lordships.

24. I cannot conclude this despatch without referring to Lieutenant Archibald Milne. His name has been frequently mentioned by me before in connection with the highly interesting and intelligent reports which he has from time to time furnished me during the war, some of which I have deemed of sufficient importance to forward direct to their Lordships. Lord Chelmsford, in writing to me of this officer, characterises him as being a most useful and intelligent aide-de-camp, and I have much pleasure in saying that a more useful and intelligent representative of the Naval Service at Head Quarters could not be desired. Lieut. Milne was directed by Lord Chelmsford to keep me fully acquainted with the progress of events during the war, and I feel sure that their Lordships will agree with me that he has ably carried out his instructions.

25. The officers and men of the ships left on the Natal coast, short of hands, deserve notice. Anxiously desiring to be at the front, their duty kept them in Durban Roads for many months; rolling on an average through an arc of 30 degrees, the vessels being always held in readiness to put to sea at short notice on the approach of bad weather. As representatives of this portion of the personnel of the squadron, I may mention Lieutenants Masterman, of the

'Boadicea' and Rainier, of the 'Shah' as deserving of the consideration of their Lordships.

I enclose, for their Lordships' information, a copy of the General Order issued by Sir Garnet Wolseley on the occasion of his inspection of the Naval Brigade, prior to embarkation at Port Durnford, and I trust their Lordships will agree that the ecomiums passed upon the service by the General were well merited.*

I have, &c.,
FREDK. W. RICHARDS,
Commodore.

*See Enclosure D, above.

The Secretary of the Admiralty,
Whitehall.

Downing Street,
15th September, 1879.

SIR,

I am directed by the Secretary of State for the Colonies to transmit to you, for the information of the Lords Commissioners of the Admiralty, the accompanying copy of a despatch from the Governor of the Cape Colony, bearing testimony to the valuable service rendered to South Africa by Captain Bradshaw, of H.M.S. 'Shah,' in bringing reinforcements to Natal from St. Helena at a critical time, after the disaster of Isandhlawana.

I am, &c.,
(Signed) R.H. MEADE.
The Secretary to the Admiralty.

Sir B. Frere to the Secretary of State for the Colonies.

No. 236.

Government House. Cape Town,
12th August, 1879.

SIR,

I am informed that Her Majesty's ship 'Shah,' Captain Bradshaw, has re-embarked the men lately forming part of the Naval Brigade in Zululand, and is under orders to proceed to England.

2. I feel assured that Lord Chelmsford and Sir Garnet Wolseley will do justice to the services of Captain Bradshaw, and his officers and men who formed a portion of the fighting force under their command.

3. But I trust it will not be forgotten that in coming here it fell to Captain Bradshaw's lot to perform a service for South Africa such as can seldom be rendered by any officer of any arm in Her Majesty's Service.

4. When he received at St. Helena the news of the disaster at Isandhlawana, Captain Bradshaw, with the Consent of the Governor and Officer Commanding the Forces in that Island, embarked nearly the whole garrison and brought them to Natal, landing at the same time a fine brigade of the seamen, marines, and artillery of his own ship.

5. The force thus brought was almost valuable addition to Lord Chelmsford's troops in the field, but the moral and political effect of the reinforcement was far greater than the number of fighting men. Few, but those who were on the spot, can realize the effect of such a disaster as that of the 22nd of January on all classes of colonists and on the natives of Natal as well as on our own men in the field.

6. At such a moment the unexpected appearance in Durban Roads of a magnificent man-of-war, bringing, as it were from out of the ocean, a large and complete body of well trained and seasoned fighting men, had a most valuable moral effect on all nationalities, classes and professions, There was not, I am convinced, a single man or woman in Natal who did not experience a sense of added security when they heard the news, not one of Her Majesty's subjects whether native, or European who did not feel that the gloomy forebodings of the inability of Her Majesty's Government to protect her subjects against the Zulu power were at least premature, and there cannot be a doubt that the influence of the impression thus created spread far beyond the border of British territory.

7. Nor, as I ventured to remark on a previous occasion, do we owe less to those who were left on board the ship, than to the officers and men who landed and did such good service in the field.

The coast of Natal has no land-locked harbours nor many secure anchorages. It is a dangerous coast for any ship short-handed, and to ensure the safety of a large man-of-war during equinoctial gales, with so many of her ship's company ashore, involves labour and anxiety not less than beset those who were serving against such an enemy as the Zulus.

8. There is some risk lest services like these should be overlooked in the excitement of brilliant military success, and I therefore venture to ask that the Lords Commissioners of the Admiralty may be informed how highly the Government and people in these Colonies estimate the value of the services rendered by Captain. Bradshaw and the officers and men under his command.

9. I learn from Captain Bradshaw that he specially notices Commander Brackenbury, who commanded the 'Shah's' men at the front, and Lieutenant Rainier, senior Lieutenant, of the ship who was in charge on board during her stay at Natal, and who had many anxious hours while lying at that dangerous and exposed anchorage.

I have, &c.,
(Signed) H..B. E. FRERE.
The Right Honourable the Secretary of State,
Colonial Office.

Horse Guards, War Office, S.W.
24th September, 1879.

SIR,
I have the honour by direction of the Field-Marshal Commanding-in-Chief, to transmit to you, for the information of the Lords Commissioners of the Admiralty, the enclosed copy of a letter from Major-General Lord Chelmsford, G.C.B., forwarding his report on the officers of the Naval Brigade engaged in the operations in South Africa and bearing testimony to the cordial co-operation and valuable assistance afforded him on all occasions by the naval service, whether on sea or on shore. His Royal Highness has perused this report with much gratification.

I have &c.,
(Signed) M.A. DILLON.
The Secretary of the Admiralty.

21, St. James' Square, Bath,
13th September, 1879.

SIR,
I have the honour to request that a copy of my report on the officers of the Naval Brigade, who afforded me such able assistance during the time that I was commanding Her Majesty's Forces in South Africa, may be forwarded for the information of the Admiralty. I feel under such obligations to the sister service for the cordial co-operation and valuable assistance which it afforded me on all occasions, whether on sea or on shore, that it is a matter to me of sincere regret that I was not able before leaving South Africa to place publicly on record, through the medium of a General Order, my hearty appreciation of those services.

It is impossible for me to speak too highly of the conduct and behaviour of the blue jackets and marines, whether in camp or under fire. Every duty which devolved upon them, no matter how long or how hard, was cheerfully and intelligently performed; and I have no hesitation in placing on record, that without their help it would have been almost impossible to have made satisfactory arrangements for the passage of troops and stores at the Lower Tugela.

The officers, as usual, set a fine example and never spared themselves when work had to be done.

To Admiral F.W. Sullivan, C.B., C.M.G., and to Commodore F.W. Richards, I am deeply indebted for the ready help and friendly assistance they at all times afforded me.

Both these officers did their utmost to facilitate the work of the military authorities at the base of operations, and their advice and suggestions were often of the greatest value.

It is with pride and satisfaction I am able to report that during the whole time that I was Commanding Her Majesty's Forces in South Africa, the Navy and Army worked together with the most perfect unanimity, and that the relations between the two services were always of the most friendly nature.

I have, &c.,
CHELMSFORD, Maj.-Gen,
Late Commanding Her Majesty's Forces
in South Africa.

The Military Secretary,
Horse Guards, War Office.

(Enclosure.)
NAVAL BRIGADE.

I am under great obligations to Rear-Admiral F.W. Sullivan, C.B., C.M.G., for the cordial assistance and willing help which he gave me during the time that I was commanding Her Majesty's Forces in South Africa – first in the Cape Colony and afterwards in Natal – at a time when much alarm prevailed in Durban. Admiral Sullivan was able by his personal influence to tranquillise the public mind, and was most useful, in advising the municipal authorities of that town regarding their public defences.

I was much indebted to him for his advice and assistance when making arrangements for the landing of the large number of troops, transport and other animals, and stores, which were sent from England so promptly after the disaster at Insandlwana.

The arrangements made at Admiral Sullivan's suggestion turned out a complete success, and I feel that the credit of the successful disembarkations is in a great measure due to the preparations which were made by his advice.

Admiral Sullivan, on promotion, was succeeded by Commodore F.W. Richards, and I cannot pay the latter a higher compliment than by saying that he was equally anxious and equally successful in affording me assistance.

Captain Bradshaw has already received well merited praise for the prompt action which he took when, on arriving at St. Helena, he heard of the disaster at Isandlwana.

The garrison of St. Helena and the naval contingent which was landed from the 'Shah' were very seasonable reinforcements at a time when every additional man was of importance.

During Commodore Richards' absence at the front Captain Bradshaw acted as senior officer at Durban, and was most useful and energetic in assisting the disembarkation of troops, horses, and stores. His popularity amongst the merchants of Durban was most useful in allaying friction and in preventing misunderstandings with regard to the delay in landing their goods, which resulted at times from the quantity of military stores which claimed precedence.

Captain Twiss was the senior naval transport officer at Port Natal, and as such deserves great credit for the successful arrangements which were carried out under his personal supervision. I should here wish to bring to notice the names of numerous officers who, on board ship or on shore, assisted so materially in the disembarkation at Port Natal. I am, however, unfortunately not in possession of them, as of course, no reports could be sent to me after I had ceased to command H.M.'s forces in South Africa. I know, however, that Captain Adeane, H.M.S. 'Tenedos,' and the officers left in charge of H.M.S. 'Shah,' 'Active,' and 'Boadicea,' exerted themselves most zealously to assist the military authorities at Durban who were charged with the duty of superintending the numerous disembarkations. Lieutenant Sidney Smith, in command of H.M.S. 'Forrester,' did excellent service in reconnoitring the coast of Zululand and in finding the landing place at Point Durnford.

Lieutenant A.B. Milne acted as my Naval A.D.C. during the time that the Naval Brigade were on shore.

He proved himself a most intelligent and trustworthy officer, and was of great assistance to me on numerous occasions.

I have mentioned this officer's name in my despatch written after Ulundi, but have thought it only fair to him that I should include it amongst others of the Naval Brigade.

Captain Campbell, H.M.S. 'Active,' Commander Brackenbury, H.M.S. 'Shah,' Lieutenant Kingscote, H.M.S. 'Tenedos,' Lieutenant Carr, H.M.S. 'Boadicea,' were respectively in command of that portion of the Naval Brigade which was landed for service in Zululand.

I cannot speak too highly of the manner in which these officers exercised their commands, or of the conduct and behaviour of those under their immediate charge.

I regret that I am not in possession of any separate reports from these officers, so that I might particularise those who had an opportunity of specially distinguishing themselves. I am glad, however, to have this opportunity of thankfully acknowledging the excellent service rendered by the Naval Brigade generally during the time that they were serving under my command.

(Enclosure.)
ROYAL MARINES.

The contingent of these excellent troops which was landed for service in Zululand was a most efficient one.

Lieutenant T.W. Dowding, R.M. was at first the senior officer in command, and advanced with the force under Colonel Pearson to Ekowe, where he remained until the garrison was relieved.

Captain J. Philips, R.M.L.I., subsequently landed with the contingent from H.M.S. 'Shah,' and was present in command of all the Marines at the battle of Ginginlhovo.

I am much indebted to both these officers for their assistance, and for the efficient manner in which they exercised their respective commands. Staff Surgeon H.F. Norbury was for a long time the senior medical officer with Colonel Pearson's column, and discharged those duties with marked ability and zeal.

Staff Surgeon W.D. Longfield was the senior medical officer with the Naval Brigade in the engagement at Gingilhovo, and was dangerously wounded.

I had previously had an opportunity of noticing the efficient manner in which this officer performed his duties when in charge of the hospital at Fort Tenedos.

Downing Street, 1st October, 1879.

SIR,

I am directed by the Secretary of State for the Colonies to transmit to you, for the information of the Lords Commissioners of the Admiralty, the accompanying copy of a despatch from the Governor of the Cape Colony, on the subject of the employment of Her Majesty's Naval Forces in Land Service.

I have, &c.
ROBERT G.W. HERBERT.
The Secretary to the Admiralty.

SIR B. FRERE TO THE SECRETARY OF STATE.

No. 253.

Government House, Cape Town,
23rd August, 1879.

SIR,

I have the honour to acknowledge your despatch No. 374, of the 24th of April last, relative to the employment of Her Majesty's Naval Forces on Land Service. I need hardly assure Her Majesty's Government that the instructions to land these men only in case of great and emergent necessity, and to re-embark them as soon as the exigencies of war would permit, have been strictly observed.

2. I understand that by this time all the officers and men of Her Majesty's Ships who were landed in Natal have been re-embarked.

3. I have already reported to Her Majesty's Government the important services performed by the bodies of Blue Jackets and Marines during the war, composed as they were of seasoned and hardy well trained and disciplined men, accustomed to turn their hands to any sort of employment, and to work in small detachments; these were far more serviceable than unseasoned troops and immature recruits.

I have, &c.,
H.B.E. FRERE, Gov. and H.C.
The Right Honourable The Secretary of State,
&c., &c., &c., Colonial Office.

The Secretary of the Admiralty to Commodore Richards.

Admiralty, 7th November, 1879.

SIR,

I have laid before my Lords Commissioners of the Admiralty your letter of the 13th September, No. 158, in which you bring generally to the notice of their Lordships the services rendered by the officers and men of the squadron under your command during the recent war in Zululand.

2. My Lords, on the arrival of H.M.S. 'Tenedos,' and on the paying off of H.M.S. 'Shah' and 'Active,' communicated to the officers and men of those ships the satisfaction which they felt in receiving from his Excellency Sir Bartle Frere, from Major-General Lord Chelmsford, and Lieutenant-General Sir Garnet Wolseley, as also from yourself and the officers in command of vessels under your orders, testimony to the discipline and efficiency of the Naval Brigade, and to the cheerfulness with which the

officers and men of the Royal Navy and Royal Marines who formed the Brigade co-operated with the Military forces, which co-operation contributed in no small degree to the successful termination of the war.

3. Their Lordships also conveyed to your predecessor, Rear-Admiral Sullivan, on his arrival in England, their appreciation of the judgment and energy with which he performed the duties which devolved upon him in connexion with the Zulu campaign. They also fully endorsed the approval expressed by the Colonial Office of the judicious step taken by Captain Bradshaw, of H.M.S. 'Shah,' in embarking the garrison of St. Helena in that vessel and taking them to Natal.

4. It now remains for me to communicate to yourself their Lordships' high sense of the zeal and discretion which has in a similar degree characterized your proceedings since you succeeded to the command of the station, and their directions that you will convey to the officers and men of the 'Boadicea' and 'Forester,' who shared either ashore or afloat in the operations of the war, to the officers and others engaged in transport services, and in the dockyard at Simons Bay, also to your clerical staff, their Lordships full approval of their exertions.

5. To mark their approbation of these services, my Lords, in addition to the promotions already made, have caused the following officers to be promoted.
    Lieutenant F.R. Carr, H.M.S. 'Boadicea,' Lieutenant R.W. Craigie, H.M.S. 'Active,' to be Commanders.
    Sub-Lieutenant James Startin, H.M.S. 'Tenedos,' Sub-Lieutenant Thomas G. Fraser, H.M.S. 'Active,' to be Lieutenants.
    Naval Sub-Lieutenant J.G. Heugh to be Navigating Lieutenant.
    Boatswain John Cotter, to be Chief Boatswain.
    And they have favourably noted the names of the other officers to whose services their Lordships' attention has been drawn in your Despatches and those of your predecessor.
    Although no necessity arose for the active service of the Battalion of Royal Marines which was sent out to Natal in H.M.S. 'Jumna,' my Lords feel assured that had they been called upon to take part in the operations they would have merited their Lordships' approval, and it was with much satisfaction that their Lordships received the testimony borne by the inhabitants of Simons Town to their good conduct whilst temporarily landed at that place.

> I am, &c.,
> ROBERT HALL.
> Commodore Richards,

H.M.S. 'Boadicea,' Cape of Good Hope.

Admiralty, 4th November, 1879.

In accordance with the provisions of Her Majesty's Order in Council of the 30th April, 1877-

Engineer Francis Andrew has been placed on the Retired List of his rank, from the 24th October last.

Royal Naval Artillery Volunteers.
Liverpool Brigade.

James Edward Hunter, Esq., Retired Captain, R.N., to be Sub-Lieutenant. Dated 4th November, 1879.

Admiralty, 6th November, 1879

The following promotions have been made from the 31st October, 1879:-

Commanders:

Arthur Hildebrand Alington,
Archer John William Musgrave,
Henry John Carr,
Charles Lister Oxley,

to be Captains in Her Majesty's Fleet.

Lieutenant Edgar Richard Mathias to be Commander in Her Majesty's Fleet.

The following promotions in Her Majesty's Fleet have this day been made for services rendered during the recent campaign in South Africa:-

Lieutenants:

Frederick Ralph Carr,
Robert William Craigie,

to be Commanders in Her Majesty's Fleet.

Sub-Lieutenants:
James Startin,
Thomas Guthrie Fraser,

to be Lieutenants in Her Majesty's Fleet.

Navigating Sub-Lieutenant John George Heugh to be Navigating Lieutenant in Her Majesty's Fleet.

Boatswain John Cotter to be Chief Boatswain in Her Majesty's Fleet.

THE ZULU WAR VICTORIA CROSSES

War Office, 2nd May, 1879.
The Queen has been graciously pleased to signify Her intention to confer the decoration of the Victoria Cross on the undermentioned Officers and Soldiers of Her Majesty's Army, whose claims have been submitted for Her Majesty's approval, for their gallant conduct in the defence of Rorke's Drift, on the occasion of the attack by the Zulus, as recorded against their names, viz.:-

Regiment	Names	Acts of Courage for which recommended
Royal Engineers	Lieutenant (now Captain and Brevet Major) J.R.M. Chard	For their gallant conduct at the defence of Rorke's Drift, on the occasion of the attack by the Zulus on the 22nd and 23rd January, 1879.
2nd Battalion 24th Regiment	Lieutenant (now Captain and Brevet Major) G. Bromhead	The Lieutenant-General commanding the troops reports that, had it not been for the fine example and excellent behaviour of these two Officers under the most trying circumstances, the defence of Rorke's Drift post would not have been conducted with that intelligence and tenacity which so essentially characterised it. The Lieutenant-General adds, that its success must, in a great degree, be attributable to the two young Officers who exercised the Chief Command on the occasion in question.
2nd Battalion 24th regiment	Private John Williams	Private John Williams was posted with Private Joseph Williams, and Private William Horrigan, 1st Battalion 24th Regiment, in a distant room of the hospital, which they held for more than an hour, so long as they had a round of ammunition left: as communication was for the time cut off, the Zulus were enabled to advance and burst open the door; they dragged out Private Joseph Williams and two of the patients, and

assagaied them. Whilst the Zulus were occupied with the slaughter of these men a lull took place, during which Private John Williams, who, with two patients, were the only men now left alive in this ward, succeeded in knocking a hole in the partition, and in taking the two patients into the next ward, where he found Private Hook.

2nd Battalion 24th Regiment	Private Henry Hook	These two men together, one man working whilst the other fought and held the enemy at bay with his bayonet, broke through three more partitions, and were thus enabled to bring eight patients.
2nd Battalion 24th Regiment	Private William Jones and Private Robert Jones	In another ward, facing the hill, Private William Jones and Private Robert Jones defended the post to the last, until six out of the seven patients it contained had been removed. The seventh, Sergeant Maxfield, 2nd Battalion 24th Regiment, was delirious from fever. Although they had previously dressed him, they were unable to induce him to move. When Private Robert Jones returned to endeavour to carry him away, he found him being stabbed by the Zulus as he lay on his bed.
2nd Battalion 24th Regiment	Corporal William Allen and Private Frederick Hitch	It was chiefly due to the courageous conduct of these men that communication with the hospital was kept up at all. Holding together at all costs a most dangerous post, raked in reverse by the enemy's fire from the hill, they were both severely wounded, but their determined conduct enabled the patients to be withdrawn from the hospital, and when incapacitated by their wounds from fighting, they continued, as soon as their wounds had been dressed, to serve out ammunition to their comrades during the night.

MEMORANDUM.

Lieutenant Melville, of the 1st Battalion 24th Foot, on account of the gallant efforts made by him save the Queen's Colour of his Regiment after the disaster at Isandlwanha, and also Lieutenant Coghill, 1st Battalion 24th Foot, on account of his heroic conduct in endeavouring to save his brother officer's life, would have been recommended to Her Majesty for the Victoria Cross had they survived.

War Office, 17th June, 1879.

The Queen has been graciously pleased to signify Her intention to confer the decoration of the Victoria Cross on the undermentioned Officers and Soldier of Her Majesty's Army, whose claims have been submitted for Her Majesty's approval, for their gallant conduct daring the recent operations in South Africa, as recorded against their names, viz.:-

Regiment	Names	Acts of Courage for which recommended
60th Rifles	Captain and Brevet Lieutenant-Colonel Redvers H. Buller C.B.	For his gallant conduct at the retreat at Inhlobana, on the 28th March, 1879, in having assisted, whilst hotly pursued by Zulus, in rescuing Captain C. D'Arcy, of the Frontier Light Horse, who was retiring on foot, and carrying him on his horse until he overtook the rear guard. Also for having on the same date and under the same circumstances, conveyed Lieutenant C. Everitt, of the Frontier Light Horse, whose horse had been killed under him, to a place of safely. Later on, Colonel Buller, in the same manner, saved a trooper of the Frontier Light Horse, whose horse was completely exhausted, and who otherwise would have been killed by the Zulus, who were within 80 yards of him.
1st Battalion 13th Regiment	Major William K. Leet	For his gallant conduct, on the 28th March, 1879, in rescuing from the Zulus Lieutenant A.M. Smith, of the Frontier Light Horse, during the retreat from the Inhlobana. Lieutenant Smith whilst on foot, his horse having been shot, was closely

pursued by the Zulus, and would have been killed had not Major Leet taken him upon his horse and rode with him, under the fire of the enemy, to a place of safety.

Army Medical Department	Surgeon-Major James Henry Reynolds	For the conspicuous bravery, during the attack at Rorke's Drift on the 22nd and 23rd January, 1879, which he exhibited in his constant attention to the wounded under fire, and in his voluntarily conveying ammunition from the store to the defenders of the Hospital, whereby he exposed himself to a cross-fire from the enemy both in going and returning.
1st Battalion 24th Regiment	Lieutenant Edward S. Browne	For his gallant conduct, on the 29th March, 1879, when the Mounted Infantry were being driven in by the enemy at Inhlobana, in galloping back and twice assisting on his horse (under heavy fire and within a few yards of the enemy) one of the mounted men, who must otherwise have fallen into the enemy's hands.
80th Regiment	Private Wassall	For his gallant conduct in having, at the imminent risk of his own life, saved that of Private Westwood, of the same regiment. On the 22nd January, 1879, when the Camp at Isandhlwana was taken by the enemy, Private Wassall retreated towards the Buffalo River, in which he saw a comrade struggling, and apparently drowning. He rode to the bank, dismounted, leaving his horse on the Zulu side, rescued the man from the stream, and again mounted his horse, dragging Private Westwood across the river under a heavy shower of bullets.

War Office, August 23, 1879.

The Queen has been graciously pleased to signify Her intention to confer the decoration of the Victoria Cross upon the undermentioned Officer of Her

Majesty's Army, whose claim has been submitted for Her Majesty's approval, for an act of bravery performed by him during the War against the Zulus, as recorded against his name:-

Regiment	Names	Acts of Courage for which recommended
9th Lancers	Captain Lord William Beresford	For gallant conduct in having at great personal risk, during the retirement of the reconnoitring party across the 'White Umvolosi River' on 3rd July last, turned to assist Sergeant Fitzmaurice, 1st Battalion 24th Foot (whose horse had fallen with him), mounted him behind him on his horse, and brought him away in safety under the close fire of the Zulus who were in great force, and coming on quickly. Lord William Beresford's position was rendered most dangerous from the fact that Sergeant Fitzmaurice twice nearly pulled him from his horse.

War Office, 9th October, 1879.

The Queen has been graciously pleased to signify. Her intention to confer the decoration of the Victoria Cross upon the undermentioned Officer and Non-Commissioned Officer of Her Majesty's Army, whose claims have been submitted for Her Majesty's approval, for their several acts of valour in endeavouring to save the lives, of soldiers during the reconnaissance made before Ulundi, on the 3rd July, 1879, as recorded against their names:-

Regiment	Names	Acts of Courage for which recommended
Frontier Light Horse	Captain (now Commandant) Cecil D'Arcy	For his gallant conduct on the 3rd July, 1879, during the reconnaissance made before Ulundi by the Mounted Corps, in endeavouring to rescue Trooper Raubenheim, of the Frontier Light Horse, who fell from his horse as the troops were retiring. Captain D'Arcy, though the Zulus were close upon them, waited for the man to mount behind him; the horse kicked them both off and though much hurt by the fall and quite

alone, Captain D'Arcy coolly endeavoured to lift the trooper, who was stunned, on to the horse and it was only when he found that he had not strength to do so that he mounted and rode off. His escape was miraculous as the Zulus had actually closed upon him.

Frontier Light Horse	Sergeant Edmund O'Toole	For his conspicuous, courage and bravery on several occasions during the campaign, and especially for his conduct on the 3rd July, 1879, at the close of the reconnaissance before Ulundi, in assisting to rescue Sergeant Fitzmaurice, 1st Battalion 24th Mounted Infantry, whose horse fell and rolled on him, as the troops retired before great numbers of the enemy. When lifted up behind him by Lord William Beresford, the man, being half stunned by the fall, could not hold on, and he must have been left had not Sergeant O'Toole, who was keeping back the advancing Zulus, given up his carbine and assisted to hold Sergeant Fitzmaurice on the horse. At the time the Zulus were rapidly closing on them, and there was no armed man between them and Sergeant O'Toole.

War Office, 17th November, 1879.

The Queen has been graciously pleased to signify Her intention to confer the decoration of the Victoria Cross upon the undermentioned Officers whose claims to the same have been submitted for Her Majesty's approval, for their gallant and courageous conduct during the recent operations in Afghanistan (*not included here*) and South Africa, as recorded against their respective names:-

Regiment	Names	Acts of Courage for which recommended
Commissariat and Transport Department	Acting Assistant (now Sub-Assistant) Commissary James Langley Dalton	For his conspicuous gallantry during the attack on Rorke's Drift Post by the Zulus on the night of the 22nd January, 1879, when he actively superintended the work of defence, and was amongst the foremost of those who received the first

attack at the corner of the hospital, where the deadliness of his fire did great execution, and the mad rush of the Zulus met its first check, and where by his cool courage he saved the life of a man of the Army Hospital Corps by shooting the Zulu, who, having seized the muzzle of the man's rifle, was in the act of assegaing him.

This Officer, to whose energy much of the defence of the place was due, was severely wounded during the contest, but still continued to give the same example of cool courage.

War Office, 29th November, 1879.

The Queen has been graciously pleased to signify Her intention to confer the decoration of the Victoria Cross upon the undermentioned Non-Commissioned Officer of the Natal Native Contingent, whose claim has been submitted for Her Majesty's approval, for his gallant conduct during the recent operations in South Africa, as recorded against his name:-

Regiment	Names	Acts of Courage for which recommended
Natal Native Contingent	Corporal Schiess	For conspicuous gallantry in the defence of Rorke's Drift Post on the night of the 22nd January, 1879, when, in spite of his having been wounded in the foot a few days previously, he greatly distinguished himself when the Garrison were repulsing, with the bayonet, a series of desperate assaults made by the Zulus, and displayed great activity and devoted gallantry throughout the defence. On one occasion when the Garrison had retired to the inner line of defence, and the Zulus occupied the wall of mealie bags which had been abandoned, he crept along the wall, without any order, to dislodge a Zulu who was shooting better than usual and succeeded in killing him, and two others, before he, the Corporal, returned to the inner, defence.

War Office, 23rd February, 1880.

The Queen has been graciously pleased to signify Her intention to confer the decoration of the Victoria Cross upon the undermentioned Non-Commissioned Officer and Men of Her Majesty's Army, whose claims have been submitted for Her Majesty's approval, for the gallant conduct displayed by them during the recent operations in South Africa, as recorded against their names:-

Regiment	Names	Acts of Courage for which recommended
80th Foot	Colour-Sergeant Anthony Booth	For the gallant conduct on the 12th March, 1879, during the Zulu attack on. the Intombi River, in having, when considerably outnumbered by the enemy, rallied a few men on the south bank of the river, and covered the retreat of fifty soldiers and others for a distance of three miles. The Officer Commanding 80th Regiment reports that, had it not been for the coolness displayed by this Non-commissioned Officer, not one man would have escaped.

War Office, 5th April, 1882.

The Queen has been graciously pleased to signify Her intention to confer the decoration of the Victoria Cross upon the undermentioned Officer and Soldier, of Her Majesty's Army, whose claims have been submitted for Her Majesty's approval, for their conspicuous bravery at the assault of the Inhlobane Mountain, in Zululand, as recorded against their names:-

Regiment	Names	Acts of Courage for which recommended
2nd Battalion, The Cameronians (Scottish Rifles)	Lieutenant Henry Lysons, Private Edmond Fowler *(Since discharged)*	On the 28th March, 1879, during the assault of the Inhlobane Mountain, Sir Evelyn Wood ordered the dislodgment of certain Zulus (who were causing the Troops much loss) from strong natural caves commanding the position in which some of the wounded were lying. Some delay occurring in the execution of the orders issued, Captain the Honourable Ronald Campbell, Coldstream Guards, followed by Lieutenant Lysons, Aide-de-Camp, and Private Fowler, ran forward

in the most determined manner, and advanced over a mass of fallen boulders, and between walls of rock, which led to a cave in which the enemy lay hidden. It being impossible for two men to walk abreast, the assailants were consequently obliged to keep in single file, and as Captain Campbell was leading, he arrived first at the mouth of the cave, from which the Zulus were firing, and there met his death, Lieutenant Lysons and Private Fowler, who were following close behind him, immediately dashed at the cave, from which led several subterranean passages, and firing into the chasm below, succeeded in forcing the occupants to forsake their stronghold. Lieutenant Lysons remained at the cave's mouth for some minutes after the attack, during which time Captain Campbell's body was carried down the slopes.

TUESDAY, 15th JANUARY, 1907.

War Office, 15th January, 1907.
The King has been graciously pleased to approve of the Decoration of the Victoria Cross being delivered to the representatives of the undermentioned Officer's and men who fell in the performance of acts of valour, and with reference to whom it was notified in the London Gazette that they would have been recommended to Her late Majesty for the Victoria Cross had they survived:-

London Gazette, 2nd May, 1879.
Lieutenant Teignmouth Melvill, 24th Foot.

Lieutenant Nevill Josiah Aylmer Coghill, 24th Foot.

'Lieutenant Melvill, of the 1st Battalion 24th Foot, on account of the gallant efforts made by him to save the Queen's Colour of his Regiment after the disaster at Isandlwanha, and also Lieutenant Coghill, 1st Battalion 24th Foot, on account of his heroic conduct in endeavouring to save his brother officer's life, would have been recommended to Her Majesty for the Victoria Cross had they survived.'

INDEX